Torts I
Workbook

A Behavioral Approach to Learning

Nelson P. Miller

Torts I Workbook–

A Behavioral Approach to Learning

Nelson P. Miller

Publisher:
Crown Management LLC – June 2018
1527 Pineridge Drive
Grand Haven, MI 49417
USA

ISBN-13: 978-1-7322387-2-5

All Rights Reserved
© 2018 Nelson P. Miller
c/o 111 Commerce Avenue S.W.
Grand Rapids, MI 49503
(616) 560-0632

Table of Contents

Introduction		1
Whole-Course Outlines		3
	Bullet Outline. Paragraph Outline.	
Week 1:	**Policy, Intent, & Battery**	17
	Bullet Outline. Paragraph Outline. Fluency Cards. Definitions Worksheet. Issue-Spotting Worksheet. Sameness Worksheet. Practice-Development Exercise. Problem-Solving Exercise.	
Week 2:	**Assault, False Imprisonment, & IIED**	30
	Bullet Outline. Paragraph Outline. Fluency Cards. Definitions Worksheet. Issue-Spotting Worksheet. Sameness Worksheet. Review Exercise. Drafting Exercise.	
Week 3:	**Trespass to Land & Chattels, & Conversion**	42
	Bullet Outline. Paragraph Outline. Fluency Cards. Definitions Worksheet. Issue-Spotting Worksheet. Discrimination Exercise. Review Exercise. Drafting Exercise.	
Week 4:	**Intentional-Tort Defenses**	54
	Bullet Outline. Paragraph Outline. Fluency Cards. Definitions Worksheet. Issue-Spotting Worksheet. Discrimination Exercise. Scenario-Generating Exercise. Drafting Exercise. Problem-Solving Exercise.	
Week 5:	**Negligence (Duty & Standard of Care)**	68
	Bullet Outline. Paragraph Outline. Fluency Cards. Definitions Worksheet. Issue-Spotting Worksheet. Example/Non-Example Worksheet. Problem-Solving Worksheet. Review Exercise. Drafting Exercise.	
Week 6:	**Qualified Duties (Contracts, Omissions, & Economic Loss)**	83
	Bullet Outline. Paragraph Outline. Fluency Cards. Definitions Worksheet. Issue-Spotting Worksheet. Comprehensiveness Worksheet. Example/Non-Example Worksheet. Sameness Exercise. Review Exercise. Drafting Exercise.	

Week 7:	**Emotional Distress, Prenatal Harm, Breach, & Proof**	99

Bullet Outline. Paragraph Outline. Fluency Cards. Definitions Worksheet. Issue-Spotting Worksheet. Comprehensiveness Worksheet. Sameness Exercises. Problem-Solving Exercise. Drafting Exercise.

Week 8:	**Res Ipsa, Statute Violation, & Causation (Cause-in-Fact)**	111

Bullet Outline. Paragraph Outline. Fluency Cards. Definitions Worksheet. Issue-Spotting Worksheet. Comprehensiveness Worksheet. Sameness Worksheet. Review Exercise. Drafting Exercise.

Week 9:	**Cause-in-Fact (continued) & Proximate or Legal Cause**	125

Bullet Outline. Paragraph Outline. Fluency Cards. Definitions Worksheet. Issue-Spotting Worksheet. Comprehensiveness Worksheet. Factors Worksheet. Review Exercise. Drafting Exercise. Problem-Solving Exercise.

Week 10:	**Intervening Causes & Professional Negligence (Duty)**	140

Bullet Outline. Paragraph Outline. Fluency Cards. Definitions Worksheet. Issue-Spotting Worksheet. Discrimination Exercise. Sameness Exercise. Problem-Solving Exercise. Drafting Exercise.

Week 11:	**Professional Negligence (continued)**	153

Bullet Outline. Paragraph Outline. Fluency Cards. Definitions Worksheet. Issue-Spotting Worksheet. Comprehensiveness Worksheet. Example/Non-Example Exercise. Review Exercise. Drafting Exercise. Problem-Solving Exercise.

Week 12:	**Premises Liability**	168

Bullet Outline. Paragraph Outline. Fluency Cards. Definitions Worksheet. Issue-Spotting Worksheet. Sameness Worksheet. Example/Non-Example Exercise. Review Exercise. Role-Play Exercise.

Week 13:	**Comparative Negligence & Assumption of Risk**	183

Bullet Outline. Paragraph Outline. Fluency Cards. Definitions Worksheet. Issue-Spotting Worksheet. Discrimination Exercise. Sameness Exercise. Drafting Exercise.

Practice Assessments   195

Introduction

This workbook is for the three-credit course Torts I, comprised of thirteen weeks of new studies, identified as Week 1, Week 2, etc., followed by a Review Week and a Final Exam Week. The workbook's topics follow the order of the casebook *The Practice of Tort Law (3rd ed.)* by Nelson Miller, Paul Sorensen, Monica Nuckolls, and Karen Chadwick.

The exercises in this workbook provide the most benefit when you complete them with other students, in pairs or small groups. The exercises' value is not only in thinking and writing but also talking and listening. The more that you can see, hear, and interact with others, and that others can see and hear you, providing you with feedback, the better these exercises are likely to serve you.

This workbook provide answers to its exercises, questions, and problems, generally on the back of the page from which you work. Immediate feedback enables you to confirm or correct your thought and expression. To use the answers for their best effect, try to complete the exercise first before referring to the answer. The value is in part in striving.

The exercises vary somewhat from week to week to increase your interest and so that you learn in different ways and practice different skills. The exercises help you start with discrete knowledge components that you gradually build into complex sequences involving applying law and solving problems. The exercises generally build from one to another, as follows:

1. The opening bullet-point outline, paragraph-format outline, and diagrams are presenting stimuli, giving you the knowledge components and their framework of relationships;

2. Fluency cards enable you to practice recall, from a brief law stimulus, the core concepts, building your fluent recall for verbal expression, although only in discrete parts;

3. Definitions worksheets enable you to practice recall, from a law-question prompt, of the discrete knowledge components, to assemble in more-complete, written sentences;

4. Framework worksheets enable you to practice recall, from abbreviated stimuli, of the assembled knowledge framework showing concept relationships;

5. Comprehensiveness worksheets enable you to examine incomplete law statements to supply the missing components, testing and confirming your recall of law detail;

6. Discrimination worksheets enable you to practice distinguishing law statements that over-generalize, under-generalize, or misconceive of the correct law;

7. Scenario-generating worksheets enable you to practice articulating illustrative scenarios of law statements, demonstrating your understanding and improving advocacy;

8. Issue-spotting worksheets enable you to practice associations, from a fact-pattern prompt, of the discrete knowledge components with fact scenarios implicating them;

9. Sameness worksheets enable you to practice associating law concepts with multiple fact scenarios, confirming critical attributes of the law and its application to facts;

10. Example/non-example worksheets enable you to practice distinguishing fact scenarios that illustrate or do not illustrate given law statements, confirming your knowledge;

11. Attributes-analysis worksheets enable you to study closely complex law statements to practice discerning their critical and variable parts, as applied to fact scenarios;

12. Factors worksheets enable you to practice recalling, choosing, and analyzing factors of law tests as you apply those factors to multiple changing fact scenarios;

13. Problem-solving worksheets enable you to practice generating new, unusual, and novel rules from fact patterns and procedural context in think-aloud problem-solving method;

14. Review worksheets enable you to recall and apply law from earlier in your studies to move knowledge from short-term to long-term memory;

15. Drafting worksheets enable you to place your law knowledge and skills in their practice context while honing your writing and drafting skills;

16. Role-play exercises enable you to place your law knowledge and skills in their practice setting while honing your interpersonal and advocacy skills;

17. Multiple-choice questions enable you to practice applying your law knowledge and skills to multiple fact patterns, one for each concept that you are learning; and

18. Essay questions enable you to practice applying your law knowledge and skills to fact patterns, while expressing your reasoning in organized and coherent written form.

The full outlines at the beginning of the book and partial outlines at the beginning of each week's exercises have superscript numbers before the law that they state. The superscript numbers correlate with the multiple-choice questions, so that you have one multiple-choice question for each bit of law that you learn.

Use this workbook to push yourself deeper into grasping, recalling, and applying the fundamental concepts of tort law. The more active that your studies are, and the more that you strive at the boundaries of your capabilities, the better you should acquire tort knowledge and skills for their practical use and benefit, to you, clients, and others. Best wishes for good studies.

Whole-Course Outlines

Bullet Format

WEEK 1 POLICY, INTENT, & BATTERY
Introduction
[1]Tort law policies (rationales, justifications)
- deter (discourage conduct that causes personal injuries and property damage)
- compensate (restore the person suffering loss to the extent able)

[2]Tort law classifications (depends on the wrongdoer's state of mind):
- intentional torts (purposeful wrongs)
    - [3]Tort practice seldom involves intentional torts
        - insurance does not ordinarily cover purposeful wrongs
- torts of negligence (carelessness, breaches of ordinary care)
    - this area is the heart of tort practice because of liability insurance
- strict liability (loss without respect to intent or fault, even with all due care)
    - Torts II subject

Intentional Torts Generally
[4]Seven intentional torts (the first five ABFiTT are traditional, the last two new):
- assault,
- battery,
- false imprisonment,
- trespass to land,
- trespass to chattels,
- intentional infliction of emotional distress (IIED), and
- conversion.

Three forms of intent:
- [5]purpose or desire to harm (not just the intent to act but the intent to harm)
    - often but not always due to ill will or malice
- [6]knowledge of substantial certainty of harm (KSC)
    - recklessness, or knowledge of high probability of harm, is intent only for IIED
- [7]transferred intent
    - transfers among the five traditional intentional torts ABFiTT
    - also transfers from victim to victim

[8]Children and the mentally ill are liable for intentional torts if they know the nature of their act.
- parents are generally not liable for a child's tort except by statute
    - statutes tend to cap parent liability at amounts around $2,500 to $5,000

[9]Mistake does not negate intent
- the actor is still liable if thinking incorrectly, even reasonably, that the act is lawful

[10]The law presumes nominal damages for four of the five traditional intentional torts (ABFiT)
- presumed damages can be nominal ($1, $10, $100) or substantial ($1,000, $10K, $100K)
- no presumed damages for trespass to chattels

- prove actual damages if you have them; don't only rely on the presumption

Assault and Battery

[11]Battery = intentional contact harmful or offensive to the reasonable person (IHOC)
- any of the three forms of intent (desire to harm, KSC, or transferred intent) will do
- [12]good motive or beneficial effect does not excuse a battery
- [13]contact with anything closely connected with the person satisfies the contact element

WEEK 2   ASSAULT, FALSE IMPRISONMENT, & IIED

[14]Assault = reasonable apprehension of an imminent battery with the apparent present ability (RAI IHOC APA)
- [15]battery can be with or without an assault, and assault with or without battery
- [16]words (threats) alone are generally not enough for an assault
    - unless combined with an overt act suggesting imminent harmful contact
- [17]learning about imminent contact after the contact occurs is not assault
    - the victim must apprehend the assault when it occurs

False Imprisonment

[18]False imprisonment = intentional unauthorized restraint against will (URAW)
- includes false arrest = refusal to release from confinement when law requires
- [19]restraint is ordinarily by force
    - restraint may also be subjecting the victim to unreasonable danger on escape
        - [20]known, reasonably safe means of escape means no false imprisonment
    - restraint could possibly involve risking loss of property (holding another's purse, for instance)
- [21]victim must know of the restraint

Intentional Infliction of Emotional Distress (IIED)

[22]IIED requires proof of *outrageous conduct* and *severe distress*
- [24]intent for IIED must be to cause the victim severe distress
    - recklessness (knowledge of a high probability of harm) will do
- [23]outrageous conduct = beyond all bounds of decency in civil society
    - [25]repetition may make the conduct more outrageous
        - so may the conduct's location and duration
        - so may the relationship between perpetrator and victim (like supervisor to subordinate)
    - [26]The conduct must be outrageous to the reasonable person
        - but knowledge that the victim is unusually susceptible can make the conduct outrageous

WEEK 3   TRESPASS TO LAND AND CHATTELS, & CONVERSION

Trespass

[27]Trespass to land = intentional interference with exclusive possession of land (IIEP)
- alternative definition = intentional unauthorized physical entry onto another's land
- the entry must be intentional
    - careless skidding off road onto land is not trespass but would be negligence
- [28]mistaken entries (boundaries unknown) are still trespass
- [33]trespass includes defendant exceeding the scope or duration of consent to entry
    - trespass also includes entry into immediate reaches above or subsurface areas beneath the land

- [29]law presumes damages from the interference
    - exception when the entry is intangible, in which case plaintiff must prove damages
    - [32]where no actual damage occurs from trespass, the law awards at least nominal damages
        - in egregious cases, punitive damages may be available (not in Michigan)
- [30]nuisance is an alternative tort to trespass
    - addresses interference with use & enjoyment (noise, smoke, light, smell) not exclusive possession
    - [31]public nuisance interferes with public enjoyment (passersby)
        - private nuisance substantially affects enjoyment of private lands (neighbors)

[34]Trespass to chattels = intentional interference with exclusive possession of personal property (IIEPPP)
- must prove some damages / loss (different from trespass to land)
    - compensated by lost-use value

Conversion

[35]Conversion = intentional dominion over personal property substantially interfering with control (IDIC)
- think of it as the civil tort for theft
- compensated by value at conversion
- [36]involves substantial deprivation or complete destruction
    - contrast with trespass to chattels = temporary or partial diminution in value
- [37]owner of converted property may recover from the original converter and subsequent holders
    - doesn't matter whether subsequent holders take in good faith
    - don't buy from thieves

WEEK 4 INTENTIONAL-TORT DEFENSES
Intentional-Tort Defenses
- ([43]defendants have the burden of proof on each element of affirmative defenses)

[38]Consent = permission expressed by words or communicative actions
- [39]determine consent from an objective rather than subjective standpoint
    - what would a reasonable person have concluded
- [40]the person must understand the conduct and risks
    - parents may give substituted consent for treatment of children
    - [41]emergency medical-care providers may treat those who are unable to give or withhold consent
        - only if the reasonable person would have consented
- [42]consent to an illegal act is invalid
- consent obtained by fraud or duress is invalid

[44]Self-defense and defense of others against physical injury authorizes reasonable force
- includes reasonable mistake
- does not include retaliation after threat ends
- [45]may require retreat before use of force likely to cause serious injury or death (retreat to the wall)
    - although possibly no retreat necessary from the home

[46]Defense of property
- only reasonable force not likely to cause death or serious injury

- no mistake permitted; must be correct

Recovery of property
- applies to fresh pursuit about the premises
  - use legal action to recover once away from the premises and no longer in fresh pursuit
  - [48]repossession allowed only without force and by agreement or summary proceedings
- [47]must make a demand before using reasonable force to recover property on or about premises in pursuit
  - no need for demand if demand would be futile

[49]Necessity
- public necessity is a complete defense to property damage
- private necessity requires payment of actual damage

[50]Authority of law, discipline, and justification
- (law must authorize or circumstances must warrant the action)
- authority of law typically involves lawful arrest
  - can include protection by medical-care providers prior to civil commitment (attempted suicide)
- discipline typically involves military, maybe school
  - watch for corporal-punishment statutes prohibiting contact for other than restraint
- justification = grab-bag / catch-all

WEEK 5   NEGLIGENCE (DUTY & STANDARDS OF CARE)

Negligence—Duty

[51]negligence = duty, breach, causation, and damages (DBCD)

[52]duty = reasonable care (reasonably prudent person / RPP)
- determined by judge rather than jury
- arises whenever acts create foreseeable risk of harm
  - can involve omissions to act when circumstances warrant duty
  - [53]controversial duty to protect against crime depends on
    - past experience of crime,
    - offers of security,
    - available means of protection,
    - foreseeability
- [54]standards of care depend on factors including
  - custom in the trade or field
  - government regulations
  - industry standards
  - likelihood, foreseeability, and seriousness of injury
- [55]emergencies alter the standard of care to the circumstances (lower the duty)
  - except not for the one who created the circumstances (duty remains ordinary, not emergency)
- [56]reasonably prudent person (RPP) assumes the actor's physical, not mental, characteristics
  - those with superior knowledge must use it
- [57]children owe the care expected of reasonable children of like age and experience
  - consider the Rule of Sevens (no duty to age 7, duty of that age to 14, adult duty beyond 14)
  - children engaged in adult activities owe adult duties
- [58]Learned Hand's formula: liability exists when

- the burden of precautions < than loss probability x loss magnitude
- theoretical formula, not practical

WEEK 6 QUALIFIED DUTIES: CONTRACTS, OMISSIONS, ECONOMIC LOSS

- [59]contract promisor owes a tort duty to a third party only when the promisor performs in part
  - misfeasance, not nonfeasance
- [60]no duty to rescue or aid another unless
  - one created the need,
  - one assumes a duty,
  - one controls the instrumentality
- [61]economic-loss doctrine limits duties to direct injury
  - bars pure economic loss claims by those who suffer no physical impact

WEEK 7 QUALIFIED DUTIES (EMOTIONAL DISTRESS, PRENATAL HARM), BREACH, & PROOF OF FAULT

- [62]duty to avoid pure emotional distress only for
  - manifestation of
  - severe distress of
  - close family members who
  - contemporaneously witness physical injury
  - or under zone-of-danger or foreseeability tests
  - [63]traditional law also allows pure-emotional-distress claims for negligent mishandling of corpses
    - and for negligent transmission of death notices
    - and for fear of illness but only with severe distress and transmission route
- [64]The law may allow prenatal-harm claims if the child is born alive or was viable at injury
  - not generally against the mother
  - [65]law may allow claims for wrongful conception (limited to the cost of pregnancy and delivery)
  - law may allow claims for wrongful birth (negligent failure to inform to abort)
    - but not wrongful life by the child except possibly for extraordinary expenses

Negligence—Breach

[67]plaintiff has burdens
- pleading breach,
- producing breach evidence, and
- proving breach by a preponderance of the evidence = 51/49 = more probable than not

[66]breach = failure to use reasonable care = violation of standard of care
- prove by direct or circumstantial evidence
  - including constructive notice
  - including presumptions from spoliation (destruction) of evidence
    - parties have a duty to preserve evidence when reasonably anticipating litigation

WEEK 8 RES IPSA LOQUITUR, VIOLATION OF STATUTE, & CAUSATION (CAUSE-IN-FACT)

- [68]may also prove breach by res ipsa loquitur providing an inference of negligence if

- o the event speaks of negligence,
- o plaintiff cannot obtain negligence evidence, and
- o defendant controls the circumstances (may need *exclusive* control)
- [69]may also prove breach by violation of safety statute protecting plaintiff's class against the injury risk
  - o negligence per se (defendant must excuse) or
  - o presumption of negligence (defendant must come forward with evidence of care) or
  - o inference of negligence (jury may find defendant negligent without further proof)
- [70]violation of industry standards permits an inference of negligence

Negligence—Causation

[71]plaintiff must show the breach was (1) a cause in fact of harm and also (2) a legal or proximate cause

- [72]remember the eggshell-skull rule = pay for all harm if at least some harm was direct and foreseeable

[73]Cause in fact

- but-for test is main test for cause in fact (but for the negligence, the injury would not have occurred)
  - o medical, legal, technical, and scientific matters may require expert testimony
    - base expertise on valid & reliable scientific methods (peer review, testing, replication)

WEEK 9 CAUSE-IN-FACT (CONTINUED) & LEGAL OR PROXIMATE CAUSE

- [74]use substantial-factor test when 2+ causes would each have caused harm independent of the other
- [75]When the plaintiff cannot determine which of two negligent actors brought about the harm, the law may shift to defendants the burden of disproving causation or even offer a market-share theory for multiple manufacturers.

[76]Legal or proximate cause (more of judge than jury question)

- asks whether the breach led in *direct sequence* to harm (traditional bang-bang test)
  - o or risk of harm was *reasonably foreseeable* (modern test) (reaches remote causes)
- [77]tests for spreading fires vary
  - o from adjoining-property and first-building rules to much larger distances in rare cases

WEEK 10 LEGAL OR PROXIMATE CAUSE (CONTINUED) & PROFESSIONAL NEGLIGENCE (DUTY)

- [78]extraordinary, unforeseeable, independent events can supersede prior negligence
  - o cuts off proximate cause
  - o especially (although not always) for intentional, criminal, and reckless acts
    - [79]if the intentional or criminal act is what makes an actor in special relationship negligent, then the intentional or criminal act is less likely to cut off proximate cause
- [80]injured rescuers may hold liable the negligent actor who created the need for rescue
  - o but not professional rescuers (firefighter rule) in many states (they get worker's compensation)
- [81]actors whose negligence create need for medical care are liable for injury from that medical care
  - o including injury from medical malpractice

- [82]intoxicated person's voluntary drinking cuts off proximate cause as to the negligent server
  - but dram-shop statutes provide liability for injury to a third party from furnishing alcohol to
    - a minor or
    - visibly intoxicated person
- [83]unpredictable forces of nature may cut off proximate cause as to prior negligence,
  - but proximate cause remains where the force was foreseeable

Malpractice (Professional Negligence)
[84]professionals are liable for harm resulting from breaches of customary practice under the same circumstances
- treat like a negligence claim (duty, breach, causation, & damages) with a special standard of care:
- Duty arises when the professional relationship forms, not just with affirmative acts
  - [85]professionals do not owe a duty to come to the aid or rescue of another
    - unless employed at that time for that purpose,
  - but Good Samaritan statutes may protect those who do
  - [86]no duty to third parties except where service is for the third party's direct benefit
    - example: lawyer's preparation of a will
    - [87]mental-health care providers owe duties to warn foreseeable victims of patients' particularized threats of imminent violence
  - [88]medical-care provider having charge of a person may owe a duty to prevent that person's suicide

WEEK 11   PROFESSIONAL NEGLIGENCE (CONTINUED)
  - [89]professional's standard of care requires a similarly qualified expert's testimony
    - except in the rare case of obvious breach.
  - [90]Professionals who breach the standard of care causing injury are liable in tort, not contract
    - unless guaranteeing the result
  - [91]testifying expert must show knowledge of practice in the same or similar locale
    - except as to defendant specialists who have a national standard (national board exams)
- [92]causation in malpractice cases ordinarily requires expert testimony
  - must show what would have happened if the defendant had complied with the standard of care
  - [93]In lawyer malpractice (legal malpractice), plaintiff proves what would have happened in the underlying case if the defendant had not committed malpractice (suit within a suit)
- [94]Medical malpractice includes failure to obtain informed consent when
  - defendant did not disclose a risk that customary practice required disclosing,
  - about which a reasonable patient would have wanted to know, and
  - to which the plaintiff would not have consented
- [95]no consent at all may be battery in addition to malpractice
- [96]medical-care providers must disclose conflicts of interest when
  - may affect their judgment and
  - about which the patient would want to know

WEEK 12   PREMISES LIABILITY

Premises Liability

[97]in most states requires classifying the plaintiff as an invitee, licensee, or trespasser
- [101]status can change depending on activities, purpose, and scope or duration of permission
- some states require reasonable care as to all, abolishing classifications
- [98]landowners may have statutory immunity as to individuals using the land for recreational purposes
- [99]tenants controlling the premises owes the duties,
  - so do landlords who retain control, contract to repair, repair negligently, fail to disclose defects

[100]Invitees = those who enter for pecuniary purposes or accompany others who do = reasonable care
- [102]reasonable care may include the duty to
  - design,
  - construct,
  - maintain,
  - repair,
  - warn, and
  - protect against unreasonably dangerous conditions on the premises
    - [103]landowners may advertise and assume duties to protect against the criminal acts
    - or owe those duties by special knowledge or relationship

[104]Licensees = non-pecuniary purposes (social guests) = warn of known hidden dangers of unreasonable risk

[105]Trespassers = no duty except as to
- children,
  - [106]but may owe children of tender years duty to protect against an attractive nuisance
    - modern formulations assess landowner's and child's relative knowledge of risk
- active operations,
- tolerated intruders,
- concealed artificial conditions, and
- discovered peril

[107]Landowners may owe limited duties to protect neighboring landowners and passersby
- from artificial or unreasonable dangers on the premises (encroaching structures, blocked vision, etc.)

WEEK 13 NEGLIGENCE DEFENSES (COMPARATIVE NEGLIGENCE & ASSUMPTION OF RISK)

Negligence—Defenses

[108]Contributory negligence = bars claims by the plaintiff at fault in any part for the plaintiff's own harm
- last-clear-chance and other doctrines soften the all-or-nothing contributory-negligence defense
- contributory negligence old, disfavored defense, replaced in 46 states by comparative negligence

[109]Comparative negligence = reduces plaintiff's damages by plaintiff's percentage fault
- pure form from 1 to 99%

- modified forms up to 49% or 50% then barring plaintiff's claim if plaintiff is equally or more at fault
- [110]statutes may further alter comparative negligence rules
    - such as by limiting the plaintiff's failure to wear a seatbelt to 5% comparative negligence (MI)
- [111]states adopting comparative negligence may abolish
    - last-clear-chance doctrine,
    - joint-and-several liability,
    - defendants' rights of contribution
- [112]some states (MI) allow factfinder to allocate fault to non-parties
    - reduces the plaintiff's damages accordingly
    - uncollectible portions plaintiff loses or some states (MI) shift in part to collectible defendants

[113]Assumption of risk bars plaintiff's claim if plaintiff voluntarily encountered known risk
- [114]express assumption of risk = statements or writings accepting a disclosed risk
    - unless adhesion contracts (unequal power or public policy prohibits)
- [115]implied assumption of risk = circumstances showing voluntary acceptance of known risk
    - some states abolish the defense with comparative negligence's adoption

Paragraph Outline

Introduction
[1]Tort law's primary policies are to deter and compensate. [2]Tort law classifies torts by the actor's state of mind, as (1) intentional torts, (2) torts of negligence, or (3) strict liability. [3]Tort practice seldom involves intentional torts because insurance does not ordinarily cover purposeful wrongs.

Intentional Torts Generally
[4]The seven intentional torts are assault, battery, false imprisonment, trespass to land and chattels, IIED, and conversion, the first five of which are traditional and the last two new. [5]The purpose or desire to harm (not just the intent to act), often but not always due to ill will or malice, is the first of three forms of intent. [6]Knowledge of substantial certainty of harm is a second form of intent, but knowledge of high probability of harm is intent only for IIED. [7]Transferred intent is a third form of intent, transferring among the five traditional intentional torts and from victim to victim. [8]Children and the mentally ill are liable for intentional torts if they know the nature of their act, but parents are generally not liable for a child's tort except by statute. [9]Mistake does not negate intent. [10]Plaintiffs prove damages that the defendant causes, but the law presumes nominal damages for assault, battery, false imprisonment, and trespass to land.

Assault and Battery
[11]Battery is an intentional contact harmful or offensive to the reasonable person. [12]Good motive or beneficial effect does not excuse a battery. [13]Contact with anything closely connected with the person satisfies the contact element of battery. [14]Assault is the reasonable apprehension of an imminent battery with the apparent present ability to carry it out. [15]Battery can be with or without an assault, and assault with or without battery. [16]Words (threats) alone are generally not enough for an assault unless combined with an overt act suggesting imminent harmful contact. [17]Learning about imminent contact after the contact occurs is not assault. The victim must apprehend the assault when it occurs.

False Imprisonment
[18]False imprisonment is intentional unauthorized restraint against will including refusal to release from confinement when law requires. [19]The restraint is ordinarily by force but may also be subjecting the victim to unreasonable danger on escape or risking loss of property. [20]A known, reasonably safe means of escape means that there is no false imprisonment. [21]The victim must know of the restraint for it to be false imprisonment.

IIED
[22]Intentional infliction of emotional distress is a newer tort requiring proof of outrageous conduct and severe distress. [23]Outrageous conduct is that which is beyond all bounds of decency in civil society. [24]The conduct for IIED must be intentional (including recklessness), meaning that it must be directed to cause the plaintiff severe distress. [25]Repetition may make the conduct more outrageous, as may the conduct's location and duration, and relationship between perpetrator and victim. [26]The conduct must be outrageous to the reasonable person, but the actor's knowledge that the victim is unusually susceptible may make the conduct more outrageous.

Trespass to Land and Chattels
[27]Trespass to land is intentional interference with exclusive possession of land or intentional unauthorized physical entry onto another's land. [28]Mistaken entries (boundaries unknown) are still trespass if intentional. [29]The law presumes damages from the interference except when the

entry is intangible, in which case plaintiff must prove damages. [30]The nuisance tort addresses interference with use and enjoyment (noise, smoke, light, smell) rather than exclusive possession. [31]A public nuisance interferes with public enjoyment, while private nuisance substantially affects enjoyment of private lands. [32]Where no actual damage occurs from trespass, the law awards nominal and in egregious cases punitive damages. [33]Trespass to land includes defendant exceeding the scope or duration of consent to entry on the land and entry into immediate reaches above or subsurface areas beneath the land. [34]Trespass to chattels is intentional interference with exclusive possession of personal property, compensated by lost-use value.

Conversion
[35]Conversion is intentional dominion over personal property substantially or totally interfering with the other's control, compensated by value at conversion. [36]Conversion involves substantial deprivation or destruction, whereas trespass to chattels involves temporary or partial diminution in value. [37]The owner of converted property may recover from the original converter and subsequent holders taking in good or bad faith.

Intentional-Tort Defenses
[38]Consent expressed by words or communicative actions is a defense to an intentional tort. [39]The law determines consent from an objective rather than subjective standpoint, meaning what a reasonable person would have concluded. [40]To consent, a person must understand the conduct and risks, although parents may give substituted consent for treatment of children. [41]Emergency medical-care providers may treat those who are unable to give or withhold consent if the reasonable person would have consented. [42]Consent to an illegal act, and consent obtained by fraud or duress, are invalid. [43]Defendants have the burden of proof on each element of affirmative defenses. [44]Self-defense and defense of others against physical injury authorizes reasonable force even likely when reasonably mistaken, although not retaliation after the threat ends. [45]The law may require retreat before use of force likely to cause serious injury or death, although possibly not from the home. [46]One may use reasonable force to defend property if the force is not likely to cause death or serious injury but not when mistaken. [47]One must make a demand before using reasonable force to recover property unless demand would be futile and only in fresh pursuit about the premises. [48]The law allows repossession from the land of another only without force and only by agreement or summary proceedings. [49]Public necessity is a complete defense to property damage, but private necessity requires payment of actual damage. [50]Authority of law, discipline, and justification are defenses, where law authorizes or circumstances warrant the action.

Negligence—Duty
[51]The elements of a negligence claim are duty, breach, causation, and damages. [52]The duty to use reasonable care (that of a reasonably prudent person), determined by judge rather than jury, arises whenever acts, omissions, or status create foreseeable risk of harm. [53]The duty to protect against depends on past experience of crime, offers of security, available means of protection, and foreseeability. [54]Standards of care depend on factors including custom, regulations, standards, experience, and likelihood and foreseeability of injury. [55]Emergencies and other circumstances alter the standard of care to the circumstances except as to the one who created the circumstances. [56]The reasonably prudent person assumes the actor's physical, not mental, characteristics, except those with superior knowledge must use it. [57]Children owe the care that we expect of reasonable children of like age and experience, except that children engaged in adult activities owe adult duties. [58]Learned Hand's formula provides that liability exists when the burden of precautions is less than loss probability times loss magnitude. [59]A contract promisor owes a tort duty to a third party only when the promisor performs the contract (misfeasance, not

nonfeasance). [60]Without special relationship, tort law imposes no duty to rescue or aid another unless one created the need, assumes a duty, or controls the instrumentality. [61]The economic-loss doctrine limits duties to direct injury, barring pure economic loss claims by those who suffer no physical impact. [62]Pure-emotion-distress claims are for manifestly severely distressed family members contemporaneously witnessing physical injury, or under zone-of-danger or foreseeability tests. [63]Traditional law also allows pure-emotional-distress claims for negligent mishandling of corpses and transmission of death notices, and fear of illness with severe distress and transmission route. [64]The law may allow prenatal-harm claims if the child is born alive or was viable at injury, but not generally against the mother. [65]The law may allow claims for wrongful conception (limited to the cost of pregnancy and delivery) and wrongful birth (negligent failure to inform to abort) but not wrongful life by the child except possibly for extraordinary expenses.

Negligence—Breach
[66]One proves breach of duty, meaning failing to use reasonable care, by direct or circumstantial evidence including constructive notice and presumptions from spoliation of evidence. [67]The plaintiff has the burden of pleading breach, producing breach evidence, and proving breach by a preponderance of the evidence. [68]Res ipsa loquitur may permit an inference of negligence if the event speaks of negligence, plaintiff cannot obtain negligence evidence, and defendant controls the circumstances. [69]Violation of safety statute is negligence per se (the majority position) or permits a presumption or inference of negligence, where the statute protects the plaintiff's class against the injury risk. [70]Violation of industry standards permits an inference of negligence.

Negligence—Causation
[71]Causation requires plaintiff to show that the breach more probably than not was a cause in fact (but-for cause) of harm and also legal or proximate cause. [72]The eggshell-skull rule requires defendant to pay for all foreseeable and unforeseeable harm if at least some harm was direct and foreseeable. [73]Cause in fact on medical, legal, technical, and scientific matters may require expert testimony based on valid and reliable scientific methods. [74]The substantial-factor test determines cause in fact when two or more causes would each have brought about the harm independent of the other. [75]When the plaintiff cannot determine which of two negligent actors brought about the harm, the law may shift to defendants the burden of disproving causation or even offer a market-share theory for multiple manufacturers. [76]Legal or proximate cause, more of a judge than jury question, asks whether the breach led in direct sequence to harm or risk of harm was reasonably foreseeable. [77]Proximate-cause tests for spreading fires vary from adjoining-property and first-building rules to much larger distances in rare cases. [78]Extraordinary, unforeseeable, independent events, including intentional, criminal, and reckless acts, can supersede prior negligence and cut off proximate cause. [79]If a foreseeable intentional or criminal act is what makes an actor in special relationship negligent, then the intentional or criminal act is less likely to cut off proximate cause. [80]An injured rescuer, other than a professional rescuer, may hold liable the negligent actor who created the need for rescue. [81]An actor whose negligence creates a need for medical care may be held liable for injury from that medical care. [82]An intoxicated person's voluntary drinking cuts off proximate cause as to the negligent server, but dram-shop statutes may provide liability for injury to a third party from furnishing alcohol to a minor or visibly intoxicated person. [83]Unpredictable forces of nature may cut off proximate cause as to prior negligence, but proximate cause remains where the force was foreseeable.

Malpractice
[84]Malpractice or professional negligence holds professionals liable for harm resulting from breaches of customary practice under the same circumstances. Duty arises when the professional

relationship forms, not just with affirmative acts. [85]Professionals do not owe a duty to come to the aid or rescue of another unless employed at that time for that purpose, but Good Samaritan statutes may protect those who do. [86]Professionals do not owe duties to third parties except where their service is for the third party's direct benefit as in a lawyer's preparation of a will. [87]Mental-health care providers owe duties to warn foreseeable victims of patients' particularized threats of imminent violence. [88]A medical-care provider or other professional having charge of a person may owe a duty to prevent that person's suicide. [89]The professional's standard of care requires a similarly qualified expert's testimony except in the rare case of obvious breach. [90]Professionals who breach the standard of care causing injury are liable in tort, not contract, unless guaranteeing the result. [91]The law may require an expert testifying in a malpractice case to show knowledge of practice in the same or similar locale except as to defendant specialists who have a national standard. [92]Causation in malpractice cases ordinarily requires expert testimony as to what would have happened if the defendant had complied with the standard of care. [93]In lawyer malpractice, the plaintiff proves what would have happened in the underlying case if the defendant had not committed malpractice. [94]Medical malpractice includes failure to obtain informed consent to a risk that the custom required disclosing, about which a reasonable patient would have wanted to know, and to which the plaintiff would not have consented. [95]A medical-care provider's failure to obtain any consent at all may be battery in addition to malpractice. [96]Medical-care providers must disclose conflicts of interest that may affect their judgment and about which the patient would want to know.

Premises Liability
[97]Premises liability in most states requires classifying the plaintiff as an invitee, licensee, or trespasser, although some states require reasonable care as to all. [98]Landowners may have limited statutory immunity from negligence claims by individuals using the land for recreational purposes. [99]A tenant controlling the premises owes the duties, but so do landlords who retain control, contract to repair, repair negligently, and fail to disclose defects. [100]Landowners owe reasonable care to invitees, meaning those who enter for pecuniary purposes or accompany others who do so. [101]A person's status can change from invitee to licensee to trespasser, depending on their activities and purpose, and scope of permission. [102]Reasonable care may include the duty to design, construct, maintain, repair, warn, and protect against unreasonably dangerous conditions on the premises. [103]Landowners may advertise and assume duties to protect against the criminal acts of others, or owe those duties by special knowledge or relationship. [104]Landowners owe licensees, meaning those who enter for their own non-pecuniary purposes, like social guests and law officers, a duty to warn of known hidden dangers creating unreasonable risk. [105]Landowners owe trespassers no duty except as to children, active operations, tolerated intruders, concealed artificial conditions, and discovered peril. [106]Landowners traditionally owed children of tender years a duty to protect against an attractive nuisance, but modern formulations assess the landowner's knowledge of the risk and child's ability to recognize it. [107]Landowners may owe limited duties to protect neighboring landowners and passersby from artificial or unreasonable dangers on the premises.

Negligence—Defenses
[108]Contributory negligence barred claims by the plaintiff at fault in part in the plaintiff's own harm, while the last-clear-chance and other doctrines softened the all-or-nothing defense. [109]Comparative negligence reduces plaintiff's damages by plaintiff's percentage fault, the pure form from 1 to 99% but modified forms up to 50% then barring the claim. [110]Statutes may further alter comparative negligence rules, such as by limiting the plaintiff's failure to wear a seatbelt to 5% comparative negligence. [111]States adopting comparative negligence may abolish the last-clear-chance doctrine, joint-and-several liability, defendants' rights of contribution, and related doctrines. [112]Some states allow the factfinder to allocate fault to non-parties, reducing the

plaintiff's damages accordingly. [113]Assumption of risk bars plaintiff's claim if plaintiff voluntarily encountered and accepted hazards of a known risk. [114]Express assumption of risk involves statements or writings accepting a disclosed risk unless barred as adhesion contracts, by unequal power, or by public policy. [115]The law may also imply assumption of risk from circumstances showing the plaintiff's voluntary acceptance of a known risk, although some states abolished the defense with comparative negligence's adoption.

Torts I Workbook

Week 1
Policy, Intent, and Battery

BULLET OUTLINE FOR WEEK 1:
POLICY, INTENT, & BATTERY
Introduction
[1]Tort law policies (rationales, justifications)
- deter (discourage conduct that causes personal injuries and property damage)
- compensate (restore the person suffering loss to the extent able)

[2]Tort law classifications (depends on the wrongdoer's state of mind):
- intentional torts (purposeful wrongs)
  - [3]Tort practice seldom involves intentional torts
    - insurance does not ordinarily cover purposeful wrongs
- torts of negligence (carelessness, breaches of ordinary care)
  - this area is the heart of tort practice because of liability insurance
- strict liability (loss without respect to intent or fault, even with all due care)
  - Torts II subject

Intentional Torts Generally
[4]Seven intentional torts (the first five ABFiTT are traditional, the last two new):
- assault,
- battery,
- false imprisonment,
- trespass to land,
- trespass to chattels,
- intentional infliction of emotional distress (IIED), and
- conversion.

Three forms of intent:
- [5]purpose or desire to harm (not just the intent to act but the intent to harm)
  - often but not always due to ill will or malice
- [6]knowledge of substantial certainty of harm (KSC)
  - recklessness, or knowledge of high probability of harm, is intent only for IIED
- [7]transferred intent
  - transfers among the five traditional intentional torts ABFiTT
  - also transfers from victim to victim

[8]Children and the mentally ill are liable for intentional torts if they know the nature of their act.
- parents are generally not liable for a child's tort except by statute
  - statutes tend to cap parent liability at amounts around $2,500 to $5,000

[9]Mistake does not negate intent
- the actor is still liable if thinking incorrectly, even reasonably, that the act is lawful

[10]The law presumes nominal damages for four of the five traditional intentional torts (ABFiT)
- presumed damages can be nominal ($1, $10, $100) or substantial ($1,000, $10K, $100K)
- no presumed damages for trespass to chattels
- prove actual damages if you have them; don't only rely on the presumption

Assault and Battery

[11]Battery = intentional contact harmful or offensive to the reasonable person (IHOC)
- any of the three forms of intent (desire to harm, KSC, or transferred intent) will do
- [12]good motive or beneficial effect does not excuse a battery
- [13]contact with anything closely connected with the person satisfies the contact element

PARAGRAPH OUTLINE FOR WEEK 1:

Introduction

[1]Tort law's primary policies are to deter and compensate. [2]Tort law classifies torts by the actor's state of mind, as (1) intentional torts, (2) torts of negligence, or (3) strict liability. [3]Tort practice seldom involves intentional torts because insurance does not ordinarily cover purposeful wrongs.

Intentional Torts Generally

[4]The seven intentional torts are assault, battery, false imprisonment, trespass to land and chattels, IIED, and conversion, the first five of which are traditional and the last two new. [5]The purpose or desire to harm (not just the intent to act), often but not always due to ill will or malice, is the first of three forms of intent. [6]Knowledge of substantial certainty of harm is a second form of intent, but knowledge of high probability of harm is intent only for IIED. [7]Transferred intent is a third form of intent, transferring among the five traditional intentional torts and from victim to victim. [8]Children and the mentally ill are liable for intentional torts if they know the nature of their act, but parents are generally not liable for a child's tort except by statute. [9]Mistake does not negate intent. [10]Plaintiffs prove damages that the defendant causes, but the law presumes nominal damages for assault, battery, false imprisonment, and trespass to land.

Battery

[11]Battery is an intentional contact harmful or offensive to the reasonable person. [12]Good motive or beneficial effect does not excuse a battery. [13]Contact with anything closely connected with the person satisfies the contact element of battery.

Fluency Cards for Week 1

Cover and uncover the response to each prompt until you fluently recall the exact response.

Tort Law Policy

Deter (encourage safety) and compensate (improve welfare).

Classes of Torts

Intentional torts, negligence, and strict liability. No insurance for intentional torts.

Intentional Torts

Assault, battery, false imprisonment, trespass to land, and trespass to chattels, and new torts IIED and conversion.

Forms of Intent

Desire to harm, knowledge of substantial certainty of harm, & transferred intent among the five traditional intentional torts.

The Mentally Ill

Liable for their intentional torts if knowing what they do.

Parent Liability

Not liable for child's tort unless by statute for a small capped amount.

Mistake	**Presumed Damages**
Mistake does not negate intent.	Damages presumed for assault, battery, false imprisonment, and trespass to land.
Damages	**Battery**
Nominal and compensatory, plus punitive in some states.	Intentional contact harmful or offensive to the reasonable person.
Battery—Motive	**Battery—Contact**
Good motive or beneficial effect does not excuse battery.	Contact with things closely connected with the person is enough.

Definitions Worksheet for Week 1

Answer each question before checking your answers against the following answer key.

1. What are tort law's two primary policies? What other policies does it serve?

2. What are the three main torts classifications? Which does practice involve?

3. Name the seven intentional torts. Which are traditional and which are new?

4. Define the three forms of intent satisfying that element of an intentional tort.

5. When are children liable for intentional torts? When are parents liable for a child's tort?

6. How does law treat mistakes relating to intentional torts? Give an example.

7. Must the plaintiff prove damages for an intentional-tort claim? When?

8. What are battery's elements (its definition)? Does motive matter?

Answer Key for Definitions Worksheet

1. *What are tort law's two primary policies? Can you think of other policies it serves?* Tort law's primary policies are to deter and compensate.

2. *What are the three main torts classifications? Which classification does practice involve?* Tort law classifies torts by the actor's state of mind, as (1) intentional torts, (2) torts of negligence, or (3) strict liability. Tort practice involves almost solely negligence claims in large part because insurance does not ordinarily cover purposeful wrongs.

3. *Name the seven intentional torts. Which are traditional and which are new?* The seven intentional torts are assault, battery, false imprisonment, trespass to land and chattels, IIED, and conversion, the first five of which are traditional and the last two new.

4. *Define the three forms of intent satisfying that element of an intentional tort.* The purpose or desire to harm (not just the intent to act), often but not always due to ill will or malice, is the first of three forms of intent. Knowledge of substantial certainty of harm is a second form of intent (knowledge of high probability of harm is intent only for IIED). Transferred intent is a third form of intent, transferring among the five traditional intentional torts and from victim to victim.

5. *When are children liable for intentional torts? When are parents liable for a child's tort?* Children and the mentally ill are liable for intentional torts if they know the nature of their act. Parents are generally not liable for a child's tort except by statute.

6. *How does law treat mistakes relating to intentional-tort claims? Give an example.* Mistake does not negate intent. Mistake is not a defense to an intentional tort. A person who mistakenly hugs and kisses someone whom they thought was their spouse would be liable for the offense to the person hugged and kissed.

7. *Must the plaintiff prove damages for an intentional-tort claim?* Not generally. Plaintiffs may prove damages that the defendant causes, but the law presumes nominal damages for assault, battery, false imprisonment, and trespass to land.

8. *What are battery's elements (its definition)? Does motive matter?* Battery is an intentional contact harmful or offensive to the reasonable person. Good motive or beneficial effect does not excuse a battery.

Issue-Spotting Worksheet for Week 1

State the law each scenario raises. No analysis. Just spot the issue and state the law.

1. You meet with a seriously injured new client who begins by saying that she isn't sure that she should be meeting with you because she doesn't think she agrees with suing anyone.

2. Satisfied with your response, your client then describes a physical altercation with her ex-boyfriend in which she suffered injury to one of her eyes. She indicates strong interest in financial recovery from the ex-boyfriend for both wage loss and medical expense.

3. Concerned with your explanation of prospects for financial recovery, your client nonetheless asks about the legal theory or claim on which she could proceed.

4. Your client then further explains that she wasn't sure that her ex-boyfriend really meant to hurt her but might just have been angry, maybe trying to scare her by damaging some furniture, and just made a mistake.

5. Your client wants to know what financial recovery she might make.

6. Your client finally wants to know exactly what information you will need to prove her claim. When you explain, your client mentions that her ex-boyfriend didn't exactly strike her but did cause her to fall and strike a table by yanking hard on her handbag.

Answer Key to Issue-Spotting Worksheet

1. ***This scenario implicates tort law policies.*** Tort law's primary policies are to deter and compensate.

2. ***This scenario implicates tort-law classifications.*** Tort law classifies torts by the actor's state of mind, as (1) intentional torts, (2) torts of negligence, or (3) strict liability. Tort practice involves almost solely negligence claims in large part because insurance does not ordinarily cover purposeful wrongs.

3. ***This scenario implicates the list of intentional torts.*** The seven intentional torts are assault, battery, false imprisonment, trespass to land and chattels, IIED, and conversion, the first five of which are traditional and the last two new.

4. ***This scenario implicates the three forms of intent and the effect of mistake.*** The purpose or desire to harm (not just the intent to act), often but not always due to ill will or malice, is the first of three forms of intent. Knowledge of substantial certainty of harm is a second form of intent (knowledge of high probability of harm is intent only for IIED). Transferred intent is a third form of intent, transferring among the five traditional intentional torts and from victim to victim. Mistake does not negate intent. Mistake is not a defense to an intentional tort.

5. ***This scenario implicates damages for an intentional tort.*** Plaintiffs may prove damages that the defendant causes, but the law presumes at least nominal damages for assault, battery, false imprisonment, and trespass to land.

6. ***This scenario implicates the elements of battery.*** Battery is an intentional contact harmful or offensive to the reasonable person. Good motive or beneficial effect does not excuse a battery. Contact can be with anything closely associated with the person.

Sameness Exercise for Week 1

Sort the fact patterns into the correct form of intent: desire to harm (DH), knowledge of substantial certainty of harm (KSC), or transferred intent (TI).

_____ All that the golfer knew when he swung the club at and hit the caddie was that he wanted to see the caddie crumple to the ground in agony.

_____ The paintball shooter expected fleeing students to get hit with paint, but all that he really wanted to do was to paint the school's entrance with bright blue paintball dots.

_____ The quarterback was trying to bonk his buddy in the back when the quarterback threw the football into the stands but instead hit his buddy's girlfriend's head.

_____ The unpaid carpenter figured that a worker would get hurt when the structure collapsed as he jury-rigged it for revenge, but he hadn't expected the worker to die.

_____ The chef had wanted to sicken the arrogant diner with the chef's special-concoction dish, but the server accidentally gave the dish to the diner's unfortunate friend.

_____ The officer had so often chased the hoodlum to no avail that when he finally caught and tackled him, the officer gave the hoodlum a vicious kick, just to hear him scream.

_____ The disturbed forester had intended to cut down a few trees on the owner's woodlands but instead mistakenly cut down trees on the neighbor's lands.

_____ The boarding-school master took sadistic pleasure in hearing his young charges scream when he caught and paddled them hard for anything or nothing.

_____ The hooded robber took no concern for whether anyone of the victims got hurt when he sprayed the bank lobby with gunfire because he expected to get away with the money.

_____ The supervisor deliberately dropped the pallet to the floor behind the worker, from high off the hydraulic lift and with a loud bang, just to see the worker jump in fright.

_____ The farmer knew that the stream that he diverted would flood and make a mess of his rancher neighbor's feedlot, but the farmer felt that he had to save his crops.

_____ The hospital meant to restrain and hold the violent patient but accidentally misidentified the patient and instead restrained, held, and medicated a peaceful patient.

_____ The terrorist left the explosive device under the bridge expecting to destroy it while not caring whether the many tourists would die or get hurt like they did.

Answer Key for Sameness Exercise

DH: All that the golfer knew when he swung the club at and hit the caddie was that he wanted to see the caddie crumple to the ground in agony. *Notice the trigger words "wanted to see" suggesting desire.*

KSC: The paintball shooter expected fleeing students to get hit with paint, but all that he really wanted to do was to paint the school's entrance with bright blue paintball dots. *Notice the "expected" trigger word, showing knowledge, contrasted with the "all that he really wanted" phrase showing no desire to harm.*

TI: The quarterback was trying to bonk his buddy in the back when the quarterback threw the football into the stands but instead hit his buddy's girlfriend's head. *Notice the trigger words "trying," suggesting desire, but then "but instead," indicating a different victim, and thus transferred intent.*

KSC: The unpaid carpenter figured that a worker would get hurt when the structure collapsed as he jury-rigged it for revenge, but he hadn't expected the worker to die. *"Figured," meaning knowledge, but "for revenge" suggesting a different desire than harm.*

TI: The chef had wanted to sicken the arrogant diner with the chef's special-concoction dish, but the server accidentally gave the dish to the diner's unfortunate friend. *"Had wanted" showing desire to harm but "accidentally gave" showing a different victim.*

DH: The officer had so often chased the hoodlum to no avail that when he finally caught and tackled him, the officer gave the hoodlum a vicious kick, just to hear him scream. *Notice how motive suggests desire to harm, here.*

TI: The disturbed forester had intended to cut down a few trees on the owner's woodlands but instead mistakenly cut down trees on the neighbor's lands. *"Had intended" and "instead mistakenly" are the key transferred-intent words.*

DH: The boarding-school master took sadistic pleasure in hearing his young charges scream when he caught and paddled them hard for anything or nothing. *"Sadistic pleasure" is a clear desire-to-harm trigger.*

KSC: The hooded robber took no concern for whether anyone of the victims got hurt when he sprayed the bank lobby with gunfire because he expected to get away with the money. *"Took no concern" eliminates desire to harm but establishes knowledge.*

DH: The supervisor deliberately dropped the pallet to the floor behind the worker, from high off the hydraulic lift and with a loud bang, just to see the worker jump in fright. *"Deliberately" and "just to see" show intent to scare (assault).*

KSC: The farmer knew that the stream that he diverted would flood and make a mess of his rancher neighbor's feedlot, but the farmer felt that he had to save his crops. *"Knew" and "but felt" rule in knowledge and rule out desire to harm.*

TI: The hospital meant to restrain and hold the violent patient but accidentally misidentified the patient and instead restrained, held, and medicated a peaceful patient. *"Meant to" and "but accidentally" are the key phrases ruling in intent but requiring transfer to unintended victim.*

KSC: The terrorist left the explosive device under the bridge expecting to destroy it while not caring whether the many tourists would die or get hurt like they did. *"Expecting to" and "not caring" rule in knowledge and rule out desire to harm.*

Practice-Development Exercise for Week 1

Working with another student as your putative law partner, decide on a practice-development plan for tort and insurance practice, by reading and completing the following guide. Do not hesitate to revisit and change your decisions as you complete the guide.

1. Tort practice involves representing injured persons or allegedly negligent parties when retained by an insurance company to do so. Working on both sides is possible but presents conflicts of interest when you make a demand for an injured person who has retained you, and the person or entity on whom you make the demand turns out to have the insurance company who *used to* assign you cases to defend. Insurance companies often promptly stop sending you cases when learning that you are working on the other side. We plan to represent (check all that apply): ___ only injured persons; ___ only allegedly negligent parties; ___ both injured persons and allegedly negligent parties.

2. Plaintiff's lawyers (also called *trial lawyers* or *personal-injury lawyers*) represent injured persons on contingency fees, meaning that the lawyer recovers a percentage, often one third, only when the injured person recovers. If no recovery, then no fee. Plaintiff's lawyers must also usually advance expenses of a case, meaning that the lawyer may expend hundreds of hours and tens of thousands of dollars before collecting any fee. Risk, though, warrants reward. Plaintiff's lawyers are typically among the highest-paid of lawyers overall, and you are doing (free) work for those who need it, making an income out of nothing but pure justice. ___ Yes or ___ No: we plan to manage the risk to earn the reward of plaintiff's work.

3. Insurance companies typically pay defense counsel a relatively lower hourly rate but tend to send multiple cases to their approved lawyers and law firms, making for steady work. Some insurers pay a fixed fee of a few thousand dollars for each assigned case, rather than an hourly rate. Insurers paying hourly fees may require a litigation budget, trying to make defense counsel answer to the budget as much or more so than the client insured's case needs. In either case (fixed or hourly rates), defense lawyers get paid whether they win or lose, making the work less risky and the revenue stream relatively constant. ___ Yes or ___ No: we like the security and consistency of defense work, even though paying less and having less control over the case.

4. Plaintiff's lawyers depend on a broad reputation to connect with one-time-claimant clients. One gets no repeat business, although good work for one client can earn a reputation to attract another client. Advertising and community visibility can be important. By contrast, defense lawyers depend on good relationships with insurance-claim representatives who assign cases to approved counsel. Some lawyers work only for a single insurer, while other lawyers or law firms work for a few different insurers, earning all or much of their revenue from those insurers. Check either that apply: ___ we are willing and able to build a broad reputation to attract plaintiff's work; or ___ we are willing and able to network into professional relationships for defense work.

5. Plaintiff's work requires creating reliable accounts of complex events, using storytelling and dramatization skills. You are the producer and director, while your client and lay and expert witnesses are your star cast. By contrast, defense work tends to require challenging allegations and evidence to find the one critical defect in plaintiff's case—reactive rather than proactive work, poking holes rather than recreating stories of loss. Check either or both that apply: ___ we have the skills and passion for plaintiff's work; or ___ we have the skills and dispassion for defense work.

6. Lawyers generally get to choose their practice field or practice mix. You don't have to do any tort or insurance practice. You could, instead, make a practice of referring tort clients whom your other law practice attracts, to plaintiff's lawyers who may be able to pay you modest referral fees that increase your law firm's revenue. While you won't survive on referral fees, you may also get referrals back of clients whose other work you are glad to do. ___ Yes or ___ No: we plan to refer tort clients rather than do any tort work.

Record concluding thoughts here: _____

_____

_____

_____

# Problem-Solving Exercise Week 1

Think-aloud problem solving (TAPS) is a proven method of using vocalization to become a more creative and better problem solver. Professionals are effective problem solvers when they speak aloud to another, speaking aloud to themselves, or let their mental operations taking the silent form of words, concepts, principles, and strategies to reach partial solutions and then chain partial solutions toward final novel solution. Read the following example (EX) and non-example (NE) of an unknown new rule (RU), one that the judges writing their opinions and orders have not expressly stated but that you must instead discern and record as your problem solution. Vocalize each mental operation taken toward a partial solution, until you reach and record the final novel rule. Check your answer against the model answer at the bottom of the next page.

EX   OPINION AND ORDER: In this battery case, the plaintiff bar patron alleges that the defendant bartender intentionally served plaintiff a poisonous drink laced with bleach, resulting in plaintiff's serious injury. Plaintiff's evidence confirms the presence of bleach in her drink. No evidence indicates the bleach's source or any action or motive on the bartender's part. Plaintiff and defendant were strangers to one another with no prior interaction. Defendant through counsel has moved to dismiss, arguing that plaintiff has no evidence of defendant's intent. The Court grants defendant's motion, dismissing plaintiff's case with prejudice.

NE   OPINION AND ORDER: In this battery case, the plaintiff catering customer alleges that the defendant caterer intentionally served plaintiff's guests a poisonous custard laced with arsenic. No evidence indicates the arsenic's source or any action defendant caterer took to introduce the arsenic. Plaintiff had disputed defendant's charges before the catered event. Defendant has moved to dismiss, arguing that plaintiff has no evidence of defendant's intent. The Court denies defendant's motion, setting plaintiff's claim for jury trial.

RU   _____

_____

_____

_____

Answer: In a battery case involving food poisoning, plaintiff must produce some evidence that defendant intended to poison the food, beyond the mere evidence that the food contained the poison. Poison alone is not enough.

Week 2

Assault, False Imprisonment, & IIED

BULLET OUTLINE FOR WEEK 2:
ASSAULT, FALSE IMPRISONMENT, & IIED

[14]Assault = reasonable apprehension of an imminent battery with the apparent present ability (RAI IHOC APA)
- [15]battery can be with or without an assault, and assault with or without battery
- [16]words (threats) alone are generally not enough for an assault
  - unless combined with an overt act suggesting imminent harmful contact
- [17]learning about imminent contact after the contact occurs is not assault
  - the victim must apprehend the assault when it occurs

False Imprisonment

[18]False imprisonment = intentional unauthorized restraint against will (URAW)
- includes false arrest = refusal to release from confinement when law requires
- [19]restraint is ordinarily by force
  - restraint may also be subjecting the victim to unreasonable danger on escape
    - [20]known, reasonably safe means of escape means no false imprisonment
  - restraint could possibly involve risking loss of property (holding another's purse, for instance)
- [21]victim must know of the restraint

Intentional Infliction of Emotional Distress (IIED)

[22]IIED requires proof of *outrageous conduct* and *severe distress*
- [24]intent for IIED must be to cause the victim severe distress
  - recklessness (knowledge of a high probability of harm) will do
- [23]outrageous conduct = beyond all bounds of decency in civil society
  - [25]repetition may make the conduct more outrageous
    - so may the conduct's location and duration
    - so may the relationship between perpetrator and victim (like supervisor to subordinate)
  - [26]The conduct must be outrageous to the reasonable person
    - but knowledge that the victim is unusually susceptible can make the conduct outrageous

PARAGRAPH OUTLINE FOR WEEK 2:

Assault. [14]Assault is the reasonable apprehension of an imminent battery with the apparent present ability to carry it out. [15]Battery can be with or without an assault, and assault with or without battery. [16]Words (threats) alone are generally not enough for an assault unless combined with an overt act suggesting imminent harmful contact. [17]Learning about imminent contact after the contact occurs is not assault. The victim must apprehend the assault when it occurs.

False Imprisonment
[18]False imprisonment is intentional unauthorized restraint against will including refusal to release from confinement when law requires. [19]The restraint is ordinarily by force but may also be subjecting the victim to unreasonable danger on escape or risking loss of property. [20]A known, reasonably safe means of escape means that there is no false imprisonment. [21]The victim must know of the restraint for it to be false imprisonment.

IIED
[22]Intentional infliction of emotional distress is a newer tort requiring proof of outrageous conduct and severe distress. [23]Outrageous conduct is that which is beyond all bounds of decency in civil society. [24]The conduct for IIED must be intentional (including recklessness), meaning that it must be directed to cause the plaintiff severe distress. [25]Repetition may make the conduct more outrageous, as may the conduct's location and duration, and relationship between perpetrator and victim. [26]The conduct must be outrageous to the reasonable person, but the actor's knowledge that the victim is unusually susceptible may make the conduct more outrageous.

Fluency Cards for Week 2

Cover and uncover the response to each prompt until you fluently recall the exact response.

Assault	**Assault v Battery**
Reasonable apprehension of imminent battery with apparent present ability to carry it out.	Battery can be with or without assault and assault with or without battery.

Assault—Words Alone	**False Imprisonment**
Words alone are not enough unless combined with acts suggesting imminent harmful contact.	Intentional unauthorized restraint against will.

False Imprisonment-- Restraint	**IIED**
Usually force but can include unreasonable danger on escape. Victim must know of restraint.	Intentional or reckless outrageous conduct beyond all bounds of decency causing severe distress.

Definitions Worksheet for Week 2

Answer each question before checking your answers against the following answer key.

1. In review, describe the three forms of intent as an intentional-tort element.

2. In review, what are the three elements of battery? Briefly define each.

3. Define assault. Be sure your definition includes each element.

4. Define false imprisonment. Be sure your definition includes all elements.

5. Define intentional infliction of emotional distress, including all its elements.

6. Extra credit: how does the intent element differ for IIED? Explain.

Answer Key for Definitions Worksheet

1. *In review, describe the three forms of intent satisfying that element of intentional torts.* Intent includes the purpose or desire to harm (as in malice), knowledge of substantial certainty of harm, or transferred intent both from victim to victim or traditional intentional tort to traditional intentional tort.

2. *In review, what are the three elements of battery? Briefly define each.* Battery's elements are intent, harm or offense, and contact. Intent may be in any of the above three forms. While either physical harm or dignitary offense will satisfy the second element, the offense must be reasonable, not just that of an unusually sensitive person. Contact must be physical but may be transmitted force rather than direct force and includes touching anything closely connected to the victim's body.

3. *Define assault. Be sure that your definition includes each element.* Assault is the reasonable apprehension of an imminent battery (intentional harmful or offensive contact) with the apparent present ability to carry it out. In effect, the victim must have a well-founded fear that the victim is about to suffer a battery, although an assault may occur without battery and battery without assault.

4. *Define false imprisonment. Once again, be sure your definition includes all elements.* False imprisonment is an intentional unauthorized restraint against will. Any of the three forms of intent will do. If law authorizes the restraint, then you have no false imprisonment. The restraint may be physical or merely coercive. If the putative victim agrees to the restraint or knows of a reasonably safe means of escape, then you do not have false imprisonment.

5. *Define intentional infliction of emotional distress, including all of its elements.* Intentional infliction of emotional distress, also known as the outrage tort, requires proof of intent, outrageous conduct beyond all bounds of decency in civil society, and severe distress, in some jurisdictions with physical manifestation of the distress. Not all jurisdictions recognize intentional infliction of emotional distress.

6. *Extra credit: how does the intent element differ for IIED? Explain.* While any one of the three traditional forms of intent (purpose or desire to harm, knowledge of a substantial certainty of harm, or transferred intent) will satisfy IIED's intent element, so will recklessness, which is knowledge of a high probability of harm.

Issue-Spotting Worksheet for Week 2
State the law each scenario raises. No analysis. Just spot the issue and state the law.

1. You meet with a new client who explains that he now suffers from severe post-traumatic stress disorder that is causing him to miss substantial work time. Having nearly exhausted his twelve weeks of medical leave, he fears that he will lose his job and needs to ensure that he can hold financially responsible the person who caused his severe distress. When you ask what happened, your client begins by saying that an apartment-complex neighbor whom he barely knew approached him late one evening looking like he was on drugs, pointing a handgun at him, and telling him to listen carefully and obey or he'd shoot.

___

2. Your client then describes that the neighbor motioned him to get in the back seat of a waiting car driven by an unknown third person. Your client obeyed, thinking that doing so was better than getting shot. The car immediately took off for parts unknown with both the driver and neighbor sitting in front silent. The car occasionally stopped at stoplights, when each time your client says he thought of jumping out and running but figured that doing so would only get him shot.

___

3. After driving around silently and what seemed aimlessly for a while, your client asked the driver and neighbor where they were going. The neighbor then explained that he and the driver were part of a satanic cult that required periodic human sacrifice and that your client was to be that sacrifice as soon as they could locate the other members of the cult. The neighbor further explained that the members would take a vote on whether to go through with the sacrifice after meeting your client and completing their incantations.

___

4. When you ask your client how the incident ended, your client explains that after driving just a little farther, the driver and neighbor burst out laughing, saying that the whole thing was a prank and that the gun was actually a toy and that they hoped he wasn't too upset. Your client was very upset and has since had recurrent nightmares, trouble sleeping, digestion troubles, and significant weight loss.

___

Answer Key for Issue-Spotting Worksheet

1. ***This scenario implicates the elements of assault.*** Assault is the reasonable apprehension of an imminent battery (intentional harmful or offensive contact) with the apparent present ability to carry it out. In other words, the victim must have a well-founded fear that the victim is about to suffer a battery. An assault may occur without battery and batter without assault.

2. ***This scenario implicates the elements of false imprisonment.*** False imprisonment is an intentional unauthorized restraint again will. Any of the three forms of intent will do. If law authorizes the restraint, then you have no false imprisonment. The restraint may be physical or merely coercive. If the putative victim agrees to the restraint or knows of a reasonably safe means of escape, then you do not have false imprisonment.

3. ***This scenario implicates the elements of intentional infliction of emotional distress.*** Intentional infliction of emotional distress, also known as the outrage tort, requires proof of intent, outrageous conduct beyond all bounds of decency in civil society, and severe distress. Not all states recognize intentional infliction of emotional distress.

4. ***This scenario implicates the lower form of intent IIED requires and IIED's physical-manifestation requirement.*** While any one of the three traditional forms of intent (purpose or desire to harm, knowledge of a substantial certainty of harm, or transferred intent) will satisfy IIED's intent element, so will recklessness, which is knowledge of a high probability of harm. Some states require physical manifestation of the severe distress. Examples would include weight gain or loss, hair loss, trembling, emesis, and even sleep disorders and nervousness.

Sameness Exercise for Week 2

Sort the fact patterns into assault (A), battery (B), false imprisonment (FI), or intentional infliction of emotional distress (IIED):

_____ Enraged at the shopper's refusal to leave at close, the clerk stepped out into the mall, closed and locked the store's entrance gate, and walked off, leaving the shopper trapped.

_____ The hunter aimed his rifle just up over the hiker's head and fired off a shot just to scare the hiker off, after the hiker ruined the hunter's three-hour wait for a deer.

_____ The drunken patron hauled back and took a wild swing at the bartender for the bartender's insult but accidentally struck the patron standing next to him.

_____ The bully dug up the fresh corpse of the neighbor kid's pet cat and propped it up on the kid's bedroom windowsill just to see the kid totally freak out.

_____ The client was so angry at the accountant's error that she stood up and flung her coffee at him, intending to douse him but just missing as he jumped back.

_____ To exact revenge, the woman paid an off-duty officer to go to her ex-boyfriend's home, arrest and handcuff him, and drive him by her home in the squad car.

_____ The rival stole her competitor's cell phone, downloaded some private selfies, and sent them to her competitor's friends to humiliate her into leaving town.

_____ The mechanic balanced a pail of used motor oil on the top of the half-open door so that it came crashing down on the supervisor's head as he left for the evening.

_____ The usher grew so tired of the patron pacing up and down the aisle that the usher slyly stuck a foot out to trip the patron, who crashed down the aisle to the usher's delight.

_____ The truant was so angry at the principal that the truant secretly took a photograph of the principal going to the bathroom and displayed it across the classroom marquees.

_____ The jealous backup, believing it would be the only way she'd ever get a chance, paid the custodian to bolt the stage star into her apartment so that she missed the show.

_____ Tired of the fan's heckling and intending to scare him off, the batter walked from the on-deck circle toward the fan with the bat raised in the batter's hand.

_____ The repairman was so angry at the bad language the stuck rider used over the emergency-service phone that the repairman had lunch before opening the elevator door.

Answer Key for Sameness Exercise

Battery (B) involves an intentional harmful or offensive contact. Assault (A) is reasonable apprehension of an imminent battery (intentional harmful or offensive contact) with the apparent present ability to carry it out. False imprisonment (FI) is intentional unauthorized restraint against will. Where recognized, intentional infliction of emotional distress (IIED) requires intent, outrageous conduct beyond all bounds of decency in civil society, and severe distress, in some jurisdictions with physical manifestation of the distress.

FI: Enraged at the shopper's refusal to leave at close, the clerk stepped out into the mall, closed and locked the store's entrance gate, and walked off, leaving the shopper trapped. *"Enraged" motive and "leaving the shopper trapped" are the key triggers.*

A: The hunter aimed his rifle just up over the hiker's head and fired off a shot just to scare the hiker off, after the hiker ruined the hunter's three-hour wait for a deer. *"Just to scare" is the key trigger phrase.*

B: The drunken patron hauled back and took a wild swing at the bartender for the bartender's insult but accidentally struck the patron standing next to him. *"Took a wild swing" and "for the bartender's insult" show intent and "but accidentally struck" show different victim.*

IIED: The bully dug up the fresh corpse of the neighbor kid's pet cat and propped it up on the kid's bedroom windowsill just to see the kid totally freak out. *"Just to see the kid totally freak out" shows intent and also confirms the outrageous nature of the conduct.*

A: The client was so angry at the accountant's error that she stood up and flung her coffee at him, intending to douse him but just missing as he jumped back. *"So angry that" shows intent, while "intending to douse but just missing" shows a different tort than the one intended.*

FI: To exact revenge, the woman paid an off-duty officer to go to her ex-boyfriend's home, arrest and handcuff him, and drive him by her home in the back of the squad car. *"To exact revenge" shows intent, while the "arrest and handcuff" in the squad car show restraint.*

IIED: The rival stole her competitor's cell phone, downloaded some private selfies, and sent them to her competitor's friends to humiliate her competitor into leaving town. *"To humiliate" shows intent, while "private selfies" and expected humiliation together show outrageousness.*

B: The mechanic balanced a pail of used motor oil on the top of the half-open door so that it came crashing down on the supervisor's head as he left for the evening. *"So that it came crashing down on the supervisor's head" shows intent to contact.*

B: The usher grew so tired of the patron pacing up and down the aisle that the usher slyly stuck a foot out to trip the patron, who crashed down the aisle to the usher's delight. *"Slyly stuck a foot out to trip" plus motive of growing tired shows intent to contact.*

IIED: The truant was so angry at the principal that the truant secretly took a photograph of the principal going to the bathroom and displayed it across the classroom marquees. *"So angry" suggests motive and therefore intent, while the bathroom and marquee suggest outrageousness.*

FI: The jealous backup, believing it would be the only way she'd ever get a chance, paid the custodian to bolt the stage star into her apartment so that she missed the show. *"Paid to bolt" and "so that she missed the show" are probably the key words here showing intent and restraint.*

A: Tired of the fan's heckling and intending to scare him off, the batter walked from the on-deck circle toward the fan with the bat raised in the batter's hand. *"Intending to scare him off" is the key phrase suggesting assault.*

FI: The repairman was so angry at the bad language the stuck rider used over the emergency-service phone that the repairman had lunch before opening the elevator door. *"So angry that" suggests purpose and therefore intent, while lunch before opening the door shows restraint.*

Review Exercise for Week 2
Match these facts with the law on the next page that the facts trigger.

Wow, what a day it had been. ____ 1. First, on her commute to work, she had seen a motorist use his large, off-road-looking vehicle as a battering ram to shove a car out of the way in what looked like a road-rage incident, hurting the car's driver. ____ 2. Then, when she got to work, she saw a boy, loosely attended by a distracted parent, mischievously trip an elderly customer, apparently causing the customer to break her leg in the fall. ____ 3. A store clerk who happened to have witnessed the tripping incident was explaining the elderly woman's legal rights to her as they waited for an ambulance. ____ 4. The boy's parent was apologizing profusely while saying something about homeowner's insurance. ____ 5. The parent was trying to explain to the elderly customer that the boy surely hadn't meant to do it, but the elderly customer wasn't so sure, and the boy also seemed to be admitting that he meant the trip, ____ 6. although he hadn't meant to hurt the elderly customer. ____ 7. When the store manager told her to interview the parent, boy, and customer, to make out an incident report, the boy explained that he had really only meant to scare the elderly customer, not to hurt her. ____ 8. The boy also indicated that he had thought that the elderly customer was his aunt with whom he often engaged in healthy horseplay. ____ 9. The boy even suggested that he was only trying to cheer up his aunt, whom he believed had been depressed lately over her husband, his uncle, passing away. ____ 10. By the time that the ambulance arrived, though, the elderly customer was feeling much better and, it turns out, hadn't broken or seriously hurt anything at all.

TORTS I WORKBOOK

Review Exercise for Week 2
Match this law with the facts on the prior page to which the law applies.

___A. Tort law's primary policies are to deter and compensate.

___B. Tort law classifies torts by the actor's state of mind, as (1) intentional torts, (2) torts of negligence, or (3) strict liability.

___C. Tort practice involves almost solely negligence claims in large part because insurance does not ordinarily cover purposeful wrongs.

___D. The purpose or desire to harm (not just the intent to act), often but not always due to ill will or malice, is the first of three forms of intent.

___E. Knowledge of substantial certainty of harm is a second form of intent (knowledge of high probability of harm is intent only for IIED).

___F. Transferred intent is a third form of intent, transferring among the five traditional intentional torts and from victim to victim.

___G. Children and the mentally ill are liable for intentional torts if they know the nature of their act. Parents are generally not liable for a child's tort except by statute.

___H. Mistake does not negate intent, as an element of an intentional tort.

___I. Tort law presumes nominal damages for assault, battery, false imprisonment, and trespass to land.

___J. Battery is an intentional contact harmful or offensive to the reasonable person. Good motive or beneficial effect does not excuse a battery.

Answer key: 1E, 2G, 3A, 4C, 5B, 6D, 7F, 8H, 9J, 10I

Torts I Workbook

Week 2 Drafting Exercise—Client Intake

Working with a seatmate, choose lawyer and client roles. The lawyer should then conduct what lawyers think of as a *client intake* or clients think of as an *initial free consultation*. Ordinarily, a first consultation with a personal-injury client takes a half hour to an hour. You will have only about ten minutes. The client's goal is to retain (for free, meaning contingency fee) the lawyer's services by relating the events giving rise to the claim. The lawyer's goal is to maintain the client's confidence to obtain a signed fee agreement (a subject for your ethics course but an example of which is in your torts book), while gathering enough information to ensure that the client has a claim. Lawyers often use intake forms or require that paralegal/legal assistant staff do so. Clients, relate information about a motor-vehicle accident that you experienced, know of, or imagine, in which someone else injured you through their fault. Lawyers, complete the intake form on the opposite side.

NEW CLIENT INTAKE FORM

PERSONAL:
NAME:_____ ALIASES/MAIDEN NAME:_____
HOME PHONE:_____ WORK PHONE:_____ CELL PHONE:_____
E-MAILS:_____/_____
HOME ADDRESS:_____
DATE OF BIRTH:_____ SOCIAL SECURITY NUMBER:_____

FAMILY:
MARRIED?___ SPOUSE'S NAME_____ SPOUSE'S EMPLOYER:_____
DIVORCED?_____ FORMER SPOUSE'S NAME:_____
CHILDREN?_____ NAME/AGE:_____ NAME/AGE:_____

EMPLOYMENT:
JOB TITLE/DESCRIPTION:_____
WAGES (HOURLY):_____ WAGES (ANNUAL):_____
EMPLOYER'S ADDRESS:_____

LEGAL SERVICE: CLAIM or DEFENSE
SUBJECT MATTER:_____
DATE CLAIM AROSE:_____ /LIMITATIONS PERIODS:_____ /EXPIRES ON:_____
OPPOSING PARTY:_____
OPPOSING PARTY'S ADDRESS:_____
OPPOSING PARTY'S LAWYER:_____
OPPOSING PARTY'S EMPLOYMENT/BUSINESS:_____
DESCRIPTION:_____

WITNESS:_____ /TELEPHONE/ADDRESS:_____
WITNESS:_____ /TELEPHONE/ADDRESS:_____
PHYSICIAN:_____ /ADDRESS:_____
BILLING: CONTINGENCY or HOURLY
REFERRING ATTORNEY:_____ REFERRAL FEE:_____
MARKETING: GOT OUR NAME FROM:_____
DISPOSITION: INSTRUCTIONS GIVEN TO CLIENT:_____
DECLINED:_____ / AT FIRST CONTACT or BY FOLLOW-UP TELEPHONE or BY CORRESPONDENCE INVESTIGATION UNDERTAKEN:_____
FILE OPENED?_____ FEE AGREEMENT?_____ CASE FILED?_____

Week 3
Trespass to Land and Chattels, & Conversion

BULLET OUTLINE FOR WEEK 3:
TRESPASS TO LAND AND CHATTELS, & CONVERSION
Trespass
[27]Trespass to land = intentional interference with exclusive possession of land (IIEP)
- alternative definition = intentional unauthorized physical entry onto another's land
- the entry must be intentional
  - careless skidding off road onto land is not trespass but would be negligence
- [28]mistaken entries (boundaries unknown) are still trespass
- [33]trespass includes defendant exceeding the scope or duration of consent to entry
  - trespass also includes entry into immediate reaches above or subsurface areas beneath the land
- [29]law presumes damages from the interference
  - exception when the entry is intangible, in which case plaintiff must prove damages
  - [32]where no actual damage occurs from trespass, the law awards at least nominal damages
    - in egregious cases, punitive damages may be available (not in Michigan)
- [30]nuisance is an alternative tort to trespass
  - addresses interference with use & enjoyment (noise, smoke, light, smell) not exclusive possession
  - [31]public nuisance interferes with public enjoyment (passersby)
    - private nuisance substantially affects enjoyment of private lands (neighbors)

[34]Trespass to chattels = intentional interference with exclusive possession of personal property (IIEPPP)
- must prove some damages / loss (different from trespass to land)
  - compensated by lost-use value

Conversion
[35]Conversion = intentional dominion over personal property substantially interfering with control (IDIC)
- think of it as the civil tort for theft
- compensated by value at conversion
- [36]involves substantial deprivation or complete destruction
  - contrast with trespass to chattels = temporary or partial diminution in value
- [37]owner of converted property may recover from the original converter and subsequent holders
  - doesn't matter whether subsequent holders take in good faith
  - don't buy from thieves

PARAGRAPH OUTLINE FOR WEEK 3:
Trespass to Land and Chattels

[27]Trespass to land is intentional interference with exclusive possession of land or intentional unauthorized physical entry onto another's land. [28]Mistaken entries (boundaries unknown) are still trespass if intentional. [29]The law presumes damages from the interference except when the entry is intangible, in which case plaintiff must prove damages. [30]The nuisance tort addresses interference with use and enjoyment (noise, smoke, light, smell) rather than exclusive possession. [31]A public nuisance interferes with public enjoyment, while private nuisance substantially affects enjoyment of private lands. [32]Where no actual damage occurs from trespass, the law awards nominal and in egregious cases punitive damages. [33]Trespass to land includes defendant exceeding the scope or duration of consent to entry on the land and entry into immediate reaches above or subsurface areas beneath the land. [34]Trespass to chattels is intentional interference with exclusive possession of personal property, compensated by lost-use value.

Conversion
[35]Conversion is intentional dominion over personal property substantially or totally interfering with the other's control, compensated by value at conversion. [36]Conversion involves substantial deprivation or destruction, whereas trespass to chattels involves temporary or partial diminution in value. [37]The owner of converted property may recover from the original converter and subsequent holders taking in good or bad faith.

Fluency Cards for Week 3

Cover and uncover the response to each prompt until you fluently recall the exact response.

Trespass to Land

Intentional interference with exclusive possession (or intentional unauthorized entry on land).

Trespass Damages

Nominal and presumed, but also prove them if you can.

Exceeding Scope

Exceeding scope of permission or duration is trespass.

Over or Under Land

Entry into immediate reaches above or beneath the land is trespass.

Trespass Mistake

Mistaking boundaries is still trespass.

Trespass to Chattels

Intentional impairment of personal property (less than full loss or destruction).

Trespass to Chattels—Damages

Lost use or diminished value (not presumed).

Conversion

Intentional full deprivation or destruction of personal property.

Subsequent Holders

Owner may recover from original converter and subsequent holders.
(Don't buy from thieves.)

Definitions Worksheet for Week 3

1. Define trespass to land. What if a person overstays a welcome or snoops?

2. How does trespass treat mistaken entries? Entries above or below the land?

3. How does law treat trespass damages? What if the owner has no damage?

4. Define nuisance in both forms. How does nuisance differ from trespass?

5. Define trespass to chattels. How does law compensate trespass to chattels?

6. Define conversion. How does conversion differ from trespass to chattels?

7. Can an owner recover stolen property from a buyer of it? What rule says so?

Answer Key for Definitions Worksheet

1. *Define trespass to land. What if a person overstays a welcome or snoops?* Trespass to land is intentional interference with exclusive possession of land or intentional unauthorized physical entry onto another's land. Trespass to land includes defendant exceeding the scope or duration of consent to entry on the land.

2. *How does trespass treat mistaken entries on land? Entries above or below the land?* Mistaken entries (boundaries unknown) are still trespass if intentional. Trespass includes entry into immediate reaches above or subsurface areas beneath the land.

3. *How does the law treat trespass damages? What if the landowner suffers no damages?* The law presumes damages from the interference except when the entry is intangible, in which case plaintiff must prove damages. Where no actual damage occurs from trespass, the law awards nominal damages. In egregious cases, law may permit punitive damages.

4. *Define nuisance in both of its forms. How is nuisance different from trespass to land?* The nuisance tort addresses interference with use and enjoyment of land (noise, smoke, light, smell) rather than interference with exclusive possession. A public nuisance interferes with public enjoyment, while private nuisance affects private lands.

5. *Define trespass to chattels. How does the law compensate trespass to chattels?* Trespass to chattels is intentional interference with exclusive possession of personal property, compensated by lost-use value.

6. *Define conversion. How does conversion differ from trespass to chattels?* Conversion is intentional dominion over personal property substantially or totally interfering with the other's control, compensated by value at conversion. Conversion involves substantial deprivation or destruction, whereas trespass to chattels involves temporary or partial diminution in value.

7. *When a person buys stolen property, can the owner recover it?* The owner of converted property may recover from the original converter and subsequent holders taking in good or bad faith.

Issue-Spotting Worksheet for Week 3

State the law each scenario raises. No analysis. Just spot the issue and state the law.

1. You meet with a new client who explains that one week when she was away on a business trip, her neighbor cut down trees, bushes, and shrubs, and other plantings that had formed a substantial privacy screen and entry barrier between their residences. Your client was sure that the vegetation had been on her land, not her neighbor's land, which she confirmed with a survey from her purchase file.

2. Your client then describes that when she confronted her neighbor, the neighbor protested that the vegetation was on his land, not hers. Your client promptly produced the survey, readily convincing the neighbor that he was wrong and that she was right.

3. Your client next explains that although her neighbor apologized, she learned from an arborist whom she consulted that replacing the vegetation would take many thousands of dollars and several years of time.

4. When you ask why your client is considering replacing the vegetation, your client explains that her neighbor has very loud parties very late at night, when she can often smell the smoke of marijuana. Strobe lights pulsating to raucous music and pops and flashes from fireworks keep her up and make her dog tremble and yowl.

5. When you ask if your client has had any other problems with her neighbor, she says that she suspects that her neighbor may have been responsible for staining her little white dog a bright yellow with hair dye, after her neighbor had complained about her dog urinating on his lawn. She also thinks that he may have stolen the dog's collar and trashed her bicycle that she may have left on his lawn.

Answer Key for Issue-Spotting Worksheet

1. ***This scenario implicates the definition of trespass to land.*** Trespass to land is intentional interference with exclusive possession of land or intentional unauthorized physical entry onto another's land. Trespass to land includes defendant exceeding the scope or duration of consent to entry on the land. Trespass also includes entry into immediate reaches above or subsurface areas beneath the land.

2. ***This scenario implicates the effect of mistaken trespasses.*** Mistaken entries, such as crossing an unknown or mistaken boundary line thinking that the property is one's own, are still trespass as long as the entry itself (the act of entering the land) is intentional. Mistake does not negate intent.

3. ***This scenario implicates trespass damages.*** The law presumes damages from the trespass except when the entry is intangible (smoke, for instance), in which case plaintiff must prove damages. Where no actual damage occurs from trespass, the law awards nominal damages. In egregious cases, law may permit punitive damages.

4. ***This scenario implicates the nuisance tort.*** The nuisance tort addresses interference with use and enjoyment of land (noise, smoke, light, smell) rather than interference with exclusive possession. A public nuisance interferes with public enjoyment, while private nuisance affects private lands.

5. ***This scenario implicates trespass to chattels or conversion.*** Trespass to chattels is intentional interference with exclusive possession of personal property, compensated by lost-use value. Conversion is intentional dominion over personal property substantially or totally interfering with the other's control, compensated by value at conversion. Conversion involves substantial deprivation or destruction, whereas trespass to chattels involves temporary or partial diminution in value.

Discrimination Worksheet for Week 3

Indicate whether each statement *overgeneralizes*, *undergeneralizes*, or *misconceives* the rule, explaining why. *Overgeneralizing* states the rule too broadly, capturing circumstances to which it does not apply. *Undergeneralizing* states the rule too narrowly, omitting circumstances to which it applies. *Misconceiving* states the rule incorrectly.

1. Trespass to land is interference with exclusive possession of land or unauthorized physical entry onto another's land.
    ____OVER/ ____UNDER/ ____MISS/ Why? _____
    _____

2. Trespass includes entry into subsurface areas beneath the land but not flyovers or other entries above the land.
    ____OVER/ ____UNDER/ ____MISS/ Why? _____
    _____

3. The law presumes trespass damages, meaning that the plaintiff needs no evidence of damage from the trespass interference.
    ____OVER/ ____UNDER/ ____MISS/ Why? _____
    _____

4. Like the trespass tort, the nuisance tort also addresses interference with exclusive possession of lands.
    ____OVER/ ____UNDER/ ____MISS/ Why? _____
    _____

5. Trespass to chattels is intentional interference with exclusive possession of vehicles or other transportation equipment, compensated by lost-use value.
    ____OVER/ ____UNDER/ ____MISS/ Why? _____
    _____

6. Conversion is intentional dominion over personal property totally depriving the owner of control, compensated by value at conversion.
    ____OVER/ ____UNDER/ ____MISS/ Why? _____
    _____

7. The owner of converted property may only recover from the original converter but not subsequent holders taking in good faith.
    ____OVER/ ____UNDER/ ____MISS/ Why? _____
    _____

Answer Key for Discrimination Worksheet

1. The statement **OVERgeneralizes** the rule. Trespass to land is *intentional* interference with exclusive possession of land or *intentional* unauthorized physical entry onto another's land. *Accidental entries are not trespass*, such as carelessly sliding a vehicle off of a slippery roadway onto land, although mistaken entries (boundary unknown) are still trespass if intentional.

2. The statement **UNDERgeneralizes** the rule. Trespass includes entry into *immediate reaches above the land* and subsurface areas beneath the land. A low-enough flyover or other entry such as shooting a gun across the land can constitute trespass.

3. The statement **OVERgeneralizes** the rule. The law presumes damages from the trespass interference *except when the entry is intangible, such as smoke, in which case plaintiff must prove damages*.

4. The statement **MISconceives** the rule. The nuisance tort addresses interference with *use and enjoyment* of land (*noise, smoke, light, smell*) rather than interference with *exclusive possession*. A public nuisance interferes with public enjoyment, while private nuisance affects private lands.

5. The statement **UNDERgeneralizes** the rule. Trespass to chattels is intentional interference with exclusive possession of *any personal property, beyond just transportation equipment*, compensated by lost-use value.

6. The statement **UNDERgeneralizes** the rule. Conversion is intentional dominion over personal property totally depriving the owner *or substantially interfering* with the owner's control, compensated by value at conversion. Conversion involves *substantial* deprivation or destruction, whereas trespass to chattels involves temporary or partial diminution in value.

7. The statement **MISconceives** the rule. The owner of converted property *may recover* from the original converter *and subsequent holders taking in good or bad faith*. The rule is *not to buy from thieves*.

Review Exercise for Week 3
Match these facts with the law on the next page that the facts trigger.

He didn't seem lately to be able to catch a break. ____ 1. First, his girlfriend—well, *ex*-girlfriend—had barred him in his bedroom after he'd said he didn't want to marry, requiring him to break down the door. ____ 2. She'd always been more-than-a-little bizarre from what she'd admitted was schizophrenia, but he hadn't thought she was *that* schizophrenic. ____ 3. He guessed he hadn't really lost that much, other than a few busted-out wood screws at the door's hinges, but he was sure angry enough to do something about it. ____ 4. She happened to work as a therapist and must have malpractice insurance, he figured, so maybe he'd make some claim against her just to settle the score and maybe get a little pocket change. ____ 5. Then, when he'd headed to the garage to get his car for work the next morning, he saw that vandals—probably that punk down the street who'd twice already been caught doing this sort of stuff—had spray painted embarrassing slurs on his garage. ____ 6. When he drove past the punk's house on his way to work and saw him sitting on the porch, he stopped and yelled at the punk that he had a shotgun in his house to take care of people who ruined his things. ____ 7. But the punk just yelled back that he had the wrong guy and, if he didn't stop, wouldn't mind messing up his face. ____ 8. When he continued his tirade, the punk got up and approached the car, shocking him that indeed, it wasn't the punk at all but someone else who looked like him. ____ 9. The man then punched him hard in the face, breaking his nose and glasses. Nope, just couldn't catch a break.

Review Exercise for Week 3

Match this law with the facts on the prior page to which the law applies.

___A. Tort practice involves almost solely negligence claims in large part because insurance does not ordinarily cover intentional wrongs. [Week 1]

___B. The purpose or desire to harm (not just the intent to act), often but not always due to ill will or malice, is the first of three forms of intent. [Week 1]

___C. The mentally ill are liable for intentional torts if they know the nature of their act. [Week 1]

___D. Mistake does not negate intent, as an element of intentional torts. [Week 1]

___E. Tort law presumes nominal damages for assault, battery, false imprisonment, and trespass to land. [Week 1]

___F. Battery is an intentional contact harmful or offensive to the reasonable person. Good motive or beneficial effect does not excuse a battery. [Week 1]

___G. Assault is the reasonable apprehension of an imminent battery with the apparent present ability to carry it out. [Week 2]

___H. False imprisonment is an intentional unauthorized restraint against will. [Week 2]

___I. Intentional infliction of emotional distress requires proof of intent, outrageous conduct beyond all bounds of decency in civil society, and severe distress, in some states with physical manifestation of the distress. [Week 2]

Answer key: 1H, 2C, 3E, 4A, 5I, 6G, 7B, 8D, 9F

Week 3 Drafting Exercise—Intake Memorandum

Dictate for voice-recognition transcription a client-intake memorandum based on the client-intake form that you completed last week.

An initial consultation is just the first step. Once a lawyer has the client's basic information, the lawyer must plan the matter's investigation and handling, and instruct law-firm staff accordingly. Lawyers often do so by dictating or typing an intake memorandum, for the file and for staff distribution. The dictation may occur in the car on the way back from the meeting outside the office or in the office immediately after the client leaves. One highly efficient lawyer to whom I referred certain cases dictated the intake memorandum *with the client present* at the consultation's end, to ensure that the lawyer has the client's information correct. One of the short stories in the book *Lawyer Storytelling: A Sacred Craft* is in the form of an intake memorandum, illustrating that these memoranda capture the stories of important events in clients' lives. Intake memoranda typically have the following information, which you should include in your dictated memorandum. Can you think of other matters to include?

- meeting date and participants;
- how the client located the lawyer;
- whether another lawyer receives a referral fee;
- who is the opposing party for conflict-check purposes;
- brief outline of the event giving rise to the matter;
- date the cause of action arose for limitation-period purposes;
- instructions on how staff should proceed including:
  - whether to open a file;
  - how to name the file (client name, matter name);
  - to check for client conflicts with other lawyers in the firm;
  - to prepare authorization forms for release of medical, employment, insurance, and academic information, for the client to sign;
  - to order the police report;
  - to get other public information like vehicle-title information, driver's license and driving history information, criminal history, and credit history;
- insurance information including liability-limits estimate;
- outline of how the lawyer intends to proceed including:
  - whether to make a demand before filing suit;
  - where to file suit;
  - when to file suit;
  - what witnesses to interview or depose;
  - what experts to retain if any;
- litigation-budget estimate;
- prediction of potential range of outcomes;
- special client-communication instructions such as to copy on all correspondence.

Week 4

Intentional-Tort Defenses

BULLET OUTLINE FOR WEEK 4:
Intentional-Tort Defenses
- ([43]defendants have the burden of proof on each element of affirmative defenses)

[38]Consent = permission expressed by words or communicative actions
- [39]determine consent from an objective rather than subjective standpoint
  - what would a reasonable person have concluded
- [40]the person must understand the conduct and risks
  - parents may give substituted consent for treatment of children
  - [41]emergency care providers may treat those unable to give or withhold consent
    - only if the reasonable person would have consented
- [42]consent to an illegal act is invalid
- consent obtained by fraud or duress is invalid

[44]Self-defense and defense of others against physical injury authorizes reasonable force
- includes reasonable mistake
- does not include retaliation after threat ends
- [45]may require retreat before using force causing serious injury/death (retreat to the wall)
  - although possibly no retreat necessary from the home

[46]Defense of property
- only reasonable force not likely to cause death or serious injury
- no mistake permitted; must be correct

Recovery of property
- applies to fresh pursuit about the premises
  - use legal action to recover once away from the premises and no longer in fresh pursuit
  - [48]repossession allowed only w/o force and by agreement or summary proceedings
- [47]make demand before using reasonable force on or about premises in fresh pursuit
  - no need for demand if demand would be futile

[49]Necessity
- public necessity is a complete defense to property damage
- private necessity requires payment of actual damage

[50]Authority of law, discipline, and justification
- (law must authorize or circumstances must warrant the action)
- authority of law typically involves lawful arrest
  - can include protection by medical-care provider before civil commitment
- discipline typically involves military, maybe school
  - watch for corporal-punishment statutes prohibiting contact for other than restraint
- justification = grab-bag / catch-all

PARAGRAPH OUTLINE FOR WEEK 4:
Intentional-Tort Defenses

[38]Consent expressed by words or communicative actions is a defense to an intentional tort. [39]The law determines consent from an objective rather than subjective standpoint, meaning what a reasonable person would have concluded. [40]To consent, a person must understand the conduct and risks, although parents may give substituted consent for treatment of children. [41]Emergency medical-care providers may treat those who are unable to give or withhold consent if the reasonable person would have consented. [42]Consent to an illegal act, and consent obtained by fraud or duress, are invalid. [43]Defendants have the burden of proof on each element of affirmative defenses. [44]Self-defense and defense of others against physical injury authorizes reasonable force even likely when reasonably mistaken, although not retaliation after the threat ends. [45]The law may require retreat before use of force likely to cause serious injury or death, although possibly not from the home. [46]One may use reasonable force to defend property if the force is not likely to cause death or serious injury but not when mistaken. [47]One must make a demand before using reasonable force to recover property unless demand would be futile and only in fresh pursuit about the premises. [48]The law allows repossession from the land of another only without force and only by agreement or summary proceedings. [49]Public necessity is a complete defense to property damage, but private necessity requires payment of actual damage. [50]Authority of law, discipline, and justification are defenses, where law authorizes or circumstances warrant the action.

Fluency Cards for Week 4

Cover and uncover the response to each prompt until you fluently recall the exact response.

Consent Defense

Objective word or action when person or guardian knows conduct and risk.

Illegal Acts

No consenting to an illegal act.

Fraud or Duress

No consent if by fraud or duress.

Substituted Consent

Emergency provider may treat one unable to consent if reasonable person would consent.

Defense of Self/Other

May use reasonable force even when reasonably mistaken but no retaliating.

Retreat

Retreat before using force likely to cause serious injury or death, except from the home.

Property Defense

Defend property only with reasonable force not likely to cause death or serious injury.

Property-Defense Mistake

No mistakes when defending property with force, but may reasonably investigate.

Recovering Property

Recover property only in fresh pursuit or or about the premises after demand.

Repossession

Only without force (no breach of peace) with agreement or summary proceeding.

Necessity

Public necessity defends trespass, but private necessity requires paying any damage.

Policy Defenses

Authority of law, discipline, and justification, where circumstances warrant act.

Definitions Worksheet for Week 4

1. List intentional-tort defenses. Which party has the proof burden on defenses?

2. How does the consent defense arise? How does one judge consent?

3. How do children consent? How do emergency-care providers get consent?

4. How does the law define and limit self-defense and defense of others?

5. How does the law define and limit defense and recovery of property?

6. What distinguishes public necessity from private necessity?

7. Name and explain other policy defenses after public or private necessity.

Answer Key for Definitions Worksheet

1. *List the defenses to intentional torts. Which party has the burden of proof on defenses?* Personal-injury intentional-tort defenses include consent, self-defense, defense of others, authority of law, discipline, and justification. Property-damage intentional-tort defenses include defense and recovery of property, and public and private necessity. Defendants have the burden of proof on each element of affirmative defenses.

2. *How does the consent defense arise? How does one judge consent?* A person expresses consent by words or communicative acts. To consent, though, a person must understand and accept the conduct and risks, meaning no fraud or duress. The law determines consent from an objective rather than subjective standpoint, meaning what a reasonable person would have understood. Consent to an illegal act is invalid.

3. *How do children consent? How do emergency-care providers get consent?* Parents may give substituted consent for treatment of children. Emergency medical-care providers may treat those who are unable to give or withhold consent if the reasonable person would have consented.

4. *How does the law define and limit self-defense and defense of others?* Self-defense and defense of others against physical injury authorizes reasonable force even when reasonably mistaken, although not retaliation after the threat ends. The law may require retreat before use of force likely to cause serious injury or death, although possibly not from the home.

5. *How does the law define and limit defense and recovery of property.* One may use reasonable force to defend property if the force is not likely to cause death or serious injury but not when mistaken. One must make a demand before using reasonable force to recover property unless demand would be futile and only in fresh pursuit about the premises. The law allows repossession from the land of another only without force and only by agreement or summary proceedings.

6. *What distinguishes public necessity from private necessity?* Public necessity is a complete defense to property damage, but private necessity requires payment of actual damage.

7. *Name and explain other policy defenses after public or private necessity.* Authority of law, discipline, and justification are policy defenses. Law may authorize restraint, such as by law enforcement or mental-health providers. Parents, teachers, and military officers may have authority to discipline physically. Justification is a catch-all policy defense.

Issue-Spotting Worksheet for Week 4

State the law each scenario raises. No analysis. Just spot the issue and state the law.

1. You meet with a new client who hands you a complaint. The client asks you to look at the complaint, cautioning you that not a word of it is true. The complaint alleges that your client beat up and badly injured another contestant in an ultimate-fighting competition. When you ask your client exactly when the process server handed him the complaint, your client's answer confirms for you that today is the last day to file an answer and defenses or suffer a default. You have thirty minutes before the court clerk's office closes.

___

2. As you are furiously typing an answer and defenses, your client explains that both he and the plaintiff in this case had signed forms releasing the competition promoter from all liability for participating in the competition. The client shows you the consent form, which doesn't mention releasing other contestants but does confirm the brutal nature of the competition. The client describes the plaintiff as his competition opponent.

___

3. Your client next explains that his opponent, the plaintiff, may have been under age eighteen and thus a minor. Your client is twenty-one years old and was an adult at the time of the event that the complaint describes. Reading the complaint further, you see that the client claims further injury from medical treatment after having been knocked unconscious.

___

4. As you are finishing typing the answer, your client explains that his opponent was actually getting the upper hand and was hurting the client to the point that the client tried to tap out. But when the opponent didn't relent, the client explains that he was forced to go all-out to stop the opponent.

___

5. Just when you are printing out the answer and defenses to file before the court closes, you are surprised when your client adds that he and his opponent had been having an argument over his opponent's having stolen your client's vehicle. Your client admits that he agreed to fight the opponent because he was going to knock him silly and then go out to the parking lot and take his vehicle back.

___

Answer Key for Issue-Spotting Worksheet

1. ***This scenario implicates the defenses to intentional torts.*** Personal-injury intentional-tort defenses include consent, self-defense, defense of others, authority of law, discipline, and justification. Defendants have the burden of pleading and proving affirmative defenses.

2. ***This scenario implicates the consent defense.*** A person expresses consent by words or communicative acts. To consent, a person must understand and accept the conduct and risks, meaning no fraud or duress. The law determines consent from an objective rather than subjective standpoint, meaning what a reasonable person would have understood. Consent to an illegal act is invalid.

3. ***This scenario implicates consent by children and consent to emergency care.*** Parents may generally give substituted consent for their children. Emergency medical-care providers may treat those who are unable to give or withhold consent if the reasonable person would have consented.

4. ***This scenario implicates self-defense and defense of others.*** Self-defense and defense of others against physical injury authorizes reasonable force even when reasonably mistaken, although not retaliation after the threat ends. The law may require retreat before use of force likely to cause serious injury or death, although possibly not from the home.

5. ***This scenario implicates defense and recovery of property.*** One may use reasonable force to defend property if the force is not likely to cause death or serious injury but not when mistaken. One must make a demand before using reasonable force to recover property unless demand would be futile and only in fresh pursuit about the premises. The law allows repossession from the land of another only without force and only by agreement or summary proceedings.

TORTS I WORKBOOK

Discrimination Exercise for Week 4

Indicate whether each statement *overgeneralizes*, *undergeneralizes*, or *misconceives* the rule, explaining why. *Overgeneralizing* states the rule too broadly, capturing circumstances to which it does not apply. *Undergeneralizing* states the rule too narrowly, omitting circumstances to which it applies. *Misconceiving* states the rule incorrectly.

1. Intentional-tort defenses include consent, authority of law, discipline, and justification.
   ____OVER/ ____UNDER/ ____MISS/ Why? _____
   _____

2. A person consents whenever, by words or communicative acts, a reasonable person would believe that the person agrees to the proposed act.
   ____OVER/ ____UNDER/ ____MISS/ Why? _____
   _____

3. Emergency medical-care providers need a court order to treat those who are unable to give consent, even if the reasonable person would have consented.
   ____OVER/ ____UNDER/ ____MISS/ Why? _____
   _____

4. Self-defense and defense of others always authorizes use of force, even when the defender is mistaken.
   ____OVER/ ____UNDER/ ____MISS/ Why? _____
   _____

5. One may use all necessary force to defend or recover one's own personal property from another who has taken it.
   ____OVER/ ____UNDER/ ____MISS/ Why? _____
   _____

6. Public necessity is a partial defense to property damage but requires payment of any actual damage.
   ____OVER/ ____UNDER/ ____MISS/ Why? _____
   _____

7. Private necessity is a complete defense to property damage, requiring no payment of any damage to the other's property.
   ____OVER/ ____UNDER/ ____MISS/ Why? _____
   _____

Answer Key for Discrimination Exercise

1. The statement **UNDERgeneralizes** the rule. Personal-injury intentional-tort defenses include consent, *self-defense, defense of others*, authority of law, discipline, and justification. ***Property-damage intentional-tort defenses include defense and recovery of property, and public and private necessity***. Defendants have the burden of proof on affirmative defenses.

2. The statement **OVERgeneralizes** the rule. While a person expresses consent by words or communicative acts agreeing to the act, to consent, a person must ***understand and accept the conduct and risks, meaning no fraud or duress***. Moreover, ***consent to an illegal act is invalid***.

3. The statement **MISconceives** the rule. Emergency medical-care providers *may* treat those who are unable to give consent, even ***without a court order***, if the reasonable person would have consented. The provider would promptly seek a court order designating a decisionmaker but may ***treat until obtaining one***.

4. The statement **OVERgeneralizes** the rule. Self-defense and defense of others against physical injury authorizes *reasonable* force even when *reasonably* mistaken, although not retaliation after the threat ends. The law ***may require retreat*** before use of force likely to cause serious injury or death, although possibly not from the home.

5. The statement **OVERgeneralizes** the rule. One may use *reasonable* force to defend property ***if the force is not likely to cause death or serious injury and when not mistaken***. One must also ***make a demand*** before using reasonable force to recover property unless demand would be futile, and recover property ***only in fresh pursuit about the premises***.

6. The statement **UNDERgeneralizes** or **MISconceives** the rule. Public necessity is a ***complete*** defense to property damage. The person or entity damaging or destroying the property for public safety or welfare ***pays no damages***.

7. The statement **OVERgeneralizes** or **MISconceives** the rule. Private necessity does authorize use or destruction of another's property to protect one's self or one's property but requires payment of any actual damage. The private actor must in effect calculate which will cause the greater loss because the private actor bears the loss.

Scenario-Generating Worksheet for Week 4
Generate a scenario demonstrating each of the following rules.

1. Defendants have the ***burdens of pleading, production, and proof*** on each element of intentional-tort affirmative defenses and defenses to other types of tort claims.

   _____
   _____

2. The law determines consent from an ***objective rather than subjective standpoint***, meaning what a reasonable person would have understood.

   _____
   _____

3. Emergency medical-care providers may treat those who are ***unable to give or withhold consent*** if the reasonable person would have consented.

   _____
   _____

4. Self-defense and defense of others against physical injury authorizes reasonable force ***even when reasonably mistaken***, although not retaliation after the threat ends. The law may require retreat before use of force likely to cause serious injury or death, although possibly not from the home.

   _____
   _____

5. One may use reasonable force to defend property ***if the force is not likely to cause death or serious injury*** but not when mistaken. One must make a demand before using reasonable force to recover property unless demand would be futile and only in fresh pursuit about the premises. The law allows repossession from the land of another only without force and only by agreement or summary proceedings.

   _____
   _____

6. Public necessity is a complete defense to property damage, but ***private necessity requires payment of actual damage***.

   _____
   _____

Example Scenarios for Scenario-Generating Worksheet

1. ***This rule calls for an example of defendant meeting the procedural burdens.*** The lawyer defending the defendant's battery claim pled with the answer that the plaintiff had consented to the touching and, responding to a summary-judgment motion as to the defense, produced defendant's deposition testimony that plaintiff consented, showing that defendant would so prove at trial.

2. ***This rule calls for an example of objective rather than subjective consent.*** Although the patron of the bar really didn't want to fight the drunk, the patron nonetheless took off his sport coat, rolled up his sleeves, raised his balled fists, and stepped forward saying "Let's see how tough you are" at the drunk's invitation to fight.

3. ***This rule calls for an example of inability to consent to medical treatment.*** The emergency physician couldn't get a response out of the unconscious patient whom EMTs had brought to the ward without accompanying family member or friend. The patient gave signs of serious internal bleeding requiring immediate exploratory surgery in the absence of which the patient faced bleeding-out death.

4. ***This rule calls for an example of reasonable mistake in self-defense or defense of others.*** The courthouse security detail received a call that an armed psychotic man was on his way to break into the courthouse to shoot a judge. The detail shot the man as he approached in a rush, shouting incoherently and waving what looked to be a handgun but turned out to be an old flip phone.

5. ***This rule calls for an example of the restriction against using force likely to cause death or serious injury when defendant property.*** A jeweler whose store had several break-ins set up a trip wire just inside the door to set off flashing lights and sounding siren, and for security call, while considering whether to add a spring gun.

6. ***This rule calls for an example of private necessity with damage.*** A boater whose yacht began to flood and sink at the dock late one night commandeered the marina's pump to keep the yacht afloat until morning rescue but burned out the pump.

TORTS I WORKBOOK

Week 4 Drafting Exercise: Demand Letter

A demand letter communicates to the wrongdoer or the wrongdoer's insurer the basis for the client's tort claim against the wrongdoer. The demand letter's goal is to promote a settlement of the claim before filing a lawsuit, by providing the information and analysis necessary for the wrongdoer and insurer to agree on liability and damages. Demand letters are typical before suit but not required except in medical-malpractice cases in certain states like Michigan and Florida. Demand letters often lead to further exchange of information and some negotiation, and occasionally even settlement, before suit. Working with the seatmate with whom you completed an intake and memorandum, dictate a demand letter for that matter, consistent with the tone, form, and content of the following fictitious example.

LAW OFFICES

FAJEN AND MILLER, P.L.L.C.

JAMES A. FAJEN
RICHARD B. BAILEY
OF COUNSEL
NELSON P. MILLER

1527 PINERIDGE DRIVE
GRAND HAVEN, MICHIGAN 49417

(616) 846-9187
FAX (616) 846-9187
E-mail: millern57@gmail.com

ANN ARBOR OFFICE:
2950 SOUTH STATE ST., #280
ANN ARBOR, MICHIGAN 48104
(734) 995-0181
FAX (734) 995-0184
fajenlaw@fajenmiller.com

February 15, 2012

Tyler Durgan, Claim Representative
State Farm Insurance Co.
1234 Meridian Road
Okemos, MI 48988

Re: Insured: ABC Trucking Co.
     Claimants: William R. Smith and Carlena J. Smith
     Claim No.:   14356789-00   Loss Date: 02/01/2011

Dear Mr. Durgan:

This correspondence constitutes the demand and offer of William R. Smith and his spouse Carlena J. Smith to resolve their claims against your insureds ABC Trucking Co. and its driver/president Justin Doe, for third-party motor-vehicle no-fault losses arising out of the motor-vehicle accident at the intersection of Main Street and Michigan Avenue in Flint, Michigan, on February 1, 2011. This demand does not offer to release Mr. and Mrs. Smith's first-party rights.

Mr. and Mrs. Smith offer to resolve their third-party liability claims against your insureds ABC and Mr. Doe for the policy-limits amount of $100,000, provided that those policy limit amounts are all of the insurance coverage ABC and Mr. Doe have relating to the claims of Mr. and Mrs. Smith. If, instead, ABC or Mr. Doe has other coverage, including excess or umbrella coverage, then this offer is null and void. We will require that Mr. Doe execute on his own behalf and for ABC an affidavit reflecting that they have no other available insurance. We will also require a recital in the settlement agreement that the parties will set aside the agreement at no cost to Mr. and Mrs. Smith if other coverage becomes available.

The basis for this demand and offer includes the following. All records to which this analysis refers are already in your possession. The UD-10 accident report confirms that your insured ABC's truck driven by your additional insured Mr. Doe struck Mr. Smith while Mr. Smith was crossing the street within a crosswalk, under circumstances where police properly ticketed Mr. Doe for violating state law. Your insureds cannot genuinely dispute, and will instead likely admit, liability. The factfinder is unlikely to ascribe any comparative negligence to Mr. Smith.

Mr. Smith suffered three broken ribs, a broken right forearm, broken right clavicle, fractures to the right wrist, and associated injuries. Mr. Smith also suffered injuries to his neck, back, and nerves in the right shoulder, arm, and wrist. The mechanism of these injuries was the crushing force of ABC's truck striking Mr. Smith at a speed fast enough to throw Mr. Smith suddenly forward and to the ground. Ambulance removed Mr. Smith from the scene to the hospital where he remained for a period of approximately 10 days for immobilization of the rib and clavicle fractures and open-reduction surgical treatment of the broken right forearm and wrist.

On Mr. Smith's release from the hospital, physicians' orders confined Mr. Smith to bed rest at home in a hospital bed in his living room for a period of approximately 10 weeks. Mr. Smith simultaneously wore a hard cast to the right arm, wrist, and hand, exposing only the right-hand fingers. He also wore bandages fixing his right arm to his torso to stabilize the clavicle fractures, or at times, sling for the same purpose. His rib and clavicle injuries meant that he was unable to move or ambulate except with exceeding care and severe pain. Physicians medicated Mr. Smith heavily for pain during this period and afterward.

It has been approximately one year since the incident. Mr. Smith has yet to return to work because of lasting and likely permanent injuries to his neck, shoulder, arm, and wrist. The injuries are neurological in nature as confirmed by treating neurosurgeon Dr. Robert Ritter. Medical records and report indicate that the right shoulder, arm, and wrist injuries severely traumatized, stretched, or severed nerves controlling Mr. Smith's right wrist, hand, and fingers. Nerves regenerate slowly over a period of one to two years. Mr. Smith's continuing numbness, loss of sensation, and loss of control to the right wrist, hand, and fingers after one year indicate a substantial probability of permanent injury.

Mr. Smith's neck, back, arm, wrist, and hand pain has been so severe that he continues to treat under physician orders, indeed pain specialists, with strong pain-killing medication. That medication interferes with his ability to drive, think, concentrate, and focus for anything more than brief periods. As a natural and probable result, Mr. Smith has been unable to continue his work as an attorney in general practice. He has not worked since the incident and does not anticipate resuming work at any foreseeable time. Mr. Smith also no longer jogs, swims, lifts weights, and does yard and household work as he was doing before the incident. His injuries have understandably affected his relationship with Mrs. Smith.

This case is certainly a policy-limits case. Litigation will only add to the expense of this matter without changing these facts. I have enclosed a summons and complaint but am extending the time for answer until two weeks from your response. Thank you for your consideration.

Sincerely,

Nelson P. Miller

cc: William R. and Carlena A. Smith
Enclosure (summons and complaint)

Problem-Solving Exercise Week 4

Think-aloud problem solving (TAPS) is a proven method of using vocalization to become a more creative and better problem solver. Professionals are effective problem solvers when they speak aloud to another, speaking aloud to themselves, or let their mental operations taking the silent form of words, concepts, principles, and strategies to reach partial solutions and then chain partial solutions toward final novel solution. Read the following example (EX) and non-example (NE) of an unknown new rule (RU), one that the judges writing their opinions and orders have not expressly stated but that you must instead discern and record as your problem solution. Vocalize each mental operation taken toward a partial solution, until you reach and record the final novel rule. Check your answer against the model answer at the bottom of the next page.

EX OPINION AND ORDER: In this battery case, the plaintiff patient alleges that the defendant surgeon removed a section of plaintiff's colon in a resection procedure, during a planned diverticulitis surgery to remove polyps. Imagery and lab results indicate that the two-inch removed section had significant bleeds that not only compromised bowel function but also created an imminent serious threat to plaintiff's life. Defendant through counsel has moved to dismiss, arguing that plaintiff impliedly consented for this beneficial procedure. The Court grants defendant's motion, dismissing plaintiff's case with prejudice.

NE OPINION AND ORDER: In this battery case, the plaintiff patient alleges that the defendant surgeon removed a tumorous kidney during a planned stomach-staple procedure. Laboratory tests of the kidney showed invasive benign tumors compromising the organ's function. All evidence indicates that the kidney would not regain function and that plaintiff would someday benefit from the kidney's removal. Defendant through counsel has moved to dismiss, arguing that plaintiff impliedly consented to this beneficial procedure. The Court denies defendant's motion, setting plaintiff's claim for jury trial.

RU _____

_____

_____

_____

Answer: While a plaintiff must ordinarily expressly consent to surgical procedures, and extending the surgery to address other non-emergency conditions, without express consent, is battery, a surgeon may address by implied consent emergency conditions that pose an imminent serious life threat.

Week 5
Negligence, Duty, & Standards of Care

BULLET OUTLINE FOR WEEK 5:
Negligence—Duty
[51] negligence = duty, breach, causation, and damages (DBCD)
[52] duty = reasonable care (reasonably prudent person / RPP)
- determined by judge rather than jury
- arises whenever acts create foreseeable risk of harm
    - can involve omissions to act when circumstances warrant duty
    - [53] controversial duty to protect against crime depends on
        - past experience of crime,
        - offers of security,
        - available means of protection,
        - foreseeability
- [54] standards of care depend on factors including
    - custom in the trade or field
    - government regulations
    - industry standards
    - likelihood, foreseeability, and seriousness of injury
- [55] emergencies alter the standard of care to the circumstances (lower the duty)
    - except not for the one who created the circumstances (duty remains ordinary, not emergency)
- [56] reasonably prudent person (RPP) assumes the actor's physical, not mental, characteristics
    - those with superior knowledge must use it
- [57] children owe the care expected of reasonable children of like age and experience
    - consider the Rule of Sevens (no duty to age 7, duty of that age to 14, adult duty beyond 14)
    - children engaged in adult activities owe adult duties
- [58] Learned Hand's formula: liability exists when
    - the burden of precautions < than loss probability x loss magnitude
    - theoretical formula, not practical

PARAGRAPH OUTLINE FOR WEEK 5:
Negligence—Duty
[51] The elements of a negligence claim are duty, breach, causation, and damages. [52] The duty to use reasonable care (that of a reasonably prudent person), determined by judge rather than jury, arises whenever acts, omissions, or status create foreseeable risk of harm. [53] The duty to protect against depends on past experience of crime, offers of security, available means of protection, and foreseeability. [54] Standards of care depend on factors including custom, regulations, standards, experience, and likelihood and foreseeability of injury. [55] Emergencies and other circumstances alter the standard of care to the circumstances except as to the one who created the

circumstances. [56]The reasonably prudent person assumes the actor's physical, not mental, characteristics, except those with superior knowledge must use it. [57]Children owe the care that we expect of reasonable children of like age and experience, except that children engaged in adult activities owe adult duties. [58]Learned Hand's formula provides that liability exists when the burden of precautions is less than loss probability times loss magnitude.

Fluency Cards for Week 5
Cover and uncover the response to each prompt until you fluently recall the exact response.

Negligence

Duty, breach, causation, and damages.

Negligence—Duty

Duty of reasonable care / prudent person arises with affirmative acts creating foreseeable risks.

Omissions

Duty to act can arise with special status or relationship.

Prevent Crime

Controversial duty may depend on crime history, security offers, and foreseeability.

Standard of Care

Depends on custom, statutes, regulations, standards, and foreseeability.

Child's Standard

Care of reasonable child of like age, except when engaged in adult activities. Consider Rule of Sevens.

Characteristics

Reasonably prudent person assumes actor's physical, not mental, characteristics.

Emergencies

Alter the standard except for the one who creates the emergency.

Definitions Worksheet for Week 5

1. List and define the four elements of a negligence claim.

2. When does a duty arise? Who determines whether a defendant owed a duty?

3. What is the general duty of care? State it in as many ways as you can recall.

4. When does a duty to protect against crime arise? What problems does the duty present?

5. What is a *standard of care*? How does law construe (define, establish) care standards?

6. How if at all would an emergency alter the standard of care?

7. How does the standard change if the actor has physical or mental anomalies, or is a child?

Answer Key for Definitions Worksheet

1. *List and define the four elements of a negligence claim.* [51]The elements of a negligence claim are duty, breach, causation, and damages. Duty involves the obligation to care for others. Breach means the violation of or departure from that obligation. Causation involves making a connection between the breach and the injury or loss that follows. Damages is that injury or loss.

2. *When does a duty arise? Who determines whether a defendant owed a duty?* [52]The duty to use reasonable care (that of a reasonably prudent person), determined by judge rather than jury, arises when affirmative acts create a foreseeable risk of harm. In certain situations, duty can also arise around omissions to or status or relationship to the one harmed.

3. *What is the general duty of care? State it in as many ways as you can recall.* The general duty of care is to act with *reasonable care*, also described as the care of a *reasonably prudent person*. Law sometimes also describes it as *ordinary care*. Substitute the defendant's role into the duty so that, for instance, a driver owes the duty of a *reasonably prudent* driver.

4. *When does a duty to protect against crime arise? What problems does the duty present?* [53]The duty to protect against crime depends on past experience of crime, offers of security, available means of protection, and foreseeability. The problem is that a police force, not private residents or business owners, ordinarily has the skill and duty to prevent crime.

5. *What is a standard of care? How does law construe (define, establish) care standards?* Standards of care articulate specifically what the defendant should have done or not done. [54]Standards of care depend on factors including custom, regulations, standards, experience, and likelihood and foreseeability of injury.

6. *How if at all would an emergency alter the standard of care?* [55]Emergencies alter the standard of care to the emergent circumstance (reasonable care *in the emergency*) except for the one who created the circumstances.

7. *How does the standard change if the actor has physical or mental anomalies, or is a child?* [56]The reasonably prudent person assumes the actor's physical, not mental, characteristics. [57]Children owe the care expected of reasonable children of like age and experience, except that children engaged in adult activities owe adult duties.

Issue-Spotting Worksheet for Week 5

State the law each scenario raises. No analysis. Just spot the issue and state the law.

1. You meet with the board of a nonprofit organization led by the executive director. The director hands you a lawyer's demand letter that you skim as the director explains that a dunk-tank volunteer got hurt at one of the nonprofit's fundraising events. The director asks you what kind of a legal claim against the nonprofit a volunteer could make in such a situation.

_____

_____

2. One of the board members cuts you off just as you are finishing your answer to the director. The board member is irate at the volunteer's *chutzpah* in asserting that the nonprofit would owe the volunteer any obligation. After all, the board member argues vehemently, the whole thing was merely a *fundraiser* for a *charity*. The director and other board members look at you expectantly, waiting to hear your answer.

_____

_____

3. Your answer settles down the irate board member. Another board member whom you later learn is an accountant asks exactly who determines what is reasonable and how.

_____

_____

_____

4. The board members take the information that you have supplied so far and begin to discuss the claim. You learn that the nonprofit rented the dunk tank and that volunteers hauled it to the fundraiser site and set it up. Most of the volunteers were women, youth, and children. They must have set it up wrong, the board members conclude, if the demand letter is accurate that the dunk-tank plank gave way suddenly as the injured volunteer was climbing onto it. One of the board members whom you later learn is a dentist asks you if it makes any difference who set it up and what were their physical capabilities, skills, and experience.

_____

_____

_____

Answer Key for Issue-Spotting Worksheet

1. ***This scenario implicates the elements of a negligence claim.*** The elements of a negligence claim are duty, breach, causation, and damages. Duty involves the obligation to care for others. Breach means the violation of or departure from that obligation. Causation involves making a connection between the breach and the injury or loss that follows. The damage element is that injury or loss.

2. ***This scenario implicates the duty element of a negligence claim.*** Duty arises whenever affirmative acts create a foreseeable risk of harm. In certain situations, duty can also arise around omissions to or status or relationship to the one harmed. The general duty of care is to act with *reasonable care*, also described as the care of a *reasonably prudent person*. Law sometimes also describes it as *ordinary care*.

3. ***This scenario implicates the standard of care.*** While judges generally decide the question of duty, juries decide reasonableness based on the standard of care. Standards of care articulate specifically what the defendant should have done or not done under the circumstances. Standards of care depend on factors including the custom or practice in the field, safety statutes, government regulations, private industry standards, the utility of the conduct, and the likelihood, severity, and foreseeability of injury.

4. ***This scenario implicates altered standards of care.*** The reasonably prudent person assumes the actor's physical, not mental, characteristics. Children owe the care expected of reasonable children of like age and experience, except that children engaged in adult activities owe adult duties. Some jurisdictions follow a *Rule of Sevens* that children up to age seven are incapable of negligence, children up to age fourteen owe duties of children of that age, and anyone older than fourteen owes the duties of an adult.

Examples/Non-Examples Exercise for Week 5

Identify whether each fact pattern is an example (E) or non-example (NE) of the **highlighted concept**. Answers follow. In the blanks, generate an additional example and non-example.

1. The elements of a **negligence claim** are duty, breach, causation, and damages. Duty involves the obligation to care for others. Breach means the violation of or departure from that obligation.

    ___ The distracted driver accidentally ran the red light, striking the pedestrian who was in the crosswalk.
    ___ The golfer took a practice swing without looking around him, accidentally striking his playing partner.
    ___ The motorist drove past the accident scene even though she could have called 911 to help the injured.

    E: _____
    N: _____

2. The duty to use reasonable care (that of a reasonably prudent person), determined by judge rather than jury, arises when **affirmative acts create a foreseeable risk of harm**.

    ___ The homeowner watched in amusement as his neighbor accidentally backed the vehicle over the mower.
    ___ The hunter professed no knowledge that the boy he mistakenly shot was hiding in the woods there.
    ___ The camp counselor didn't know when he tipped over her canoe for fun that the girl couldn't swim well.

    E: _____
    N: _____

3. In certain situations, duty can also arise around omissions toward another or status or **relationship with the one harmed**.

    ___ The emergency-room doctor refused to treat the drunken patient when the patient arrived in critical need.
    ___ No one knew that the patron right behind the man who choked was a doctor who could have saved him.
    ___ The prison guard saw the inmate bleeding profusely from the mouth and nose but did nothing.

    E: _____
    N: _____

4. The general duty of care is to act with **reasonable care**, also described as the care of a reasonably prudent person. Law sometimes also describes it as ordinary care.

    ___ He checked the battery, gas, and oil before taking the motorboat out to be sure it would keep running.
    ___ The foreman tossed the hammer across the open rafters without even seeing if the apprentice was looking.
    ___ She read the directions over again until she was sure how to put the guards on the machine properly.

    E: _____
    N: _____

5. The **duty to protect against crime** depends on experience of crime, offers of security, available means of protection, and foreseeability.

___ The bed-and-breakfast host had never heard of a break-in and theft in the neighborhood before.
___ The casino advertised lit, fenced, and guarded parking structures to ensure patron safety late at night.
___ The ballpark had so many fights in the stands that it cut off beer after seven innings and hired guards.

E: _____
N: _____

6. **Standards of care** articulate what defendant should have done or not done. Standards of care depend on factors including custom, government regulations, industry standards, and likelihood and foreseeability of injury.

___ The riverboat pilot had trained in the tricky docking maneuver and even had to perform it for his license.
___ The grocer tried to follow the grocery association's guides for customer safety but could barely keep up.
___ No one had ever led a hiking tour of that kind, and no one had any idea of what hazards it might entail.

E: _____
N: _____

7. **Emergencies alter the standard of care** to the emergent circumstance (reasonable care in the emergency) except for the one who created the circumstances.

___ The ambulance driver ran one red light after another, although with his sirens and lights on.
___ The nurse rushed sloppily through the dangerous procedure even though the patient had stabilized.
___ In haste to get the unconscious guest to shore, the motorboat operator sped down the no-wake channel.

E: _____
N: _____

8. The reasonably prudent person **assumes the actor's physical characteristics**, not the actor's mental characteristics.

___ The foster adult hadn't known that his actions could seriously injure the aide who had tried to help him.
___ The little woman was simply unable to lift the beam that she accidentally knocked over onto her friend.
___ He would have done CPR on the stricken guest if he could have made it up the steps in his wheelchair.

E: _____
N: _____

9. Children owe the care expected of reasonable children of like age and experience, except that **children engaged in adult activities** owe adult duties.

___ The boy loved driving the cart at high speeds over blind hills, even though his dad had told him not to.
___ The girl pulled back on her mom's compound bow, aiming the arrow wildly in the neighbor's direction.
___ The children in the pool tossed the plastic ball back and forth over the net strung across the pool's center.

E: _____
N: _____

Answers: 1 EEN; 2 NEE; 3 ENE; 4 ENE; 5 NEE; 6 EEN; 7 ENE; 8 NEE; 9 EEN

Problem-Solving Exercise Week 5 (Problem 1)

Think-aloud problem solving (TAPS) is a proven method of using vocalization to become a more creative and better problem solver. Professionals are effective problem solvers when they speak aloud to another, speaking aloud to themselves, or let their mental operations taking the silent form of words, concepts, principles, and strategies to reach partial solutions and then chain partial solutions toward final novel solution. Read the following example (EX) and non-example (NE) of an unknown new rule (RU), one that the judges writing their opinions and orders have not expressly stated but that you must instead discern and record as your problem solution. Vocalize each mental operation taken toward a partial solution, until you reach and record the final novel rule. Check your answer against the model answer at the bottom of the next page.

EX   OPINION AND ORDER: In this negligence case, the plaintiff diabetic alleges that defendant negligently designed, marketed, and sold a prescription diabetic-drug product that, although reasonably safe at the time of sale, interacted catastrophically with another drug product a non-party later designed and marketed, and that plaintiff diabetic also took under later prescription, the interaction causing brain hemorrhage and permanent loss of cognitive function. Defendant through counsel assigned by defendant's insurer has moved to dismiss, arguing that defendant owed plaintiff no duty. The Court grants defendant's motion, dismissing plaintiff's case with prejudice.

NE   OPINION AND ORDER: In this negligence case, the plaintiff painter alleges that defendant negligently designed, marketed, and sold a breathing-filter product that, although reasonably safe for filtering most paint solvents then on the market, was not reasonably safe for the paint solvent that plaintiff painter was using when plaintiff painter purchased the filter product, resulting in inhalation of solvent fumes and permanent brain damage. Defendant has moved to dismiss, arguing that defendant owed plaintiff no duty. The Court denies defendant's motion, setting plaintiff's claim for jury trial.

RU   _____

_____

_____

_____

Answer for problem on next page: While acts creating foreseeable risks of harm ordinarily give rise to a duty, some harm must be of the type that makes the action a foreseeable risk, not entirely of some other, unforeseeable type.

Problem-Solving Exercise Week 5 (Problem 2)

Think-aloud problem solving (TAPS) is a proven method of using vocalization to become a more creative and better problem solver. Professionals are effective problem solvers when they speak aloud to another, speaking aloud to themselves, or let their mental operations taking the silent form of words, concepts, principles, and strategies to reach partial solutions and then chain partial solutions toward final novel solution. Read the following example (EX) and non-example (NE) of an unknown new rule (RU), one that the judges writing their opinions and orders have not expressly stated but that you must instead discern and record as your problem solution. Vocalize each mental operation taken toward a partial solution, until you reach and record the final novel rule. Check your answer against the model answer at the bottom of the next page.

EX   OPINION AND ORDER: In this negligence case, the plaintiff homeowner alleges that defendant negligently manufactured and sold a lead-based paint, the lead levels of which substantially exceeded federal and state safety regulations relating to ingestion and brain damage, and that the paint, although safe for every known wood floor, when applied to plaintiff's rare African-hardwood floor interacted with its sap or resin in a manner that destroyed the floor. Defendant has moved to dismiss, arguing no duty. The Court grants defendant's motion and dismisses plaintiff's case with prejudice.

NE   OPINION AND ORDER: In this negligence case, the plaintiff restaurant owner alleges that defendant negligently manufactured and sold a table wax that included unlawfully high levels of carcinogenic materials, and that once the restaurant had applied the wax to its tables and only then learned of the hazard, the restaurant had to remove and replace the tables at substantial cost and business-interruption loss. Defendant has moved to dismiss, arguing no duty. The Court denies defendant's motion, bringing this case on for jury trial as to defendant's negligence and the amount of resulting damages.

RU   _____

Answer for problem on prior page: Although acts creating foreseeable risks of harm give rise to a duty of reasonable care, the risk must have been foreseeable at the time of the action, not after the defendant acted.

Review Exercise for Week 5

Match these facts with the law on the next page that they trigger.

Her life lately had been like a bad dream. ____ 1. She had awoken in the pre-dawn morning once again smelling that awful smell from the tannery down the street. ____ 2. Sickened, she had rolled out of bed, thrown on the first thing she could find, and stumbled out of her tiny house toward the coffee shop a few blocks away, only to have a scruffy man suddenly step in front of her, pointing something at her while demanding her purse. ____ 3. She had at first said *no, just take this money for yourself*, hoping that he'd take the wadded $20 bill that she had pulled from her pocket on instinct. ____ 4. But the man had instead jerked her purse off her shoulder and dashed off with it—only for her to find it a few minutes later in the happy clutches of a patron at the coffee shop with whom she had argued for its immediate return. ____ 5. When she headed back to her tiny house just after dawn, she was stunned to find asleep on her couch her neighbor who, when awaken, protested loudly that he was drunk and had thought that he had entered his own tiny house. ____ 6. She had rousted him off her couch at first with a few shoves and finally with a few good, swift kicks. ____ 7. Her neighbor had then accidentally knocked her over, breaking her wrist, when trying to get him up and out of her house. ____ 8. She was of course outraged, especially when he made no effort to help her up and instead just poured profanity down on her as she struggled with her injury. ____ 9. In the end, she thought of seeing a lawyer but wondered, like a bad dream, *what good would it do?*

TORTS I WORKBOOK

Review Exercise for Week 5
Match this law with the facts on the prior page to which the law applies.

___A. Tort law's twin policies are to deter (discourage wrongs) and compensate (restore the injured).^{Week 1}

___B. Intent transfers from intended to actual victim and among the five traditional intentional torts.^{Week 1}

___C. While purpose or desire to harm, knowledge of a substantial certainty of harm, or transferred intent will satisfy IIED's intent element, so will recklessness, which is knowledge of a high probability of harm.^{Week 2}

___D. Assault is the reasonable apprehension of an imminent battery with the apparent present ability to carry it out.^{Week 2}

___E. Mistaken entries are still trespass if intentional.^{Week 3}

___F. The nuisance tort addresses interference with use and enjoyment of land (noise, smoke, light, smell) rather than interference with exclusive possession, as for trespass.^{Week 3}

___G. The owner of converted property may recover from the original converter and subsequent holders taking in good or bad faith.^{Week 3}

___H. To consent, a person must understand and accept the conduct and risks, meaning no fraud or duress.^{Week 4}

___I. One may use reasonable force to defend property if the force is not likely to cause death or serious injury.^{Week 4}

Answer key: 1F, 2D, 3H, 4G, 5E, 6I, 7B, 8C, 9A

Week 5 Drafting Exercise—Caption

Draft the caption of a personal-injury complaint. A tort claimant's lawyer will typically make a written demand on the wrongdoer whose insurer will reply. If the claimant and insurer do not resolve the claim, then the claimant's lawyer may start a lawsuit by filing a complaint. Every complaint must have a caption providing the court and parties with certain information. The requirements differ from state to state and between the federal and state courts. This exercise follows rules common to Michigan state courts. Following the guide below, on the next page, draft the caption of the following complaint filling in the blanks corresponding to the following numbered instructions.

1. You must choose the court in which to file the complaint, usually for tort cases the court of the county in which the accident occurred. Your client, who lives in Ottawa County, suffered serious injury in a motor-vehicle accident in Kent County.

2. You must state your client's legal name. Your client is Marcellus Q. Cluse.

3. You must state the defendant's legal name. Sabrina P. Carter drove her vehicle through a red light, striking Marcellus as a pedestrian in the crosswalk.

4. You must put the last two digits of the year when you file the complaint as the first part of the case number.

5. You must leave a blank for the court to assign the case number.

6. You must choose the correct two-letter case code. Your client claims that Sabrina Carter was negligent, causing your client's injury. Motor-vehicle negligence claims bear an NI case code. Slip-and-fall negligence claims bear an NO case code. Medical-malpractice claims bear an NM case code.

7. You must leave a blank for the court to randomly assign the case judge.

8. You must list your name, bar number, address, telephone, and party whom you represent.

9. Every court paper must bear an appropriate title.

10. Every court paper would begin with a basic statement of its form including the party filing the paper and the party against whom the filing party seeks relief.

STATE OF MICHIGAN

IN THE [1]_____ COUNTY CIRCUIT COURT

```
_____
                              )
[2]_____,        )   No. [4]____--[5]_____--[6]____
        Plaintiff,            )
            v                 )   Hon.[7]_____
[3]_____,        )
        Defendant.            )
_____)
```

[8]_____ (P_____)
_____
_____
_____
_____

Attorneys for _____
_____)

[9] _____

Plaintiff _____ complains against defendant _____ stating:

PARTIES, VENUE, AND JURISDICTION
[Numbered paragraphs alleging the claim follow.]
ALLEGATIONS OF FACT
[Numbered paragraphs alleging the claim follow.]
COUNT I
[Numbered paragraphs alleging the claim follow.]

Week 6
Qualified Duties: Contracts, Omissions, & Economic Loss

BULLET OUTLINE:
QUALIFIED DUTIES: CONTRACTS, OMISSIONS, AND ECONOMIC LOSS
- [59]contract promisor owes a tort duty to a third party only when the promisor performs in part
    - misfeasance, not nonfeasance
- [60]no duty to rescue or aid another unless
    - one created the need,
    - one assumes a duty,
    - one controls the instrumentality
- [61]economic-loss doctrine limits duties to direct injury
    - bars pure economic loss claims by those who suffer no physical impact

PARAGRAPH OUTLINE:
Qualified Duties: Contracts, Omissions, and Economic Loss
[59]A contract promisor owes a tort duty to a third party only when the promisor performs the contract (misfeasance, not nonfeasance). [60]Without special relationship, tort law imposes no duty to rescue or aid another unless one created the need, assumes a duty, or controls the instrumentality. [61]The economic-loss doctrine limits duties to direct injury, barring pure economic loss claims by those who suffer no physical impact.

Fluency Cards for Week 6
Cover and uncover the response to each prompt until you fluently recall the exact response.

Duty—Contracts

Duty only when promisor negligently performs (misfeasance), not fails to perform (nonfeasance).

Duty to Rescue

No duty to rescue unless creating need, assuming duty, controlling instrumentality, or in special relationship.

Economic Loss

No pure-economic-loss claims by those who suffer no physical impact.

Definitions Worksheet for Week 6

1. [Review:] When does duty arise? Who says whether defendant owed duty?

2. [Review:] What is a *standard of care*? How does law define standards?

3. How does a promise to perform a contract affect tort duties to non-parties?

4. Does tort law impose a duty to rescue another? If so, then when?

5. Give examples of when tort law would impose a rescue duty.

6. What is the economic-loss doctrine? What function (policy) does it serve?

Answer Key for Definitions Worksheet

1. *[Review:] When does a duty arise? Who determines whether a defendant owed a duty?* The duty to use reasonable care (that of a reasonably prudent person), determined by judge rather than jury, arises when affirmative acts create a foreseeable risk of harm. In certain situations, duty can also arise around omissions, status, or relationship with the one harmed.

2. *[Review:] What is a standard of care? How does law define care standards?* Standards of care articulate specifically what the defendant should have done or not done. Standards of care depend on factors including custom, regulations, standards, experience, and likelihood and foreseeability of injury.

3. *How does a party's promise to perform a contract affect tort duties to third parties?* A contract promisor owes a tort duty to a third party only when the promisor performs the contract at least in part (misfeasance, not nonfeasance).

4. *Does tort law impose a duty to rescue another? If so, then when?* Tort law imposes no duty to rescue or aid another unless the actor has a special relationship to the one needing rescue or the actor created the need, assumed a duty, or controlled the instrumentality from which the other needs rescue.

5. *Give examples of each of the situations in which tort law would impose a rescue duty.* A ship captain bears a special relationship to the ship's passengers to, for instance, rescue one who falls overboard. A motorist who carelessly forces another vehicle off the road would owe a duty to aid the vehicle's injured occupants. A business that advertises and supplies security would owe a duty to deploy it reasonably for the safety of customers. A property owner that offers tenants an elevator would owe a duty to rescue occupants trapped in the elevator.

6. *What is the economic-loss doctrine? What function (policy) does it serve?* The economic-loss doctrine limits duties to direct injury, barring pure economic loss claims by those who suffer no physical impact. The doctrine's purpose or function is to keep liability within management (insurable) bounds. Without the doctrine, some accidents could produce liability so extensive as to exhaust the insurance of and bankrupt actors whose carelessness alone would not warrant such penalty. Liability would lose its deterrent effect.

Torts I Workbook

Issue-Spotting Worksheet for Week 6
State the law each scenario raises. No analysis. Just spot the issue and state the law.

1.   The liability insurer for your small-business client, a lawn-mowing service that plows driveways and shovels walks in the winter, forwards to you a complaint that alleges that your client neglected to shovel, salt, and sand a snowy and icy walkway in front of a convenience store, with the result that the plaintiff slipped, fell, and suffered serious injury. Before you answer the complaint, the liability insurer wants you to report to it whether you might instead move to dismiss for no duty.

_____

_____

2.   After replying to the insurer, you read the complaint in detail in order to draft and file a timely answer. The complaint alleges that your client owed a duty to remove all snow and ice so as to make the sidewalk completely safe for any user under any circumstance. You mull how you should answer that allegation consistent with the state's tort law. [Hint: review from last week.]

_____

_____

3.   The complaint further alleges that your client owed the injured plaintiff a duty to provide first aid and call 911 or otherwise summon emergency personnel promptly once the plaintiff fell but that your client breached that duty when its driver drove past, saw the plaintiff, and did not stop to fulfill any of the alleged duties.

_____

_____

4.   For damages, the complaint alleges the usual medical expense, wage loss, and pain and suffering that you have seen alleged in other complaints. Yet the complaint also alleges that the plaintiff's employer lost revenue and profits when the plaintiff could not show up for work to perform the special operations that only the plaintiff could perform.

Answer Key for Issue-Spotting Worksheet

1. ***This scenario implicates when a tort duty arises under a contract.*** A contract promisor owes a tort duty to a third party only when the promisor performs the contract at least in part (misfeasance, not nonfeasance).

2. ***This scenario implicates the standard of care under the duty element of a negligence claim.*** The general duty of care is to act with *reasonable care*, also described as the care of a *reasonably prudent person*. Law sometimes also describes it as *ordinary care*. For example, one does not have an absolute duty to make a condition safe for all users and purposes, only a duty to make a condition *reasonably* safe for *reasonable* uses and *reasonably anticipated* users.

3. ***This scenario implicates whether one has a duty to aid or rescue.*** Tort law imposes no duty to rescue or aid another unless the actor has a special relationship to the one needing rescue or the actor created the need, assumed a duty, or controlled the instrumentality from which the other needs rescue.

4. ***This scenario implicates the economic-loss doctrine.*** The economic-loss doctrine limits duties to direct injury, barring pure economic loss claims by those who suffer no physical impact. The doctrine's purpose or function is to keep liability within management (insurable) bounds. Without the doctrine, some accidents could produce liability so extensive as to exhaust the insurance of and bankrupt actors whose carelessness alone would not warrant such penalty. Liability would lose its deterrent effect.

COMPREHENSIVENESS EXERCISE—WEEK 6

Insert words at the ^ mark that would make for a more-accurate or more-detailed law statement. Follow the italicized hints for help. Suggested answers are on the next page.

1. [Review:] The duty to use reasonable care, ^ determined by judge rather than jury, arises with ^ a foreseeable risk of harm. *[State another way to define "reasonable care." And is a foreseeable risk enough on its own to create a duty?]*

2. [Review:] Standards of care ^ articulate specifically what the defendant should have done ^ . *[Connect a standard of care with the duty to use reasonable care. And do standards only say what to do?]*

3. Standards of care depend on factors including ^ ^ regulations, ^ standards, and likelihood ^ and foreseeability of injury. *[Missed the first big one. And whose regulations? Whose standards? And then injury's likelihood is only half the equation.]*

4. A contract promisor owes a tort duty to a third party only when the promisor performs ^ the contract (misfeasance^). *[Full performance? And what's the alternative to misfeasance?]*

5. Tort law imposes no duty to rescue or aid another unless the actor has a special relationship to the one needing rescue or the actor ^ assumed a duty ^ . *[Left out two other ways the actor could create a duty where none would otherwise exist.]*

6. The economic ^ doctrine limits duties to ^ direct injury, barring economic loss claims by those who suffer no ^ impact. *[The economic-what doctrine? And "duties to direct injury"? One owes duties to persons, not injuries. And what kind of impact?]*

ANSWER KEY FOR COMPREHENSIVENESS EXERCISE

1. The duty to use reasonable care *(that of a reasonably prudent person)*, determined by judge rather than jury, arises with *affirmative acts creating* foreseeable risk of harm.

2. Standards of care, *a more specific statement of the duty of reasonable care,* articulate specifically what the defendant should have done *or not done under the circumstances then existing*.

3. Standards of care depend on factors including *custom*, *government* regulations, *industry* standards, and likelihood, *severity,* and foreseeability of injury.

4. A contract promisor owes a tort duty to a third party only when the promisor performs the contract *at least in part* (misfeasance, *not nonfeasance*).

5. Tort law imposes no duty to rescue or aid another unless the actor has a special relationship to the one needing rescue or the actor *created the need,* assumed a duty, *or controlled the instrumentality from which the other needs rescue*.

6. The economic-*loss* doctrine limits duties to *those who suffer* direct injury, barring *pure* economic loss claims by those who suffer no *direct, physical* impact.

Torts I Workbook

Examples/Non-Examples Exercise for Week 6

Identify whether each fact pattern is an example (E) or non-example (NE) of the **highlighted concept**. Answers follow. In the blanks, generate an additional example and non-example.

1. A contract promisor owes a tort duty to a third party only *when the promisor performs the contract at least in part (misfeasance*, not nonfeasance).
   ___ The pedestrian tripped and fell over the asphalt ridge that the paving contractor had left in the crosswalk.
   ___ The guest remained trapped in the elevator overnight after the repairman carelessly flipped the circuit.
   ___ The cement contractor never showed up to pour the concrete slab, where the woman fell into the ditch.
   ___ The snow-removal company made only a quick pass at the ice, leaving the patch where the shopper fell.
   ___ The security company never managed to send a guard to the new account where the robbery happened.
   ___ The inspector had a heart attack before even beginning, leaving the homeowners unaware of the defect.
   ___ The lab ran the tests for the medical clinic but misprinted the results, leaving the patients misdiagnosed.
   E: _____
   N: _____

2. ***Tort law ordinarily imposes no duty to rescue or aid another***. Moral duty may exist, but tort law would not hold liable the person who refuses to aid or rescue.
   ___ The drunken driver drove the vehicle straight through the red light into the path of the oncoming vehicle.
   ___ The motorist saw the horrific accident happen, including the rollover, but just kept on driving.
   ___ The physician remained seated quietly in the theater as attendants called frantically for medical help.
   ___ The physician misread the lab results, overlooking the danger sign that led to the patient's demise.
   ___ The neighbor just watched from her window as the homeowner dangled upside down from the tree.
   ___ The family friend suspected that someone, probably the uncle, was abusing the child but said nothing.
   ___ The daycare aide just watched as the children ran out the daycare's open gate and into the roadway.
   ___ The teen saw that the shopper had dropped her crutches and would fall without them but didn't move.
   E: _____
   N: _____

3. While tort law ordinarily imposes no duty to rescue or aid another, *a duty arises when the actor creates the need for aid or rescue*.
   ___ The carpenter accidentally bumped the roofer over the roof's edge, the fall knocking him unconscious.
   ___ The vacationing emergency medical technician didn't want to get involved with the guest's heart attack.
   ___ The worker who lowered the inspector into the tank hadn't expected fumes to overcome the inspector.
   ___ The driver felt awful that she had unwittingly run the car off the road into the creek but kept driving.
   ___ The hunting guide could see the fishermen trapped at the bottom of the canyon but just kept walking.
   ___ The canoeist carelessly ran into the submerged stump, tipping the youth out into the frothing water.
   ___ The hi-lo operator hadn't meant to drop the laden pallet on the clerk's foot but jumped off and ran away.
   E: _____
   N: _____

TORTS I WORKBOOK

4. While tort law ordinarily imposes no duty to rescue or aid another, *a duty arises when the actor has a special relationship to the one needing aid or rescue*.
    ___ The hotel manager saw the fire spreading toward the occupied rooms but fled without giving warning.
    ___ The pedestrian saw the alley fight and saw the victim get stabbed but out of fear kept on walking.
    ___ The aide saw the suicidal patient prying at the hospital's third-floor window but figured he wouldn't jump.
    ___ The river pilot knew kids were jumping from the upper deck into the swirling river but said nothing.
    ___ The dorm's resident assistant left the binge-drunk and passed out freshman in the hall and went to bed.
    ___ The physician suspected that her neighbor was having transient ischemic attacks but quietly ignored them.
    ___ The dentist knew that the indigent patient's infection was critical but sent her away with a patched tooth.

E: _____

N: _____

5. While tort law ordinarily imposes no duty to rescue or aid another, *a duty arises when an actor offers and assumes a duty*.
    ___ The officer had told the resident that he could not remain to see if the suspect returned to do more harm.
    ___ The retailer had posted signs in the parking lot that cameras surveilled and secured it against such attacks.
    ___ The motorist called out his window an offer to call 911, which the relieved crash victim gladly accepted.
    ___ The manager told the patient that the clinic was not an emergency facility and to go instead to the hospital.
    ___ The lawyer grudgingly said he'd take a look at the neighbor's will but missed the underage witness.
    ___ The tour operator had advertised that it employed armed guards to protect guests, but none were evident.
    ___ The trainer could see the rider struggling with her unruly mount but knew better than to get involved.

E: _____

N: _____

6. While tort law ordinarily imposes no duty to rescue or aid another, *a duty arises when the actor controls the instrumentality from which the other needs rescue*.
    ___ The engineer started to pull back on the train's throttle but didn't want to be late and so just took the risk.
    ___ The clerk saw that the shopper's coat was caught in the escalator but was too horrified to shut it off.
    ___ The hose kept filling the flooding pit in which the worker struggled to stay afloat, as passersby watched.
    ___ The captain liked to see the helpless dinghies flip in his ship's wake and so refused to change course.
    ___ The demolition continued despite that the tourist could see that a youth had snuck into the building.
    ___ The operator continued to bulldoze the huge pile even though knowing that the kids were playing on it.
    ___ The keeper saw the man enter the enclosure but figured he'd climb out when the keeper let the gorilla out.

E: _____

N: _____

Answers: 1 EENENNE; 2 NEENEENE; 3 ENEENEE; 4 ENEEENE; 5 NEENEEN; 6 EENENEE

TORTS I WORKBOOK

Sameness Exercise for Week 6

Deductive legal reasoning applies a rule to a fact pattern to determine the outcome. Analogic legal reasoning (reasoning by analogy) compares a hypothetical scenario to the real scenario to suggest an outcome. A policy argument construes a larger public interest from the recommended outcome of a private dispute. Working with a seatmate, sort the following fact patterns into deductive (D) or analogic (A) reasoning, or a policy (P) argument. Answers are on the next page.

____: Because the defendant drove a motor vehicle, and duties arise on acts creating foreseeable risk of harm, defendant owed a duty because driving forseeably risks harm.

____: The defendant driving is like a person shooting off a gun or a person chopping wood with an ax, where one would surely owe a duty of reasonable care not to hurt someone.

____: The defendant driver should owe a duty of care because duties of care and liability for breaches of care discourage drivers from driving carelessly, thus reducing injuries.

____: The driver owed a duty to keep a sharp lookout because a state statute required keeping a sharp lookout, and the statute was a safety statute for protecting a class against a risk.

____: The driver should have kept a sharp lookout because the driver controlled the risk, and when we internalize risks to those who control them, we get better-managed risk.

____: The driver should have kept a sharp lookout because keeping a sharp lookout is watching what you are doing, and everyone knows watching what you are doing is common sense.

____: The repair service owed a duty because it had contracted to perform but then misperformed, and misfeasance gives rise to a tort-based duty, not just contract breach like nonfeasance.

____: The repair service owed a duty because not doing a bad repair is like running a red light or selling an unreasonably dangerous product, where one would obviously owe a duty.

____: The repair service owed a duty because imposing a duty for sloppy repair should not only make repair services more reliable but would also shift the loss to the one who created it.

____: The physician owed no duty to come to the diner's aid because forcing a physician to help would be like making a neighbor cook your dinner every night or do your laundry.

____: The physician owed no duty to aid the diner because duties arise only through acts creating foreseeable risks or special relationships or status, and we had none of those here.

____: The physician owed no duty to come to the diner's aid because the physician did not create the diner's need for aid, and only those who create the need for rescue owe a duty to rescue.

____: The physician owed no duty to aid the diner because requiring strangers to aid would discourage people from acquiring valuable skills or going out in public with them.

Answer Key

Deductive legal reasoning applies a rule to a fact pattern to state determine the outcome. Analogic legal reasoning (reasoning by analogy) compares a hypothetical scenario to the real scenario to suggest an outcome. A policy argument construes a larger public interest from the recommended outcome of a private dispute. Working with a seatmate, sort the following fact patterns into deductive (D) or analogic (A) reasoning, or a policy (P) argument. Answers are on the next page.

D: Because the defendant drove a motor vehicle, and duties arise on acts creating foreseeable risk of harm, defendant owed a duty because driving forseeably risks harm.

A: The defendant driving is like a person shooting off a gun or a person chopping wood with an ax, where one would surely owe a duty of reasonable care not to hurt someone.

P: The defendant driver should owe a duty of care because duties of care and liability for breaches of care discourage drivers from driving carelessly, thus reducing injuries.

D: The driver owed a duty to keep a sharp lookout because a state statute required keeping a sharp lookout, and the statute was a safety statute for protecting a class against a risk.

P: The driver should have kept a sharp lookout because the driver controlled the risk, and when we internalize risks to those who control them, we get better-managed risk.

A: The driver should have kept a sharp lookout because keeping a sharp lookout is watching what you are doing, and everyone knows watching what you are doing is common sense.

D: The repair service owed a duty because it had contracted to perform but then misperformed, and misfeasance gives rise to a tort-based duty, not just contract breach like nonfeasance.

A: The repair service owed a duty because not doing a bad repair is like running a red light or selling an unreasonably dangerous product, where one would obviously owe a duty.

P: The repair service owed a duty because imposing a duty for sloppy repair should not only make repair services more reliable but would also shift the loss to the one who created it.

A: The physician owed no duty to come to the diner's aid because forcing a physician to help would be like making a neighbor cook your dinner every night or do your laundry.

D: The physician owed no duty to come to the diner's aid because duties arise only through acts creating foreseeable risks or special relationships or status, and we had none of those here.

D: The physician owed no duty to come to the diner's aid because the physician did not create the diner's need for aid, and only those who create the need for rescue owe a duty to rescue.

P: The physician owed no duty to aid the diner because requiring strangers to aid would discourage people from acquiring valuable skills or going out in public with them.

Review Exercise for Week 6
Match these facts with the law on the next page that they trigger.

His life lately had been a roller-coaster ride, more roll than coast. ____ 1. When a loud noise from his garage awoke him in the middle of the night, he had grabbed his gun from the drawer and headed out to investigate. ____ 2. When he opened the door to the garage, someone struck the gun out of his hand. ____ 3. He then heard a frightened voice say in quavering words, "Close the door, or I'll shoot." ____ 4. Thinking the voice sounded familiar, he had said, "George! Is that you?!" ____ 5. His neighbor George had replied in a shaky voice, "Yes… I was just going to borrow a few dollars from your wallet in your car but return it before you woke up in the morning." ____ 6. But George had then collapsed, clutching his chest, so he had called emergency personnel who, when they arrived, had asked him for permission to defibrillate George, to which he had replied he didn't know. ____ 7. Apparently, they decided to go ahead anyway but just when he had reached down to take George's cell phone from him to call his wife next door, resulting in a severe shock to him from the defibrillator. ____ 8. When he regained his senses from the shock, he had yelled, "Are you trying to kill me, you fools?!" ____ 9. One of the emergency technicians had apologized profusely, saying that they should have yelled to "Clear!" before shocking George but had forgotten in the excitement.

Review Exercise for Week 6
Match this law with the facts on the prior page to which the law applies.

___A. The purpose or desire to harm (not just the intent to act), often but not always due to ill will or malice, is the first of three forms of intent.[Week 1]

___B. Contact with anything closely connected with the person satisfies the contact element of battery.[Week 1]

___C. Words (threats) alone are generally not enough for an assault unless combined with an overt act suggesting imminent harmful contact.[Week 2]

___D. Trespass to land is intentional interference with exclusive possession of land or intentional unauthorized physical entry onto another's land.[Week 3]

___E. Conversion is intentional dominion over personal property substantially or totally interfering with the other's control, compensated by value at conversion.[Week 3]

___F. Emergency medical providers may treat those who are unable to give or withhold consent if the reasonable person would have consented.[Week 4]

___G. One may use reasonable force to defend property if the force is not likely to cause death or serious injury but not when mistaken.[Week 4]

___H. The duty to use reasonable care (that of a reasonably prudent person) arises whenever acts create foreseeable risk of harm.[Week 5]

___I. Standards of care depend on factors including custom, regulations, standards, experience, and likelihood and foreseeability of injury.[Week 5]

Answer key: 1G, 2B, 3C, 4D, 5E, 6F, 7H, 8A, 9I

Week 6 Drafting Exercise—Fact Allegations

Draft the fact allegations of this complaint for motor-vehicle negligence. Fact allegations are short and plain statements alerting defendant to events giving rise to liability. A model answer follows.

[Caption omitted.]

Complaint

Plaintiffs Pamela S. Bertrand and Johnnie P. Bertrand complain against defendant Jonathan Q. Carter saying:

PARTIES, JURISDICTION, AND VENUE

1. Mrs. Bertrand resides in Rockville, Glen County, Michigan.
2. Mr. Bertrand also resides in Rockville, Glen County, Michigan.
3. Mrs. Bertrand and Mr. Bertrand are husband and wife.
4. Mr. Carter resides in Wayfair, Glen County, Michigan.
5. This case is for damages in excess of $25,000 exclusive of interest and costs.
6. This cause of action arose in Riverview Township, Glen County, Michigan.
7. This Court has jurisdiction over the parties in this case.
8. This Court is a proper venue and the only convenient venue for this case.

FACT ALLEGATIONS

9.
10.
11.
12.
13.
14.
15.
16.
17.
18.
19.
20.
21.
22.
23.
24.
25.

COUNT I: MOTOR-VEHICLE NEGLIGENCE, MCL §500.3135

26. This reference incorporates the above paragraphs into this count.

27. Mr. Carter owed Mrs. Bertrand a duty of ordinary and reasonable care, that of the reasonably prudent motor-vehicle driver.

28. Mr. Carter further owed Mrs. Bertrand the duty to comply with all traffic laws, rules, and regulations including but not limited to the duties to: (a) obey all traffic signs and signals; (b) yield to other vehicles already in the intersection; (c) keep a sharp lookout; (d) maintain reasonable control of the vehicle; and (e) observe and avoid other vehicles.

29. Mr. Carter breached his above duties of reasonable care, did not act as a reasonably prudent motor-vehicle driver under the circumstances, and violated each of the above statutory duties such that the law presumes him negligent, in that he: (a) failed to obey the stop sign; (b) failed to yield to Mrs. Bertrand's through vehicle entering the intersection; (c) failed to keep a sharp lookout so as to observe and avoid Mrs. Bertrand's vehicle; (d) failed to maintain reasonable control of his vehicle so as to avoid Mrs. Bertrand's vehicle, and (e) failed to observe and avoid Mrs. Bertrand's vehicle, all if and when in the exercise of reasonable care and complying with his statutory duties Mr. Bertrand would and should have.

30. Mrs. Bertrand suffered the above injuries, loss, and damage as a factual and legal or proximate result of Mr. Carter's negligence.

31. Mrs. Bertrand further suffered serious impairment of body function from those above injuries, as MCL §500.3135 and interpreting case law defines that threshold, in that she suffered objectively manifested impairment of important body function generally affecting her ability to lead her normal life.

32. Mrs. Bertrand's injuries are permanent and her damages will continue into the future until the end of her life.

33. Mrs. Bertrand has suffered non-economic loss and excess economic loss compensable loss under Michigan's No-Fault Act, MCL §§500.3101 et seq., as a third-party claim under MCL §500.3135, for which Mr. Carter is liable.

COUNT II: LOSS OF CONSORTIUM

34. This reference incorporates the above paragraphs into this count.

35. The duties that Mr. Carter owed to Mrs. Bertrand Mr. Carter also owed derivatively and by extension to Mrs. Bertrand's husband Mr. Bertrand.

36. Mr. Carter breached each of those duties in the ways alleged above and was the factual and legal or proximate cause of Mr. Bertrand's loss of consortium.

ON THESE GROUNDS, plaintiffs Pamela S. Bertrand and Johnnie P. Bertrand pray for judgment in their favor and against defendant Jonathan Q. Carter for all amounts to which the Court finds them entitled, together with costs and attorney's fees most wrongfully sustained.

[Jury demand and signature block omitted.]

Model answer (condensed format): 9. A collision of motor vehicles driven by Mrs. Bertrand and Mr. Carter occurred. 10. The collision occurred at the intersection of Wagner and Fruitdale Roads. 11. The collision occurred at or about 8:26 a.m. on April 14, 2016. 12. Mrs. Bertrand was a belted driver of her 2011 Subaru Forester motor vehicle. 13. Mr. Carter was driving his 2008 Jeep Wrangler motor vehicle. 14. Mrs. Bertrand's vehicle was eastbound on Wagner Road, a through intersection. 15. Mr. Carter's vehicle was northbound on Fruitdale Road, a stop intersection. 16. Mr. Carter pulled his vehicle out from the stop sign into Mrs. Bertrand's vehicle. 17. Mr. Carter received and acknowledged traffic citations for causing the collision. 18. The collision's force damaged and disabled both vehicles. 19. The collision further seriously injured Mrs. Bertrand inside her vehicle. 20. Emergency technicians backboarded and removed Mrs. Bertrand by ambulance. 21. The ambulance took Mrs. Bertrand to Riverview Hospital for treatment. 22. Mrs. Bertrand suffered an unstable fracture of the thoracic spine, paraspinal hematoma, cervical strain, rib fractures, pulmonary and multiple other contusions, multiple abrasions, and other traumatic injury, requiring hospitalization, neurosurgery operative repair, clamshell bracing, physical therapy, pain control, and other extensive medical treatment, examination, services, and care. 23. Mrs. Bertrand further incurred pain, suffering, disability, fear, fright, shock, embarrassment, mortification, scarring, lost enjoyment of life, and mental and emotional distress. 24. Mrs. Bertrand has further been unable since the accident to work at her full-time employment as a medical-office manager and as a consequence has incurred work loss in excess of the limited work-loss benefits provided for under Michigan's No-Fault Act, MCL 500.3101 et seq. 25. Mr. Bertrand suffered loss of Mrs. Bertrand's love, society, companionship, services, and support that the law recognizes as loss of consortium.

Week 7

Emotional Distress, Prenatal Harm, Breach, & Proof of Fault

BULLET-POINT OUTLINE FOR WEEK 7:
QUALIFIED DUTIES (EMOTIONAL DISTRESS, PRENATAL HARM), BREACH, & PROOF OF FAULT
Qualified Duties (continued)
- [62]duty to avoid pure emotional distress only for
  - manifestation of
  - severe distress of
  - close family members who
  - contemporaneously witness physical injury
    - or under zone-of-danger or foreseeability tests
    - [63]traditional law also allows pure-emotional-distress claims for negligent mishandling of corpses
      - and for negligent transmission of death notices
      - and for fear of illness but only with severe distress and transmission route
- [64]The law may allow prenatal-harm claims if the child is born alive or was viable at injury
  - not generally against the mother
  - [65]law may allow claims for wrongful conception (limited to the cost of pregnancy and delivery)
  - law may allow claims for wrongful birth (negligent failure to inform to abort)
    - but not wrongful life by the child except possibly for extraordinary expenses

Negligence—Breach
[67]plaintiff has burdens
- pleading breach,
- producing breach evidence, and
- proving breach by a preponderance of the evidence = 51/49 = more probable than not

[66]breach = failure to use reasonable care = violation of standard of care
- prove by direct or circumstantial evidence
  - including constructive notice
  - including presumptions from spoliation (destruction) of evidence
    - parties have a duty to preserve evidence when reasonably anticipating litigation

PARAGRAPH-FORMAT OUTLINE FOR WEEK 7:
[62]Pure-emotion-distress claims are for manifestly severely distressed family members contemporaneously witnessing physical injury, or under zone-of-danger or foreseeability tests. [63]Traditional law also allows pure-emotional-distress claims for negligent mishandling of corpses and transmission of death notices, and fear of illness with severe distress and transmission route. [64]The law may allow prenatal-harm claims if the child is born alive or was viable at injury, but

not generally against the mother. [65]The law may allow claims for wrongful conception (limited to the cost of pregnancy and delivery) and wrongful birth (negligent failure to inform to abort) but not wrongful life by the child except possibly for extraordinary expenses.

Negligence—Breach
[66]One proves breach of duty, meaning failing to use reasonable care, by direct or circumstantial evidence including constructive notice and presumptions from spoliation of evidence. [67]The plaintiff has the burden of pleading breach, producing breach evidence, and proving breach by a preponderance of the evidence.

Fluency Cards for Week 7
Cover and uncover the response to each prompt until you fluently recall the exact response.

Pure Emotional Distress

Only for manifest severe distress of family members witnessing serious injury or within zone of danger.

Death Duties

Duty for negligent mishandling of corpses and transmission of death notices.

Duty to Unborn

Wrongful conception for cost of pregnancy/delivery, wrongful birth for failure to inform to abort, but not wrongful life.

Evidence of Breach

Direct or circumstantial evidence, constructive notice, or presumption from spoliation.

Definitions Worksheet for Week 7

1. When may law allow claims for pure distress without physical impact?

2. What are some categories where law may recognize pure-distress claims?

3. When does law allow prenatal-harm claims on the infant's behalf?

4. Define *wrongful conception, wrongful birth,* and *wrongful life.* Which does law allow?

5. With what kind of evidence does a claimant prove breach of duty?

6. Who has procedural burdens on breach? What are those burdens?

Answer Key for Definitions Worksheet

1. *When may law allow claims for pure emotional distress without physical impact?* Pure-emotion-distress claims are generally for manifested severe distress to family members who contemporaneously witness physical injury, or possibly under zone-of-danger or foreseeability tests.

2. *What are some special categories where law may recognize pure-distress claims?* Traditional law also allows pure-emotional-distress claims for negligent mishandling of corpses and transmission of death notices, and fear of illness with severe distress and transmission route.

3. *When does law allow prenatal-harm claims on the infant's behalf?* The law may allow prenatal-harm claims if the child is born alive or was viable at injury, but not generally against the mother.

4. *Define **wrongful conception**, **wrongful birth**, and **wrongful life**. Which does law allow?* A *wrongful-conception* claim is against a physician whose malpractice (failure to sterilize) allowed the claimant to conceive, *wrongful-birth* claim for failing to advise of test results on which the claimant would have aborted, and *wrongful-life* claim by the congenitally abnormal child for failing to abort. The law may allow claims for wrongful conception (limited to the cost of pregnancy and delivery) and wrongful birth (negligent failure to inform to abort) but not wrongful life by the child except possibly for extraordinary expenses.

5. *With what evidence does a claimant prove breach of duty?* One proves breach of duty, meaning failing to use reasonable care, by direct or circumstantial evidence (including constructive notice) and by presumptions from spoliation of evidence.

6. *Who has the procedural burdens on the breach element? What are those burdens?* The plaintiff has the burden of pleading breach, producing breach evidence, and proving breach by a preponderance of the evidence.

Issue-Spotting Worksheet for Week 7

State the law each scenario raises. No analysis. Just spot the issue and state the law.

1. A married couple visits you in your office expressing concern that the husband, the family's sole income earner, is unable to work. When you ask what happened, they explain that the husband grew so upset over the wife's motor-vehicle-accident injury that the husband's emotional distress and depression have prevented the husband from working. They want to know whether the husband can sue the negligent driver who caused the motor-vehicle accident.

_____

_____

2. The couple further explains that the wife was pregnant when the accident and her injury occurred three months ago, complicating the pregnancy and putting the baby at risk. They want to know whether their baby, due any day now, will also have a claim against the negligent driver if the accident caused the baby a serious injury.

_____

_____

3. The couple further explains that they hadn't planned the wife's pregnancy. In fact, the husband had a sterilization procedure not long before the wife's pregnancy because both the wife's family and husband's family carried genes for significant risk of birth defect. Test results, though, have shown that the baby should be born without the genetic condition.

_____

_____

4. After discussing potential legal issues arising out of the pregnancy, the couple explain the motor-vehicle accident's circumstances. The wife was asleep in her friend's vehicle when her friend says the other driver ran a red light while on a cell phone. The other driver says his light was green and the friend's light red and that he has since lost the phone and closed his phone account. The couple wants to know how you'd prove the case and who wins a close dispute.

_____

_____

Answer Key for Issue-Spotting Worksheet

1. ***This scenario implicates when tort law may recognize a pure-emotional-distress claim.*** Pure-emotion-distress claims are generally for manifested severe distress to family members who contemporaneously witness physical injury, or possibly under zone-of-danger or foreseeability tests. Traditional law also allows pure-emotional-distress claims for negligent mishandling of corpses and transmission of death notices, and fear of illness with severe distress and transmission route.

2. ***This scenario implicates when tort law may allow prenatal-harm claims.*** The law may allow prenatal-harm claims if the child is born alive or was viable at injury but not generally against the mother.

3. ***This scenario implicates when tort law may allow claims against medical providers for enabling conception and failing to inform to allow abortion.*** A *wrongful-conception* claim is against a physician whose malpractice (failure to sterilize) allowed the claimant to conceive, *wrongful-birth* claim for failing to advise of test results on which the claimant would have aborted, and *wrongful-life* claim by the congenitally abnormal child for failing to abort. The law may allow claims for wrongful conception (limited to the cost of pregnancy and delivery) and wrongful birth (negligent failure to inform to abort) but not wrongful life by the child except possibly for extraordinary expenses.

4. ***This scenario implicates the evidence with which to prove breach and the burden of proof.*** One proves breach of duty, meaning failing to use reasonable care, by direct or circumstantial evidence (including constructive notice) and by presumptions from spoliation of evidence. The plaintiff has the burden of pleading breach, producing breach evidence, and proving breach by a preponderance of the evidence.

Torts I Workbook

COMPREHENSIVENESS WORKSHEET—WEEK 7

Insert words at the ^ mark that would make for a more-accurate or more-detailed law statement. Follow the italicized hints for help. Suggested answers are on the next page.

1. Pure-emotion-distress claims are generally for ^ severe distress for those who contemporaneously witness physical injury ^, or possibly under ^ foreseeability test. *[What kind of severe distress? And an injury to anyone? And doesn't law offer another test?]*

2. Traditional law also allows ^ emotional-distress claims for negligent mishandling of corpses ^ and fear of illness with severe distress ^. *[Emotional distress alone and with physical injury? And missing one more category? And fear of illness alone or with something else?]*

3. The law may allow prenatal-harm claims if the child is born alive ^ ^. *[Another alternative? And a limitation?]*

4. The law may allow claims for wrongful conception and wrongful birth (negligent failure to inform to abort) ^ ^ but not wrongful life by the child. *[Doesn't law limit recovery? Any option for more?]*

5. One proves breach of duty, meaning failing to use ^ care, by direct ^ evidence including constructive notice ^. *[Doesn't care have a qualifier? And only direct evidence? And when may law presume breach?]*

6. The plaintiff has the burden of pleading breach ^ and proving breach by ^ evidence. *[Missed one of the three burdens. And the proof burden is more specific than just evidence.]*

ANSWERS FOR COMPREHENSIVENESS WORKSHEET

1. Pure-emotional-distress claims are generally for **physically manifested** severe distress for those who contemporaneously witness physical injury **to a close family member**, or possibly under **zone-of-danger or** foreseeability test.

2. Traditional law also allows **pure**-emotional-distress claims for negligent mishandling of corpses **or transmission of death notices,** and fear of illness with severe distress **and transmission route**.

3. The law may allow prenatal-harm claims if the child is born alive **or was viable at injury but not generally against the mother**.

4. The law may allow claims for wrongful conception and wrongful birth (negligent failure to inform to abort), **limited to the cost of pregnancy and delivery, and possibly extraordinary expenses,** but not wrongful life by the child.

5. One proves breach of duty, meaning failing to use **reasonable** care, by direct **or circumstantial** evidence, including constructive notice, **or by presumptions from spoliation of evidence**.

6. The plaintiff has the burden of pleading breach, **producing breach evidence**, and proving breach by **a preponderance of the** evidence.

Sameness Exercises for Week 7

Determine whether the fact pattern supports a pure-emotional-distress claim under the immediate-family-member (IFM), zone-of-danger (ZOD), directly involved (DI), mishandled-corpse (MC), or transmitted-death-notice (TDN) exceptions, or supports no claim (N). Answers are at the bottom.

1_____ Motorist driving home one evening happens to witness fatal vehicle-bicycle accident involving decapitation, suffer recurrent nightmares and severe weight loss.

2_____ Pedestrian, standing next to and jumping back from killed pedestrian struck by wandering truck, suffers severe shaking, depression, and disorienting flashbacks.

3_____ Emergency personnel call severely distressed wife to hospital to identify her deceased husband from vehicle accident when husband was instead safely at work.

4_____ Husband waving goodby to wife at urban bus stop sees approaching bus skid into, strike, and kill wife, with husband suffering chronic depression and weight gain.

5_____ Medical care provider mistakenly informs severely distressed patient that she must undergo chemotherapy and surgery for late-stage cancer that patient does not have.

6_____ Funeral home mistakenly leaves body of severely distressed adult daughter's mother outside rear of funeral home where vandals steal body to hang it from bridge.

7_____ Basketball fan sitting in front row experiences player dying from heart attack at fan's feet due to team's lacking defibrillator, with fan suffering tremors and flashbacks.

8_____ SeaWorld orca snatches spectator from poolside, causing crushing and drowning death, leaving adjacent spectator suffering nightmares and seizures.

9_____ Hospital mistakenly informs transfusion patient that HIV tainted donated and transfused blood, causing patient to isolate self severely in chronic depression.

10_____ Parent suffers vomiting, uncontrollable shaking, and nightmares after medical examiner carelessly permits local media to film and broadcast autopsy on deceased child.

11_____ Sea-film producer notifies missing worker's severely distressed spouse that rogue wave swept worker to his death, when worker was instead on drinking binge.

12_____ News website posts spoof notice that famous entertainer has died suddenly while recording a music video, severely distressing the entertainer's most-ardent fan.

13_____ Summer-camp counselor causes severe campfire-burn injuries to child camper in front of crowd of parents including child's severely distressed parents.

1N 2ZOD 3TDN 4IFM 5DI 6MC 7N 8ZOD 9DI 10MC 11TDN 12N 13IFM

More Sameness Exercises for Week 7

Determine whether the fact pattern supports a child's claim for death or injury (CDI), or assuming the jurisdiction recognizes it then a parent's claim for wrongful conception (WC) or wrongful birth (WB), or instead alleges only a child's claim for wrongful life (WL) recognized in no jurisdiction or otherwise supports no claim (N). Answers are at the end.

1_____ Pregnant vehicle passenger suffers seatbelt injury in negligent driver's vehicle collision, bearing **child claimant** with resulting disabling spine and limb defects.

2_____ Pregnant vehicle passenger suffers seatbelt injury in negligent driver's vehicle collision, causing miscarriage of **claimant child** at three months' gestational age.

3_____ Pregnant vehicle passenger suffers seatbelt injury in negligent driver's vehicle collision, causing prompt premature birth of **claimant child** dying days later as a result.

4_____ Lab carelessly swaps test results incorrectly indicating to **claimant parents** that they will bear a normal rather than Downs child, when parents would have aborted.

5_____ Lab carelessly swaps test results incorrectly indicating to parents that they will bear a normal rather than Downs **child claimant**, when parents would have aborted.

6_____ Physician performs substandard vasectomy causing **claimant father** to father healthy but unwanted child.

7_____ Physician performs substandard hysterectomy causing **claimant mother** to conceive unwanted child with special needs requiring extraordinary expense.

8_____ Clinic carelessly swaps pregnancy-test results indicating to **claimant mother** that she was not pregnant when she was pregnant.

1CDI 2N 3CDI 4WB 5WL 6WC 7WC 8WB

Determine whether the fact pattern describes the plaintiff's burden of PLEADING, PRODUCTION, or PROOF. Answers are below.

1_____ As the lawyer sat down to draft her client's negligence complaint, she wasn't sure whether law supported that defendant owed a duty to her client plaintiff or not.

2_____ Defense counsel needed to draft jury instructions to submit to the trial judge before counsel gave closing arguments in the medical-malpractice trial the next day.

3_____ Plaintiff's counsel gulped as he read defendant's motion to dismiss the plaintiff's case for lack of standard-of-care evidence in the negligence case.

4_____ Defense counsel went over and over plaintiff's trial proofs, looking for a hole to poke in the evidence in closing argument, to take advantage of the plaintiff's burden.

5_____ Defense counsel was delighted when plaintiff's expert admitted she didn't know how the accident happened because now counsel could file that motion to dismiss.

1PLEADING 2PROOF 3PRODUCTION 4PROOF 5PRODUCTION

Problem-Solving Exercise Week 7 (1)

Think-aloud problem solving (TAPS) is a proven method of using vocalization to become a more creative and better problem solver. Professionals are effective problem solvers when they speak aloud to another, speaking aloud to themselves, or let their mental operations taking the silent form of words, concepts, principles, and strategies to reach partial solutions and then chain partial solutions toward final novel solution. Read the following example (EX) and non-example (NE) of an unknown new rule (RU), one that the judges writing their opinions and orders have not expressly stated but that you must instead discern and record as your problem solution. Vocalize each mental operation taken toward a partial solution, until you reach and record the final novel rule. Check your answer against the model answer at the bottom of the next page.

EX   OPINION AND ORDER: In this negligence case, the plaintiff elderly dementia sufferer alleges that the defendant nursing-care provider owed plaintiff a duty to protect the plaintiff against mental and emotional distress but failed in that duty, causing plaintiff severe emotional disability, when defendant's staff repeatedly exposed plaintiff to violent and terrifying R-rated films. Defendant has moved to dismiss, arguing that defendant owed plaintiff no duty. The Court denies defendant's motion, setting plaintiff's claim for jury trial.

NE   OPINION AND ORDER: In this negligence case, the plaintiff minor, through his next-friend parents, alleges that the defendant video-game store owed plaintiff a duty to protect the plaintiff against mental and emotional distress but failed in that duty, causing plaintiff severe emotional disability, when defendant premises and products repeatedly exposed plaintiff to violent and terrifying R-rated video games. Defendant through counsel assigned by defendant's insurer has moved to dismiss, arguing that defendant owed plaintiff no duty. The Court grants defendant's motion, dismissing plaintiff's case with prejudice.

RU   _____

_____

_____

_____

Answer to problem on next page: The mother of a child owes no duty to protect the child against in utero harm except when voluntarily undertaking a duty by special relationship, such as when a surrogate mother specifically contracts to carry the child of another.

Problem-Solving Exercise Week 7 (2)

Think-aloud problem solving (TAPS) is a proven method of using vocalization to become a more creative and better problem solver. Professionals are effective problem solvers when they speak aloud to another, speaking aloud to themselves, or let their mental operations taking the silent form of words, concepts, principles, and strategies to reach partial solutions and then chain partial solutions toward final novel solution. Read the following example (EX) and non-example (NE) of an unknown new rule (RU), one that the judges writing their opinions and orders have not expressly stated but that you must instead discern and record as your problem solution. Vocalize each mental operation taken toward a partial solution, until you reach and record the final novel rule. Check your answer against the model answer at the bottom of the next page.

EX   OPINION AND ORDER: In this negligence case, the plaintiff child, through a conservator, alleges that the defendant surrogate mother was negligent and caused the child permanent brain damage when the surrogate consumed substantial quantities of alcohol while carrying the unborn child in utero under contract with the child's parents. Defendant has moved to dismiss, arguing no duty. The Court denies defendant's motion, bringing this case on for jury trial as to defendant's negligence and the amount of resulting damages.

NE   OPINION AND ORDER: In this negligence case, the plaintiff infant, through the father as next friend, alleges that the defendant mother was negligent in causing the child developmental delays and permanent neurological damage by unlawfully using illicit cocaine, heroin, and opioid drugs on frequent occasion and against physician's advice while pregnant with the unborn infant. Defendant has moved to dismiss, arguing no duty. The Court grants defendant's motion and dismisses plaintiff's case with prejudice.

RU   _____

_____

_____

_____

Answer to problem on prior page: Although one ordinarily has no duty to prevent emotional distress without impact, a duty may arise out of a special relationship in which a skilled service provider agrees to protect a special ward against such distress.

Week 7 Drafting Exercise—Negligence Count

Draft the negligence count of this complaint for motor-vehicle negligence. A negligence count must allege duty, breach, causation, and damage. The duty paragraph should allege specific standards of care implicating defendant's fault as the fact allegations suggest. The breach paragraph should allege specific breaches of that standard of care. A model answer appears at the end.

[Caption omitted.]

Complaint

Plaintiffs Pamela S. Bertrand and Johnnie P. Bertrand complain against defendant Jonathan Q. Carter saying:

PARTIES, JURISDICTION, AND VENUE

1. Mrs. Bertrand resides in Rockville, Glen County, Michigan.
2. Mr. Bertrand also resides in Rockville, Glen County, Michigan.
3. Mrs. Bertrand and Mr. Bertrand are husband and wife.
4. Mr. Carter resides in Wayfair, Glen County, Michigan.
5. This case is for damages in excess of $25,000 exclusive of interest and costs.
6. This cause of action arose in Riverview Township, Glen County, Michigan.
7. This Court has jurisdiction over the parties in this case.
8. This Court is a proper venue and the only convenient venue for this case.

FACT ALLEGATIONS

9. A collision of motor vehicles driven by Mrs. Bertrand and Mr. Carter occurred.
10. The collision occurred at the intersection of Wagner and Fruitdale Roads.
11. The collision occurred at or about 8:26 a.m. on April 14, 2016.
12. Mrs. Bertrand was a belted driver of her 2011 Subaru Forester motor vehicle.
13. Mr. Carter was driving his 2008 Jeep Wrangler motor vehicle.
14. Mrs. Bertrand's vehicle was eastbound on Wagner Road, a through intersection.
15. Mr. Carter's vehicle was northbound on Fruitdale Road, a stop intersection.
16. Mr. Carter pulled his vehicle out from the stop sign into Mrs. Bertrand's vehicle.
17. Mr. Carter received and acknowledged traffic citations for causing the collision.
18. The collision's force damaged and disabled both vehicles.
19. The collision further seriously injured Mrs. Bertrand inside her vehicle.
20. Emergency technicians backboarded and removed Mrs. Bertrand by ambulance.
21. The ambulance took Mrs. Bertrand to Riverview Hospital for treatment.
22. Mrs. Bertrand suffered an unstable fracture of the thoracic spine, paraspinal hematoma, cervical strain, rib fractures, pulmonary and multiple other contusions, multiple abrasions, and other traumatic injury, requiring hospitalization, neurosurgery operative repair, clamshell bracing, physical therapy, pain control, and other extensive medical treatment, examination, services, and care.
23. Mrs. Bertrand further incurred pain, suffering, disability, fear, fright, shock, embarrassment, mortification, scarring, lost enjoyment of life, and mental and emotional distress.
24. Mrs. Bertrand has further been unable since the accident to work at her full-time employment as a medical-office manager and has incurred work loss exceeding the limited work-loss benefits provided for under Michigan's No-Fault Act, MCL 500.3101 et seq.
25. Mr. Bertrand suffered loss of Mrs. Bertrand's love, society, companionship, services, and support that the law recognizes as loss of consortium.

COUNT I: MOTOR-VEHICLE NEGLIGENCE, MCL §500.3135

26. This reference incorporates the above paragraphs into this count.

27.

28.

29.

30.

31.

32.

33.

COUNT II: LOSS OF CONSORTIUM

34. This reference incorporates the above paragraphs into this count.
35. The duties that Mr. Carter owed to Mrs. Bertrand Mr. Carter also owed derivatively and by extension to Mrs. Bertrand's husband Mr. Bertrand.
36. Mr. Carter breached each of those duties in the ways alleged above and was the factual and legal or proximate cause of Mr. Bertrand's loss of consortium.

ON THESE GROUNDS, plaintiffs Pamela S. Bertrand and Johnnie P. Bertrand pray for judgment in their favor and against defendant Jonathan Q. Carter for all amounts to which the Court finds them entitled, together with costs and attorney's fees most wrongfully sustained.
[Jury demand and signature block omitted.]

Model answer (condensed format): 27. Mr. Carter owed Mrs. Bertrand a duty of ordinary and reasonable care, that of the reasonably prudent motor-vehicle driver. 28. Mr. Carter further owed Mrs. Bertrand the duty to comply with all traffic laws, rules, and regulations including but not limited to the duties to: (a) obey all traffic signs and signals; (b) yield to other vehicles already in the intersection; (c) keep a sharp lookout; (d) maintain reasonable control of the vehicle; and (e) observe and avoid other vehicles. 29. Mr. Carter breached his above duties of reasonable care, did not act as a reasonably prudent motor-vehicle driver under the circumstances, and violated each of the above statutory duties such that the law presumes him negligent, in that he: (a) failed to obey the stop sign; (b) failed to yield to Mrs. Bertrand's through vehicle entering the intersection; (c) failed to keep a sharp lookout so as to observe and avoid Mrs. Bertrand's vehicle; (d) failed to maintain reasonable control of his vehicle so as to avoid Mrs. Bertrand's vehicle, and (e) failed to observe and avoid Mrs. Bertrand's vehicle, all if and when in the exercise of reasonable care and complying with his statutory duties Mr. Bertrand would and should have. 30. Mrs. Bertrand suffered the above injuries, loss, and damage as a factual and legal or proximate result of Mr. Carter's negligence. 31. Mrs. Bertrand further suffered serious impairment of body function from those above injuries, as MCL §500.3135 and interpreting case law defines that threshold, in that she suffered objectively manifested impairment of important body function generally affecting her ability to lead her normal life. 32. Mrs. Bertrand's injuries are permanent and her damages will continue until the end of her life. 33. Mrs. Bertrand has suffered non-economic loss and excess economic loss compensable loss under Michigan's No-Fault Act, MCL §§500.3101 et seq., as a third-party claim under MCL §500.3135, for which Mr. Carter is liable.

Week 8
Res Ipsa Loquitur, Violation of Statute, Causation, & Cause-in-Fact

Bullet Outline for Week 8:
RES IPSA, VIOLATION OF STATUTE, & CAUSATION (CAUSE-IN-FACT)
Proof of Breach (continued)
- [68]may also prove breach by res ipsa loquitur providing an inference of negligence if
  - the event speaks of negligence,
  - plaintiff cannot obtain negligence evidence, and
  - defendant controls the circumstances (may need *exclusive* control)
- [69]may also prove breach by violation of safety statute protecting plaintiff's class against the injury risk
  - negligence per se (defendant must excuse) or
  - presumption of negligence (defendant must come forward with evidence of care) or
  - inference of negligence (jury may find defendant negligent without further proof)
- [70]violation of industry standards permits an inference of negligence

Negligence—Causation
[71]plaintiff must show the breach was (1) a cause in fact of harm and also (2) a legal or proximate cause
- [72]remember the eggshell-skull rule = pay for all harm if at least some harm was direct and foreseeable

[73]Cause in fact
- but-for test is main test for cause in fact (but for the negligence, the injury would not have occurred)
  - medical, legal, technical, and scientific matters may require expert testimony
    - base expertise on valid & reliable scientific methods (peer review, testing, replication)

Paragraph Outline for Week 8:
Proof of Breach (continued)
[68]Res ipsa loquitur may permit an inference of negligence if the event speaks of negligence, plaintiff cannot obtain negligence evidence, and defendant controls the circumstances. [69]Violation of safety statute is negligence per se (the majority position) or permits a presumption or inference of negligence, where the statute protects the plaintiff's class against the injury risk. [70]Violation of industry standards permits an inference of negligence.

Negligence—Causation
[71]Causation requires plaintiff to show that the breach more probably than not was a cause in fact (but-for cause) of harm and also legal or proximate cause. [72]The eggshell-skull rule requires

defendant to pay for all foreseeable and unforeseeable harm if at least some harm was direct and foreseeable.

Fluency Cards for Week 8

Cover and uncover the response to each prompt until you fluently recall the exact response.

Res Ipsa Loquitur

Infer negligence if speaks of negligence, plaintiff cannot get evidence, and defendant controls.

Statute Violation

Negligence per se or a presumption or inference of negligence if protects plaintiff's class from risk.

Cause in Fact

But for the breach, plaintiff would not have been injured.

Definitions Worksheet for Week 8

1. What does *res ipsa loquitur* accomplish and when does it apply?

2. How does violating a safety statute support a negligence claim? What is a safety statute?

3. How would violating an industry standard prove negligence? What is an industry standard?

4. Causation requires considering not one but two questions. Name and define them.

5. How would you prove cause in fact on medical, legal, technical or scientific matters?

Answer Key for Definitions Worksheet

1. *What does res ipsa loquitur accomplish and when does it apply?*

Res ipsa loquitur may permit an inference of negligence if the event speaks of negligence, plaintiff cannot obtain negligence evidence, and defendant controls the circumstances.

2. *How does violating a safety statute support a negligence claim? What is a safety statute?*

Violating a safety statute is negligence per se or permits a presumption or inference of negligence, depending on the jurisdiction. A safety statute is one that protects the plaintiff's class against the specific risk of injury that occurred in the actual event.

3. *How would violating an industry standard prove negligence? What is an industry standard?*

Violating an industry standard permits the jury to draw an inference of negligence. An industry standard represents the custom or practice within a certain field.

4. *Causation requires considering not one but two questions. Name and define them.*

Causation requires plaintiff to show both cause-in-fact and legal or proximate cause. Cause in fact is scientific or logical cause (typically but-for cause, meaning that but for the breach, the plaintiff would not have suffered injury), while legal or proximate cause represents a policy judgment on how far liability should extend.

5. *How would you prove cause in fact on medical, legal, technical or scientific matters?*

Cause in fact on medical, legal, technical, and scientific matters may require expert testimony based on valid and reliable scientific methods.

TORTS I WORKBOOK

Issue-Spotting Worksheet for Week 8
State the law each scenario raises. No analysis. Just spot the issue and state the law.

1.   A new client explains that he suffered serious injury when his work required him to inspect a customer's plant. An explosion occurred when he opened a door to a storage closet. The explosion and following fire left no evidence. The customer won't say what happened.

_____

_____

_____

2.   After hearing your first thoughts, the client pulls from his pocket a crumpled printout of a code section that prohibits storage of certain chemicals in workplaces. He says the rumor is that the customer was storing those chemicals in the closet.

_____

_____

_____

3.   Impressed at your eloquence, the client admits that he isn't sure that those chemicals are combustible. In fact, while he's pretty sure that the customer had several code violations ongoing, the client isn't sure that any of them had anything to do with the explosion, which he thinks instead may have just been a freak accident.

_____

_____

_____

4.   After quickly looking up the chemicals online in your office, you and the client see that the information raises a significant technical issue over the chemicals' properties.

_____

_____

_____

Answer Key for Issue-Spotting Worksheet

1. ***This scenario implicates the conditions for when res ipsa loquitur may permit an inference of negligence.*** Res ipsa loquitur may permit an inference of negligence if the event speaks of negligence, plaintiff cannot obtain negligence evidence, and defendant controls the circumstances.

2. ***This scenario implicates how tort law treats the defendant's having violated a statute.*** Violating a safety statute is negligence per se or permits a presumption or inference of negligence, depending on the jurisdiction. A safety statute is one that protects the plaintiff's class against the specific risk of injury that occurred in the actual event.

3. ***This scenario implicates what tort law requires the plaintiff to prove in connecting the defendant's breach to the plaintiff's damages.*** Causation requires plaintiff to show both cause-in-fact and legal or proximate cause. Cause in fact is scientific or logical cause (typically but-for cause, meaning that but for the breach, the plaintiff would not have suffered injury), while legal or proximate cause represents a policy judgment on how far liability should extend.

4. ***This scenario implicates how the plaintiff would prove cause in fact on technical issues.*** Cause in fact on medical, legal, technical, and scientific matters may require expert testimony based on valid and reliable scientific methods.

COMPREHENSIVENESS EXERCISE—WEEK 8

Insert words at the ^ mark that would make for a more-accurate or more-detailed law statement. Follow the italicized hints for help. Suggested answers are on the next page.

1. Res ipsa ^ may permit an inference of negligence if the event speaks of negligence and plaintiff cannot obtain negligence evidence ^ . *[Missed one of the three conditions.]*

2. Violating a ^ statute is negligence per se or permits ^ an inference of negligence ^ . *[Any statute? Just an inference? And who decides?]*

3. To be a safety statute, the statute must protect the plaintiff's class ^ . *[That's half of it, but what's the other condition?]*

4. Violating an industry ^ standard permits the jury to draw ^ negligence. *[What kind of standard? And does law draw negligence or draw something else?]*

5. Causation requires plaintiff to show ^ cause in fact ^ . *[Didn't you leave out something else plaintiff must prove?]*

6. Cause in fact is ^ logical cause. Plaintiff must show that ^ the plaintiff would not have suffered injury. *[Just logical or something else, too? And just suffering injury is enough? Didn't you leave out the connection?]*

7. Cause in fact on ^ ^ technical matters may require expert testimony based on ^ scientific methods. *[Just technical matters? And any scientific method?]*

ANSWERS TO COMPREHENSIVENESS EXERCISE

1. Res ipsa *loquitur* may permit an inference of negligence if the event speaks of negligence and plaintiff cannot obtain negligence evidence, *and defendant controls the circumstances*.

2. Violating a *safety* statute is negligence per se or permits a *presumption or* inference of negligence, *depending on the jurisdiction*.

3. To be a safety statute, the statute must protect the plaintiff's class *against the specific risk of injury like that of the actual event*.

4. Violating an industry *safety* standard permits the jury to draw *an inference of* negligence.

5. The causation element requires plaintiff to show *both* cause in fact *and legal or proximate cause*.

6. Cause in fact is *scientific or* logical cause. Plaintiff must show that *but for the breach*, the plaintiff would not have suffered injury.

7. Cause in fact on *medical, legal, scientific, and* technical matters may require expert testimony based on *valid and reliable* scientific methods.

TORTS I WORKBOOK

Sameness Exercises for Week 8

Sort the fact patterns based on whether *res ipsa loquitur* (RIL), **violation of safety statute** (SS), or **violation of industry standard** (IS) would apply. Answers are at the bottom of the next page. The next page has a similar exercise.

1. _____ No one could tell how, but the hitch had clearly come undone without the safety chains hooked.
2. _____ Ignoring the flashing yield sign, the driver drove her car out right into the oncoming truck's path.
3. _____ The punch press was the only one of its kind that didn't have the customary two-hand controls.
4. _____ The bartender slipped the 17-year-old a drink, figuring the teen wouldn't be so stupid as to drive.
5. _____ In the explosion's aftermath, investigators could only trace the source to the motorist's gas can.
6. _____ The barge-association rules called for two deck hands, but the owner figured doing with one.
7. _____ The fire left no sign of an accelerant, but the manager admitted he had been using turpentine there.
8. _____ The chemist knew better than to work without the eye shield that her profession recommended.
9. _____ The gas-pump sign said law prohibited filling non-approved containers, but the worker still did it.
10. _____ The engineering guide said to use hardened steel, but the bridge's designer rejected it as too pricey.
11. _____ The law prohibited sales of handguns to minors, but the shop owner needed the youth's cash.
12. _____ No one was talking and nothing showed in the medical records explaining the burn during surgery.
13. _____ The unbelted passenger had his head slam into the windshield when the vehicles collided.
14. _____ The university had none despite that the conference required a defibrillator courtside at all games.
15. _____ State law prohibited returning to the ring within 30 days of knockout, but the fighter needed money.
16. _____ The submerged vehicle no longer showed any evidence of its sudden mechanical failure.
17. _____ The officer calculated from skid marks that the motorcyclist was going about ten over the limit.
18. _____ The medical association's published guide was for CT scan, but the doctor opted only for x-ray.
19. _____ The banker knew industry publications advised against security workaround but used one anyway.
20. _____ The executive blew just a tick over the legal limit in the post-accident roadside sobriety test.
21. _____ The maker claimed it mistakenly destroyed the failed product its injured customer sent to it to test.
22. _____ Federal law required clearance before landing, but the pilot set the craft down without it anyway.
23. _____ The pool cleaner ignored the manufacturers' association guidelines against using the chemical.
24. _____ The general contractor was unaware of the trade association's advisory to include tie-off safety.

Answer Key to Reverse Side: Cause in fact is scientific or logical cause, typically determined as ***but-for cause*** (BFC), meaning that but for the breach, the plaintiff would not have suffered injury. Cause in fact on medical, legal, technical, and scientific matters may require ***expert testimony*** (ET) based on valid and reliable scientific methods. Use the ***substantial-factor test*** (SFT) rather than but-for causation when each of two or more independent acts would alone have caused the harm. 1.BF 2.SF 3.ET 4.SF 5.BF 6.ET 7.BF 8.SF 9.ET 10.SF 11.BF 12.ET 13.BF 14.ET 15.SF 16.BF 17.ET 18.BF 19.SF 20.ET 21.BF 22.SF 23.ET 24.BF

Sameness Exercise for Week 8

Sort the fact patterns based on whether **but-for cause** (BFC), **expert testimony** (ET) as to causation, or the **substantial-factor test** (SFT) for causation would apply. Answers are at the bottom of the prior page.

1. _____ The mechanic forgot to tighten fittings on the leaking brake lines, after which the brakes failed.
2. _____ Either guest's campfire would clearly have caused the campground's unfortunate conflagration.
3. _____ The standard of care clearly called for twice the dosage that the nurse mistakenly administered.
4. _____ Both manufacturers had sold asbestos-laden insulation to contractors retrofitting the plant.
5. _____ The surgeon accidentally left the cotton packing in the wound, requiring a second surgery.
6. _____ The failing metal was clearly a new composite rather than the standard steel.
7. _____ The crew so seriously overloaded the airplane that it never got off the ground by runway's end.
8. _____ The river toxins clearly came from both industrial sources, with way too much to go around.
9. _____ The office neglected to schedule the blood draw for two months before the results showed cancer.
10. _____ Ballistics showed that both hunters had accidentally shot the hiker in the head at the same moment.
11. _____ The stoplight had already turned red, when the driver judged poorly that he could make it anyway.
12. _____ The medical records showed an eight-minute delay in the staff's administering ordered oxygen.
13. _____ The shopper never saw the slippery pool of cleaning fluid that the custodian left in the aisle.
14. _____ Nothing was obviously wrong with the engineering, and yet the roof span had clearly failed.
15. _____ Each of the five pharmacies had sold doses of the defective drug to the unfortunate decedent.
16. _____ The builder admitted using the wrong adhesive that caused all of the panels to fall off.
17. _____ The literature showed strong exposure correlation and yet high incidence under non-exposure.
18. _____ The electrician acknowledged she had accidentally reversed poles on the circuit that caught fire.
19. _____ Autopsy showed the patient would have died from either the defective device or unrelated poison.
20. _____ Evidence was unclear if the defective door had ejected occupants or if they came out the windows.
21. _____ Electronics showed the officer was typing on the onboard computer when striking the pedestrian.
22. _____ Both machines, one made by each manufacturer, had accidentally irradiated the injured workers.
23. _____ Several patients in that hospital wing died just about the time the virus infected the cooling towers.
24. _____ The boat operator forgot to hook the paraglider cable's end before hauling the tourist aloft.

Answer Key to Other Side: *Res ipsa loquitur* (RIL) may permit an inference of negligence if the event speaks of negligence, plaintiff cannot obtain negligence evidence, and defendant controls the circumstances. Violating a *safety statute* (SS) is negligence per se or permits a presumption or inference of negligence, depending on the jurisdiction. A safety statute is one that protects the plaintiff's class against the specific risk of injury that occurred in the actual event. Violating an *industry standard* (IS) permits the jury to draw an inference of negligence. An industry standard represents the custom or practice within a certain field. 1.RIL 2.SS 3.IS 4.SS 5.RIL 6.IS 7.RIL 8.IS 9.SS 10.IS 11.SS 12.RIL 13.SS 14.IS 15.SS 16.RIL 17.SS 18.IS 19.IS 20.SS 21.RIL 22.SS 23.IS 24.IS

Review Exercise for Week 8
Match these facts with the law on the next page that they trigger.

Wow, he'd been having a rough time of it lately. ____ 1. First, an accident had closed the industrial park's entrance so that his workers couldn't get to his plant, shutting his business down for a week. ____ 2. Then, the plant owner next door refused to move his truck off the lot where he'd let him park it for what he thought would just be a couple days, when he had a big new shipment come in. ____ 3. Then, a bicyclist who got hit at the park's entrance hired a lawyer who sent a demand letter to him saying that his sign at the entrance had blocked traffic sight lines. ____ 4. He'd gone in for a regular dental cleaning that same day, only to find out afterward, when he looked in the mirror, that the hygienist had on her own applied a cheap-looking white paint sort of material to his front teeth—yikes! ____ 5. That night a police officer had come to his door saying that his kid had been killed at college, which, after nearly having a heart attack, he was fortunately able to confirm with a cell-phone call to his kid was not the case. ____ 6. Then, a stranger notified him that she was going to sue him for every penny he had for not having promptly delivered one of his business's defibrillators to a local school that had just ordered it, when her kid's heart stopped at a school athletic event. ____ 7. He'd then noticed a ladder up against his building, and so he'd taken it down when he left for the night, only to find out that service person was on the roof where he'd had to spend the night. ____ 8. He'd then gone out to his car at the bar, where a drunk had nearly shot him mistakenly thinking that he was stealing his car. ____ 9. Finally, his engineer had told him that his industry was adopting new defibrillator standards that were going to cost them a ton of money if they wanted to comply. Ugh. Good thing one must only deal with each day's trouble because each day brings plenty.

Review Exercise for Week 8
Match this law with the facts on the prior page that the facts trigger.

___A. Good motive or beneficial effect does not excuse a battery.^{Week 1}

___B. False-imprisonment's restraint, ordinarily by force, may also be subjecting the victim to unreasonable danger or lost property on escape.^{Week 2}

___C. Trespass to land includes exceeding the scope or duration of consent to entry on the land.^{Week 3}

___D. One may use reasonable force to defend property if the force is not likely to cause death or serious injury but not when mistaken.^{Week 4}

___E. Duty to use reasonable care arises whenever acts create foreseeable risk of harm.^{Week 5}

___F. Standards of care depend on things like custom, regulations, standards, experience, and likelihood and foreseeability of injury.^{Week 5}

___G. A contract promisor owes a tort duty to a third party only when the promisor performs the contract (misfeasance, not nonfeasance).^{Week 6}

___H. The economic-loss doctrine limits duties to direct injury, barring pure economic loss claims by those who suffer no physical impact.^{Week 6}

___I. Traditionally, law allows pure-emotional-distress claims for negligent mishandling of corpses and transmission of death notices.^{Week 7}

Answer key: 1H, 2C, 3E, 4A, 5I, 6G, 7B, 8D, 9F

TORTS I WORKBOOK

Week 8 Drafting Exercise—Interrogatories

Outline the interrogatories that you, as counsel for the defendant motor-vehicle driver Jonathan Carter, would serve on the plaintiff motor-vehicle driver Pamela Bertrand who suffered injury due to Mr. Carter's negligent operation of his motor vehicle, based on last week's complaint. Interrogatories are questions that the party must answer in writing under oath. A model answer is at the end.

[Caption omitted.]
DEFENDANT'S FIRST INTERROGATORIES TO PLAINTIFF PAMELA BERTRAND

Defendant Jonathan Q. Carter serves the following interrogatories on plaintiff Pamela S. Bertrand through her attorneys, under MCR 2.309, for answer under oath within 28 days after service. Your answers must include all information reasonably available to you, your attorneys, and your agents or employees. You must also supplement your answers within a reasonable time after receiving new or different information:

1.

2.

3.

4.

5.

6.

7.

8.

9.

10.

11.

12.

13.

14.

15.

16.

17.

18.

19.

20.

21.

22.

23.

[Signature block omitted.]

Model answer (condensed format): INTERROGATORIES: 1. As to your driving privileges, state: all states of licensure; dates of licensure; license numbers; name on license; nature and duration of any license restrictions; whether you were complying with restrictions at the time of the incident. 2. As to your driving history, state: nature of any license discipline (suspension, revocation, etc.); date and duration of any license discipline; grounds for any license discipline (alcohol, moving violations, etc.); terms of any license restoration. 3. If you have been an involved driver in prior accidents, state: dates; locations; convictions for or acknowledgment of legal violations (statutory, ordinances, etc.); any injuries you suffered; title, case number, and court for any associated civil actions. 4. If you have been an involved passenger in prior accidents, state: dates; locations; any injuries you suffered; title, case number, and court for any associated civil actions. 5. State the point of departure, intended destination, and all purposes for your driving at the time of the alleged incident. 6. State whether you reached your intended destination and, whether or not so, the route you took and distance you drove concluding your trip that day. 7. Describe any conditions (lighting, road surface, weather, etc.) in any way affecting the occurrence. 8. Describe each observation you made of the other vehicle before the collision. 9. Describe verbatim or as close as you can recall any statement made by the other driver after the collision. 10. Describe in as much detail as you can recall the precise actions you took to avoid the collision. 11. State the name, address, telephone, and relationship to you of any occupant of your vehicle at the time of the collision, and the observations that they claim to have made of the occurrence. 12. Describe any communications you made to any law enforcement officer or other emergency personnel following the collision about its occurrence. 13. Identify by name, address, telephone, and email any person who you believe witnessed any part of the incident including its immediate aftermath. 14. Describe your injuries from the incident. 15. Describe the treatment for your injuries including: a. the name, address, and specialty of each medical care provider; b. the treatment each rendered; c. the dates on which the treatment was rendered; and d. how it affected your recovery. 16. Describe the course of your recovery from the standpoint of your ability to sit, stand, walk, do household chores, work, and engage in recreation, including the periods during which you were disabled from any of those activities or other physical activities, and the date you resumed each. 17. Give the name, address, and qualifications of any expert witness who will or may testify on your behalf in this case, and for each state the substance of the facts and opinions to which you expect them to testify. Include accident reconstruction or other liability experts, rehabilitation or other damages experts, and medical experts including treating physicians and other care providers. 18. Itemize all loss and damage you claim, including a description and amount. 19. Itemize by date, provider, and amount any medical expenses you claim to have incurred relating to this matter, and which you claim as an element of damages in this case. 20. Identify by name, address, telephone number, policy number, claim number, and claim representative any motor-vehicle insurer, health insurer, disability insurer, medical care insurer, or other insurer of any kind who was, is, or may become obligated to reimburse you or to pay on your behalf for any expense of any kind relating to this incident, and for each such insurer identify the charges and amounts reimbursed or paid on your behalf. 21. State whether you have made any other claim for money or any benefit of any kind from any other person or company relating to the injuries or illness you claim to have sustained, and if so, state that person or company's name, address, and telephone number, the basis for your claim, and the results including any amounts paid. Also identify counsel if counsel was assigned. 22. State whether you were employed at the time of the matter you complain of in your complaint, and if so, give the name, address, and telephone number of your employer, your job title, your job duties, and your pay rate. 23. If you lost any income from work due to the matter alleged in your complaint, state the amount and calculation for that amount, as well as whether you were paid by any source for the same, and the name of any medical care provider who indicated or you believe will indicate that you were disabled from that work during those periods. 24. Give the name, address, telephone number, treatment dates, and treatment type (modalities) for each medical care provider of any kind, for any medical condition existing before the matter alleged in the complaint, within the previous five years, and describe that condition. Be sure to include your back condition and surgery. 25. Give the name, address, telephone number, treatment dates, and treatment type (modalities) for each medical care provider of any kind, for any medical condition existing after the matter alleged in the complaint unrelated to the injuries you claim from the motor-vehicle collision, and describe that condition. 26. Describe any medical condition which you admit pre-existed the matter alleged in your complaint, but which you claim was aggravated or exacerbated by the matter alleged in your complaint, and give the name, address, and qualifications of any medical care provider who will so testify. 27. Describe any accident or other injury you suffered after the date of your alleged injury in this case. 28. Describe the damage to the motor vehicle you were driving at the time of the collision. Include in your answer the cost of repair, place of repair (name, address, and telephone number), and nature of repair. 29. Describe any damage you claim to have observed of the other vehicle involved in the collision.

Week 9

Cause-in-Fact (continued) & Proximate or Legal Cause

Bullet Outline for Week 9:

CAUSE-IN-FACT (CONTINUED) & LEGAL OR PROXIMATE CAUSE
- [74]use substantial-factor test when 2+ causes would each have caused harm independent of the other
- [75]When the plaintiff cannot determine which of two negligent actors brought about the harm, the law may shift to defendants the burden of disproving causation or even offer a market-share theory for multiple manufacturers.

[76]Legal or proximate cause (more of judge than jury question)
- asks whether the breach led in *direct sequence* to harm (traditional bang-bang test)
    - or risk of harm was *reasonably foreseeable* (modern test) (reaches remote causes)
- [77]tests for spreading fires vary
    - from adjoining-property and first-building rules to much larger distances in rare cases

Paragraph Outline for Week 9:

Negligence—Causation (continued)
[73]Cause in fact on medical, legal, technical, and scientific matters may require expert testimony based on valid and reliable scientific methods. [74]The substantial-factor test determines cause in fact when two or more causes would each have brought about the harm independent of the other. [75]When the plaintiff cannot determine which of two negligent actors brought about the harm, the law may shift to defendants the burden of disproving causation or even offer a market-share theory for multiple manufacturers. [76]Legal or proximate cause, more of a judge than jury question, asks whether the breach led in direct sequence to harm or risk of harm was reasonably foreseeable. [77]Proximate-cause tests for spreading fires vary from adjoining-property and first-building rules to much larger distances in rare cases.

Fluency Cards for Week 9

Cover and uncover the response to each prompt until you fluently recall the exact response.

Technical Cause

May require expert testimony.

Multiple Causes

Use the substantial-factor test.

Which of Two?

Shift the burden when plaintiff cannot show which of two caused the harm.

Causation Forms

Must show both cause in fact and proximate or legal cause.

Proximate Cause

Judge rather than jury says whether law recognizes the factual connection.

Proximate-Cause Tests

Direct sequence or modern foreseeability.

Definitions Worksheet for Week 9

1. When would you use the *substantial-factor test* for cause in fact?

2. What is the *eggshell-skull rule*?

3. What is the traditional test for proximate or legal cause? Give an example.

4. What is the modern test for proximate or legal cause? Give an example.

5. Who decides proximate cause? Which side usually seeks the decision?

6. What proximate-cause rules do the courts apply to spreading fires?

Answer Key for Definitions Worksheet

1. *When would you use the substantial-factor test for cause in fact?*

   Use the substantial-factor test rather than but-for causation when each of two or more independent acts would alone have caused the harm.

2. *What is the **eggshell-skull rule**?*

   The eggshell-skull rule requires defendant to pay for all foreseeable and unforeseeable harm if at least some harm was direct and foreseeable.

3. *What is the traditional test for proximate or legal cause? Give an example.*

   The traditional test for proximate or legal cause is whether the breach led in *direct sequence* to the harm. One looks at how close the connection is between the breach and harm, in time, place, and events. A motor-vehicle accident shows proximate cause in direct sequence. Running the red light instantly causes the harm, very close in time, place, and event.

4. *What is the modern test for proximate or legal cause? Give an example.*

   The modern test for proximate cause is whether the wrongdoer should reasonably have foreseen that harm would flow from the wrong. One looks at how predictable the harm would have been before it happened. Carelessly pouring toxic waste into water system show proximate cause under the modern foreseeability test. One should reasonably expect some harm, although the harm might be relatively remote in time, place, or event.

5. *Who decides proximate cause? Which side usually seeks the decision?*

   Judges rather than juries typically decide proximate cause as a matter of law or policy rather than as a matter of fact. Defendants are usually the parties who move for dismissal of the claim based on the lack of proximate cause, seeking a judge's order that the case has no merit.

6. *What proximate-cause rules do the courts apply to spreading fires?*

   When someone starts a fire carelessly, that wrongdoer may pay only for harm to adjoining property, or to the first building burned, or in rare cases for harm at much greater distances. Proximate-cause rules vary.

Issue-Spotting Worksheet for Week 9

State the law each scenario raises. No analysis. Just spot the issue and state the law.

1. The client says that he has also heard that the explosion and fire may actually have come from two different causes.

2. The client finally admits that he wouldn't have been injured hardly at all except that he just happened to have had a prior concussion and also an unusual stress reaction to the event.

3. Unsure of the effect of your law explanation about *legal cause* on the client's claim against the driver, the client asks how a court would traditionally decide whether the driver's fault in not putting the car in park and turning off the car might be a legal cause of the client's serious injury.

4. After the client leaves, your very-senior law partner reminds you of some new case law indicating that the state's appellate courts have *updated* the law of proximate cause. While you're not sure what your law partner means by *updated*, you think you know.

5. The partner grumbles in response about how a jury would ever figure out the new law.

6. As the partner leaves your office, she tosses a file on your desk asking what you think about suing a camper who started a fire that eventually spread to a new client's motorhome. The partner thinks that the camper's homeowner's insurance might pay.

Answer Key for Issue-Spotting Worksheet

1. ***This scenario implicates how tort law would treat liability when two or more independent acts each would have caused the harm.*** Use the substantial-factor test rather than but-for causation when each of two or more independent acts would alone have caused the harm.

2. ***This scenario implicates the eggshell-skull rule.*** The eggshell-skull rule requires defendant to pay for all foreseeable and unforeseeable harm if at least some harm was direct and foreseeable.

3. ***This scenario implicates the traditional test for proximate cause.*** The traditional test for proximate or legal cause is whether the breach led in direct sequence to the harm. One looks at how close the connection is between the breach and harm, in time, place, and events.

4. ***This scenario implicates the modern test for proximate cause.*** The modern test for proximate cause is whether the wrongdoer should reasonably have foreseen that harm would flow from the wrong. One looks at how predictable the harm would have been before it happened.

5. ***This scenario implicates who decides proximate cause.*** Judges typically decide proximate cause as a matter of law and policy rather than juries deciding proximate cause as a matter of fact.

6. ***This scenario implicates proximate cause rules for spreading fires.*** When someone starts a fire carelessly, that wrongdoer may pay only for harm to adjoining property, or to the first building burned, or in rare cases for harm at much greater distances.

COMPREHENSIVENESS EXERCISE FOR WEEK 9

Insert words at the ^ mark that would make for a more-accurate or more-detailed law statement. Follow the italicized hints for help. Suggested answers are on the next page.

1. [Review:] Violating a safety statute can be negligence ^ or in some states only give rise to ^ an inference of negligence. *[Can be negligence what? And just an inference?]*

2. Proximate ^ cause is a ^ question of how far liability should extend given that the breach in fact led to harm. *[Proximate cause sometimes goes by another name. And what kind of question?]*

3. The traditional test for proximate or legal cause is whether the breach led ^ to the harm, close in ^ place and event. *[Just led to the harm, any way? And just close in pace and event, or something else?]*

4. The modern test for proximate cause is whether the wrongdoer saw ^ that harm would flow from the wrong. *[Only saw coming harm, or something else, too?]*

5. Judges ^ typically decide proximate cause ^. *[Judges rather than who? And how do they decide?]*

6. When someone starts a fire carelessly, that wrongdoer may pay only for harm to adjoining property ^. *[Can you name a couple other rules some states follow?]*

ANSWER KEY FOR COMPREHENSIVENESS EXERCISE

1. [Review:] Violating a safety statute can be negligence *per se* or in some states only give rise to ***a presumption or*** inference of negligence.

2. Proximate ***or legal*** cause is a ***policy*** question of how far liability should extend given that the breach in fact led to harm.

3. The traditional test for proximate or legal cause is whether the breach led ***in direct sequence*** to the harm, close in ***time***, place, and event.

4. The modern test for proximate cause is whether the wrongdoer saw ***or should reasonably have foreseen*** that harm would flow from the wrong.

5. Judges ***rather than juries*** typically decide proximate cause ***as a matter of law or policy rather than as a matter of fact***.

6. When someone starts a fire carelessly, that wrongdoer may pay only for harm to adjoining property, ***or to the first building burned, or in rare cases for harm at much greater distances***.

Factors Exercise for Week 9

Whether proximate cause exists can depend on factors. The are direct sequence or modern foreseeability, plus (next week) intervening or superseding cause. But factors determine how any test comes out. For each scenario, choose which one of these factors (1) close in time, (2) close in place, (3) frequency of prior similar events, (4) notice or knowledge of actor, (5) predictability, (6) seriousness of loss or injury, and (7) reprehensibility of conduct, would weigh most heavily in favor of one or the other party, and analyze the factor filling in the blanks.

1. The moment the dockhand tightened the winch, the frayed cable gave way, dropping the fragile load to the deck with a shattering crash, destroying the shipper's expensive stock.
    The [_choose a factor_] favors the [_choose a party_] when [_state relevant facts_] because [_explain your reasoning_].

2. The foreman had seen girders loosen and fall under the tack welds even though he didn't expect this girder to do so, when it struck and seriously injured the inspector.
    The [_choose a factor_] favors the [_choose a party_] when [_state relevant facts_] because [_explain your reasoning_].

3. Although the toxic waste took years to poison the landowner's well and child, prosecutors convicted the remediation company for illegally dumping it on the land instead of taking it to the treatment site as contracted and required.
    The [_choose a factor_] favors the [_choose a party_] when [_state relevant facts_] because [_explain your reasoning_].

4. Although the chemist failed to meet testing standards for the facial-cream product, the cream produced only temporary irritation even in the worst example found in the plaintiff class.
    The [_choose a factor_] favors the [_choose a party_] when [_state relevant facts_] because [_explain your reasoning_].

5. Although notes showed that the wing's designers had considered that failure mode, it had never happened, and nothing showed that it possibly could, until the freakish accident.
    The [_choose a factor_] favors the [_choose a party_] when [_state relevant facts_] because [_explain your reasoning_].

Example Answers for Factors Exercise

These answers are only examples. You may have chosen other relevant factors. Each fact pattern may implicate more than one, or indeed several, factors for which you could make good arguments.

1. *The moment the dockhand tightened the winch, the frayed cable instantly gave way, dropping the fragile load to the deck with a shattering crash.* **THE** close-in-time **FACTOR FAVORS** the plaintiff shipper **WHEN** the cable gave way the instant the dockhand tightened the winch **BECAUSE** under the direct-sequence test, the fault of tightening the frayed cable led directly and instantly to the destructive crash.

2. *The foreman had seen girders loosen and fall under the tack welds even though he didn't expect this girder to do so, when it struck and seriously injured the inspector.* **THE** notice-or-knowledge **FACTOR FAVORS** the plaintiff inspector **WHEN** the foreman had seen girders loosen and fall under tack welds **BECAUSE** under the modern-foreseeability test, prior knowledge that the action could lead to harm would make the harm foreseeable or predictable, even if, as here, the actor subjectively didn't believe that the harm would happen.

3. *Although the toxic waste took years to poison the landowner's well and child, prosecutors convicted the remediation company for illegally dumping it on the land instead of taking it to the treatment site as contracted and required.* **THE** reprehensibility-of-conduct **FACTOR FAVORS** the plaintiff landowner's child **WHEN** the company dumped the waste illegally and in breach of contract **BECAUSE** the severe reprehensibility of the act, indeed its criminality and moral repugnance for not doing as paid to do, would make judges more likely to find proximate cause and juries more likely to decide fact issues against the company.

4. *Although the chemist clearly failed to meet testing standards for the facial-cream product, fortunately the cream produced only temporary irritation even in the worst example found in the plaintiff class.* **THE** seriousness-of-loss **FACTOR FAVORS** the defendant chemist or product seller **WHEN** the cream only temporarily irritated the class member suffering the greatest harm in the class **BECAUSE** temporary irritation is not a serious loss compared to burns, scarring, depigmentation, and other longer-lasting or permanent injury.

5. *Although notes showed that the wing's designers had considered that failure mode, it had never happened, and nothing showed that it possibly could, until the freakish accident.* **THE** predictability **FACTOR FAVORS** the defendant designers or product seller **WHEN** the "freakish" failure mode had never happened and nothing showed it possibly could **BECAUSE** although the designers considered the possibility, they appear to have properly rejected it when they had nothing to show that it had ever happened and no way of knowing or discerning that it possibly could.

Review Exercise for Week 9
Match these facts with the law on the next page that they trigger.

Yikes. She wasn't sure how much more she could take. ____ 1. First, she was driving home from the store when a motorist pulled right out in front of her, requiring her to slam on her brakes, pulling her seatbelt sharply across her unborn baby. ____ 2. She'd stopped, alarmed, but the motorist, who'd also stopped, just got out, kicked her vehicle leaving an ugly dent, swore at her, and drove off. ____ 3. While she was still stopped, gathering her breath, another motorist ran off the rode and into the ditch, trying to avoid her vehicle. ____ 4. When she got home, she learned that the neighbor's teen had accidentally broken her stained-glass window, one the huge value of which her insurer had refused to cover. ____ 5. The odd thing was, while the teen admitted breaking the window, the teen wouldn't say how. ____ 6. Later, she'd been at a restaurant when a diner started to choke on something, with everyone just standing around staring at him as he passed out, and she'd run out. ____ 7. When she opened her mail back at home and found a note from her boyfriend saying that he was leaving her because of her pregnancy, she'd taken her handgun over to his house and sat outside in her car aiming it at him through his front window before finally driving off, figuring she'd sent a note to him later telling him that she'd nearly killed him. ____ 8. When she approached her home, though, police stopped her saying that escaped convicts had holed up in her home and that they were about to shoot in canisters of choking agent to flush them out but likely badly damaging her home. ____ 9. Finally, as she spoke roadside with police, a drunk driver nearly ran her over, if she hadn't just jumped out of harm's way. When would it all end?

Review Exercise for Week 9
Match this law with the facts on the prior page that the facts trigger.

___A. Parents are generally not liable for a child's tort except by statute, usually capped at a relatively low amount. Week 1

___B. The victim claiming assault must have apprehended the assault when the action occurred, not learned of it later. Week 2

___C. Trespass to chattels is intentional interference with exclusive possession of personal property compensated by lost-use value. Week 3

___D. Public necessity is a complete defense to property damage, but private necessity requires payment of actual damage. Week 4

___E. Emergencies alter the standard of care to the circumstances except as to the one who created the emergency. Week 5

___F. Pure-emotional-distress bystander claims may arise under a zone-of-danger test. Week 6

___G. Without special relationship, law imposes no duty to aid or rescue unless one created the need, assumes a duty, or controls the instrumentality. Week 6

___H. Law may allow prenatal-harm claims if the child is born alive or was viable at injury, but not generally against the mother. Week 7

___I. Res ipsa loquitur permits an inference of negligence if the event speaks of negligence, plaintiff cannot obtain negligence evidence, and defendant controls the circumstances. Week 8

Answer key: 1H, 2C, 3E, 4A, 5I, 6G, 7B, 8D, 9F

Week 9 Drafting Exercise—Production Requests

Outline the production requests that you, as counsel for the defendant motor-vehicle driver Jonathan Carter, would serve on the plaintiff motor-vehicle driver Pamela Bertrand who suffered injury allegedly due to Mr. Carter's negligent operation of his motor vehicle, based on the earlier complaint. Production requests require the party to produce documents and things that may be evidence in the case. A model answer appears at the end.

[Caption omitted.]

DEFENDANT'S FIRST PRODUCTION REQUESTS TO PLAINTIFF

Defendant Jonathan Q. Carter serves the following production requests on plaintiff Pamela S. Bertrand through her attorneys, under MCR 2.310, for response within 28 days after service. Your answers must include all documents and other things reasonably available to you, your attorneys, and your agents or employees.

1.

2.

3.

4.

5.

6.

7.

8.

9.

10.

11.

12.

[Signature block omitted.]

Model answer (condensed format): PRODUCTION REQUESTS: 1. The insurance policy and any declaration sheet and addenda reflecting any motor vehicle, health, disability, or other insurance covering you at the time of the matter complained of in your complaint. 2. The complete claim file for any motor vehicle, health, disability, or other insurance claim you made relating to the matter complained of in your complaint. 3. Bills or invoices, receipts, and any other documentation for all loss and damage you claim in this case. 4. Any settlement agreement, release, or other paper reflecting your receipt of any other recovery relating to the matter complained of in your complaint, together with any claims, complaints, or demands under which that recovery was made. 5. A curriculum vitae and report from any expert you will call in this case. 6. Your complete medical records for the injuries described in the complaint, including medical invoicing. 7. Your complete medical records pre-dating and post-dating the matter complained of in the complaint. 8. Any work records for the five years prior to the accident, and post-accident. 9. Any incident reports relating to the matter alleged in your complaint. 10. Any records including photographs, drawings, estimates, and billings relating to the damage to the vehicle you were driving and its repair. 11. The vehicle itself for inspection, if not repaired. 12. Any photographs, drawings, diagrams, or other illustrations or depictions of any kind relating in any way to the matters alleged in your complaint.

Problem-Solving Exercise Week 9

Think-aloud problem solving (TAPS) is a proven method of using vocalization to become a more creative and better problem solver. Professionals are effective problem solvers when they speak aloud to another, speaking aloud to themselves, or let their mental operations taking the silent form of words, concepts, principles, and strategies to reach partial solutions and then chain partial solutions toward final novel solution. Read the following example (EX) and non-example (NE) of an unknown new rule (RU), one that the judges writing their opinions and orders have not expressly stated but that you must instead discern and record as your problem solution. Vocalize each mental operation taken toward a partial solution, until you reach and record the final novel rule. Check your answer against the model answer at the bottom of the next page.

EX OPINION AND ORDER: In this negligence case, the plaintiff project owner alleges that the defendant contractor negligently used panel adhesive that failed within a few years, requiring extensive repairs at exorbitant cost. Evidence shows that the adhesive manufacturer, now bankrupt, learned of its adhesive product's defects shortly after this use, from new industry testing not previously available, after which it sent a product alert to all customers including defendant contractor. Defendant through counsel has moved to dismiss, arguing no proximate cause under the jurisdiction's modern foreseeability test. The Court grants defendant's motion, dismissing plaintiff's case with prejudice.

NE OPINION AND ORDER: In this negligence case, the plaintiff developer alleges that the defendant installer negligently used siding fasteners that failed within a few years, requiring extensive repairs at exorbitant cost. Evidence shows that the fastener manufacturer, now bankrupt, knew of the fasteners' weakness and issued product alerts that reached defendant installer before its fastener use, although defendant denies that it was aware of the product alerts. Defendant through counsel has moved to dismiss, arguing no proximate cause under the jurisdiction's modern foreseeability test. The Court denies defendant's motion, setting plaintiff's claim for jury trial.

RU _____

_____

_____

_____

Answer: While under the modern test for proximate cause, a defendant is liable in negligence for damage resulting from a risk that the defendant foresaw or reasonably should have foreseen, the risk must have been foreseeable at the time of defendant's negligent action, not later.

Week 10
Intervening Causes & Malpractice (Duty)

Bullet Outline for Week 10:
Legal or Proximate Cause (continued)
- [78]extraordinary, unforeseeable, independent events can supersede prior negligence
  - cuts off proximate cause
  - especially (although not always) for intentional, criminal, and reckless acts
    - [79]if the intentional or criminal act is what makes an actor in special relationship negligent, then the intentional or criminal act is less likely to cut off proximate cause
- [80]injured rescuers may hold liable the negligent actor who created the need for rescue
  - but not professional rescuers (firefighter rule) in many states (they get worker's compensation)
- [81]actors whose negligence create need for medical care are liable for injury from that medical care
  - including injury from medical malpractice
- [82]intoxicated person's voluntary drinking cuts off proximate cause as to the negligent server
  - but dram-shop statutes provide liability for injury to a third party from furnishing alcohol to
    - a minor or
    - visibly intoxicated person
- [83]unpredictable forces of nature may cut off proximate cause as to prior negligence,
  - but proximate cause remains where the force was foreseeable

Malpractice (Professional Negligence)
[84]professionals are liable for harm from breach of customary practice under same circumstances
- treat like negligence (duty, breach, causation, & damages) with a special standard of care
- Duty arises when the professional relationship forms, not just with affirmative acts
  - [85]professionals do not owe a duty to come to the aid or rescue of another
    - unless employed at that time for that purpose,
  - but Good Samaritan statutes may protect those who do
  - [86]no duty to third parties except where service is for the third party's direct benefit
    - example: lawyer's preparation of a will
    - [87]mental-health care providers owe duties to warn foreseeable victims of patients' particularized threats of imminent violence
  - [88]medical-care provider having charge of a person may owe a duty to prevent that person's suicide

Paragraph Outline for Week 10:
Legal or Proximate Cause (continued)
[78]Extraordinary, unforeseeable, independent events, including intentional, criminal, and reckless acts, can supersede prior negligence and cut off proximate cause. [79]If a foreseeable intentional or criminal act is what makes an actor in special relationship negligent, then the intentional or

criminal act is less likely to cut off proximate cause. [80]An injured rescuer, other than a professional rescuer, may hold liable the negligent actor who created the need for rescue. [81]An actor whose negligence creates a need for medical care may be held liable for injury from that medical care. [82]An intoxicated person's voluntary drinking cuts off proximate cause as to the negligent server, but dram-shop statutes may provide liability for injury to a third party from furnishing alcohol to a minor or visibly intoxicated person. [83]Unpredictable forces of nature may cut off proximate cause as to prior negligence, but proximate cause remains where the force was foreseeable.

Malpractice

[84]Malpractice or professional negligence holds professionals liable for harm resulting from breaches of customary practice under the same circumstances. Duty arises when the professional relationship forms, not just with affirmative acts. [85]Professionals do not owe a duty to come to the aid or rescue of another unless employed at that time for that purpose, but Good Samaritan statutes may protect those who do. [86]Professionals do not owe duties to third parties except where their service is for the third party's direct benefit as in a lawyer's preparation of a will. [87]Mental-health care providers owe duties to warn foreseeable victims of patients' particularized threats of imminent violence. [88]A medical-care provider or other professional having charge of a person may owe a duty to prevent that person's suicide.

Fluency Cards for Week 10
Cover and uncover the response to each prompt until you fluently recall the exact response.

Superseding Cause	**Rescuer Claim**
Extraordinary, unforeseeable, intentional, and criminal acts can supersede and cut off proximate cause.	Hold liable the negligent actor who created the need for rescue.

Dram-Shop Claim

Hold liable the person who furnishes alcohol to minor or visibly intoxicated person.
Intoxicated person has no claim.

Malpractice

Liability for breaches of customary practice under the same circumstances.

Volunteers

No duty to volunteer aid to another.

Duty to Others

No duties to third parties except for their direct benefit as in lawyer preparing will.

Warning Others

Mental-health providers must warn foreseeable victims of specific imminent threats of serious harm.

Definitions Worksheet for Week 10

1. How do intervening events affect proximate cause?

2. When might an intentional or criminal intervening act not cut off proximate cause?

3. Is an actor whose negligence required rescue liable to an injured rescuer?

4. Who is liable to whom for serving alcohol to a minor or visibly intoxicated person?

5. What is malpractice, and to whom do professionals owe duties the breach of which gives rise to a malpractice action?

6. When if ever would a professional owe a duty to a third party?

7. Must professionals come to the aid or rescue of another?

Answer Key for Definitions Worksheet

1. *How do intervening events affect proximate cause?* Extraordinary, unforeseeable, independent events, including intentional, criminal, and reckless acts, can supersede prior negligence and cut off proximate cause.

2. *When might an intentional or criminal intervening act not cut off proximate cause?* If a foreseeable intentional or criminal act is what makes negligent a respondent in special relationship with the claimant, then the intentional or criminal act is less likely to cut off proximate cause.

3. *Is an actor whose negligence required rescue liable to an injured rescuer?* An injured rescuer, other than a professional rescuer, may hold liable the negligent actor who created the need for rescue. Similarly, an actor whose negligence creates a need for medical care may be held liable for injury from that medical care.

4. *Who is liable to whom for serving alcohol to a minor or visibly intoxicated person?* An intoxicated person's voluntary drinking cuts off proximate cause as to the negligent server, but dram-shop statutes may provide liability for injury to a third party from furnishing alcohol to a minor or visibly intoxicated person.

5. *What is **malpractice**, and to whom do professionals owe duties the breach of which gives rise to a malpractice action?* Malpractice or professional negligence holds professionals liable for harm to their patients or clients resulting from breaches of customary practice under the same circumstances. Professionals owe duties to their patients or clients, not generally to others.

6. *When if ever would a professional owe a duty to a third party?* Professionals do not owe duties to third parties except where their service is for the third party's direct benefit as in a lawyer's preparation of a will. Mental-health care providers owe duties to warn foreseeable victims of patients' particularized threats of imminent violence. A medical-care provider or other professional having charge of a person may owe a duty to prevent that person's suicide.

7. *Must professionals come to the aid or rescue of another?* Professionals do not owe a duty to come to the aid or rescue of another unless employed at that time for that purpose, but Good Samaritan statutes may protect those who do.

Issue-Spotting Worksheet for Week 10

State the law each scenario raises. No analysis. Just spot the issue and state the law.

1. A potential new client called asking if you were interested in suing the client's neighbor for the client. An unusual 90-mph straight-line wind blew the neighbor's tall tree over onto the client's uninsured but previously highly valuable classic motor vehicle.

___

2. Another potential new client called asking if you were interested in suing a security company whose guard failed to show up one night to protect the client's business, resulting in substantial uninsured business theft loss.

___

3. You and your senior law partner meet with a new client who was hit by an uninsured driver when the client stopped along the freeway to help two motorists whose vehicles collided when one failed to yield to the other. You learn during the consultation that the client's emergency-room treatment worsened the injuries.

___

4. That evening, a family member asks if you can help a friend who suffered severe injury when hit by a drunken driver. The driver was a minor who had gotten drunk at a kegger party.

___

5. A couple comes in asking about suing the husband's physician for failing to diagnose the husband's hepatitis, which they believe worsened considerably for the lack of treatment.

___

6. The husband and wife are also concerned that the wife may now also have contracted the disease.

___

7. You quickly learn that the physician whom the couple wishes to sue was not the husband's doctor but instead the couple's neighbor.

___

Answer Key for Issue-Spotting Worksheet

1. ***This scenario implicates how intervening events affect proximate cause.*** Extraordinary, unforeseeable, independent events, including intentional, criminal, and reckless acts, can supersede prior negligence and cut off proximate cause.

2. ***This scenario implicates when an intervening act might NOT cut off proximate cause.*** If a foreseeable intentional or criminal act is what makes negligent a respondent in special relationship with the claimant, then the intentional or criminal act is less likely to cut off proximate cause.

3. ***This scenario implicates the rescue doctrine.*** An injured rescuer, other than a professional rescuer, may hold liable the negligent actor who created the need for rescue. Similarly, an actor whose negligence creates a need for medical care may be held liable for injury from that medical care.

4. ***This scenario implicates how serving and drinking alcohol affect proximate cause.*** An intoxicated person's voluntary drinking cuts off proximate cause as to the negligent server, but dram-shop statutes may provide liability for injury to a third party from furnishing alcohol to a minor or visibly intoxicated person.

5. ***This scenario implicates the duties that professionals owe.*** Malpractice or professional negligence holds professionals liable for harm to their patients or clients resulting from breaches of customary practice under the same circumstances. Professionals owe duties to their patients or clients, not generally to others.

6. ***This scenario implicates whether professionals owe duties to third parties.*** Professionals do not owe duties to third parties except where their service is for the third party's direct benefit as in a lawyer's preparation of a will. Mental-health care providers owe duties to warn foreseeable victims of patients' particularized threats of imminent violence. A medical-care provider or other professional having charge of a person may owe a duty to prevent that person's suicide.

7. ***This scenario implicates whether professionals must aid voluntarily.*** Professionals do not owe a duty to come to the aid or rescue of another unless employed at that time for that purpose, but Good Samaritan statutes may protect those who do.

TORTS I WORKBOOK

Discrimination Exercise for Week 10

Indicate whether each statement *overgeneralizes*, *undergeneralizes*, or *misconceives* the rule, explaining why. *Overgeneralizing* states the rule too broadly, capturing circumstances to which it does not apply. *Undergeneralizing* states the rule too narrowly, omitting circumstances to which it applies. *Misconceiving* states the rule incorrectly.

1. Extraordinary, unforeseeable, independent events, including intentional, criminal, and reckless acts, do not supersede prior negligence to cut off proximate cause.
   ____OVER/ ____UNDER/ ____MISS/ Why? _____
   _____

2. If a foreseeable intentional or criminal act occurs involving respondent's relationship with the claimant, then the intentional or criminal act is less likely to cut off proximate cause.
   ____OVER/ ____UNDER/ ____MISS/ Why? _____
   _____

3. An injured rescuer may hold liable the negligent actor who created the need for rescue.
   ____OVER/ ____UNDER/ ____MISS/ Why? _____
   _____

4. An intoxicated person's voluntary drinking cuts off proximate cause as to the negligent server, but dram-shop statutes may provide liability for injury to a third party from furnishing alcohol to a minor.
   ____OVER/ ____UNDER/ ____MISS/ Why? _____
   _____

5. Malpractice or professional negligence holds professionals liable for harm to their patients or clients resulting from lack of reasonable care under the same circumstances.
   ____OVER/ ____UNDER/ ____MISS/ Why? _____
   _____

6. Professionals do not owe duties to third parties.
   ____OVER/ ____UNDER/ ____MISS/ Why? _____
   _____

Answer Key for Discrimination Exercise

1. The statement **MISconceives** the rule. Extraordinary, unforeseeable, independent events, including intentional, criminal, and reckless acts, *can* supersede prior negligence to cut off proximate cause.

2. The statement **OVERgeneralizes** the rule. If a foreseeable intentional or criminal act *is what makes negligent* a respondent in *special* relationship with the claimant, then the intentional or criminal act is less likely to cut off proximate cause.

3. The statement **OVERgeneralizes** the rule. An injured rescuer, *other than a professional rescuer,* may hold liable the negligent actor who created the need for rescue. Similarly, an actor whose negligence creates a need for medical care may be held liable for injury from that medical care.

4. The statement **UNDERgeneralizes** the rule. An intoxicated person's voluntary drinking cuts off proximate cause as to the negligent server, but dram-shop statutes may provide liability for injury to a third party from furnishing alcohol to a minor *or visibly intoxicated person*.

5. The statement **MISconceives** the rule. Malpractice or professional negligence holds professionals liable for harm to their patients or clients resulting from *breaches of customary practice* under the same circumstances. Professionals owe duties to their patients or clients, not generally to others.

6. The statement **OVERgeneralizes** the rule. Professionals do not owe duties to third parties *except where their service is for the third party's direct benefit as in a lawyer's preparation of a will*. Mental-health care providers owe duties to warn foreseeable victims of patients' particularized threats of imminent violence. A medical-care provider or other professional having charge of a person may owe a duty to prevent that person's suicide.

Sameness Exercise for Week 10

Working with a seatmate, sort the following fact patterns into the best test of proximate cause: direct sequence (DS), modern foreseeability (MF), or intervening/superseding cause (ISC):

____: The winch gave way the moment that the worker carelessly overtightened it, causing the chain to snap and load to drop right on top of the truck's cab, killing its operator.

____: The vehicle crash into the pumping station cracked the containment wall, causing a slow but unstoppable fuel leak into the ground that gradually contaminated soil and water.

____: The lightning strike set the carelessly stacked boxes ablaze, destroying both the valuable boxed products and the facility against which the transporter had stacked them.

____: The manufacturer had test results suggesting the wing's weakness but installed the wing anyway, causing the wing's failure and the plane's crash five years later.

____: The moment that the worker carelessly struck the match inside the empty old fuel-storage tank, the tank exploded in a flash from old vapors, causing four deaths.

____: The contractor had seen the problem before but went ahead painting in the bitterly cold weather, resulting a year later in the paint peeling free, requiring expensive repainting.

____: The trespasser climbed onto the building's roof planning to break in to steal but fell through a carelessly guarded skylight, breaking his back in the fall.

____: The valet roared off in the customer's vehicle, carelessly skidding into a temporary stanchion supporting a new section of the garage's roof, which collapsed causing damage.

____: A hundred-year flood inundated the plant through the carelessly placed drain, destroying substantial inventory and valuable equipment.

____: As soon as the aide dropped the vial, its vapors ignited from the heating element along the floor, causing the hospital bedding to catch fire, causing smoke damage.

____: The clinic manager had seen several patients stagger and almost fall as they encountered the odd step but figured they'd learn, until one patient fell breaking a hip.

____: The lab had reports of its sending out inaccurate test results but kept the same protocol, until one customer died from an inaccurate test result.

Answers are on the back, but please do not turn this sheet over until you have answered all questions fully and conferred with a seatmate to complete and correct your answers.

Answer Key for Sameness Exercise

Proximate cause's direct-sequence test judges how close in time and place the breach and damage were. Proximate cause's modern-foreseeability test judges how foreseeable or predictable the damage was at the time of the breach. Proximate cause's intervening/superseding cause test examines the quality of the other causes that came between the breach and damage. Intervening causes are natural, probable, and predictable, and thus do not cut off proximate cause, while superseding causes are unnatural, unusual, and extraordinary, and thus do cut off proximate cause.

DS: The winch gave way the moment that the worker carelessly overtightened it, causing the chain to snap and load to drop right on top of the truck's cab, killing its operator. *Notice the immediacy of the death following closely to the carelessness.*

MF: The vehicle crash into the pumping station plainly cracked the containment wall, causing a slow but unstoppable fuel leak into the ground that gradually contaminated soil and water. *Notice the plain crack and unstoppable leak, suggesting foresight or foreseeability.*

ISC: The lightning strike set the carelessly stacked boxes ablaze, destroying both the valuable boxed products and the facility against which the transporter had stacked them. *Isn't a lightning strike the classic extraordinary unpredictable and thus superseding event?*

MF: The manufacturer had test results suggesting the wing's weakness but installed the wing anyway, causing the wing's failure and the plane's crash five years later. *Test results suggest foreseeability.*

DS: The moment that the worker carelessly struck the match inside the empty old fuel-storage tank, the tank exploded in a flash from old vapors, causing four deaths. *Immediate explosion may have been unforeseen and unforeseeable, but it is in direct sequence.*

MF: The contractor had seen the problem before but went ahead painting in the bitterly cold weather, resulting a year later in the paint peeling free, requiring expensive repainting. *See the problem before = foreseeability.*

ISC: The trespasser climbed onto the building's roof planning to break in to steal but fell through a carelessly guarded skylight, breaking his back in the fall. *Criminal acts are extraordinary and thus often seen as superseding—and the plaintiff's own acts may supersede.*

DS: The valet roared off in the customer's vehicle, carelessly skidding into a temporary stanchion supporting a new section of the garage's roof, which collapsed causing damage. *Immediate and thus direct sequence even if odd and unpredictable.*

ISC: A hundred-year flood inundated the plant through the carelessly placed drain, destroying substantial inventory and valuable equipment. *A hundred-year flood is another classic extraordinary and likely superseding event.*

DS: As soon as the aide dropped the vial, its vapors ignited from the heating element along the floor, causing the hospital bedding to catch fire, causing smoke damage. *Immediate and thus direct sequence.*

MF: The clinic manager had seen several patients stagger and almost fall as they encountered the odd step but figured they'd learn, until one patient fell breaking a hip. *Seen it before, can foresee it again.*

MF: The lab had reports of its sending out inaccurate test results but kept the same protocol, until one customer died from an inaccurate test result. *Put on notice means foreseeable again.*

TORTS I WORKBOOK

Problem-Solving Exercise Week 10 (Problem 1)

Think-aloud problem solving (TAPS) is a proven method of using vocalization to become a more creative and better problem solver. Professionals are effective problem solvers when they speak aloud to another, speaking aloud to themselves, or let their mental operations taking the silent form of words, concepts, principles, and strategies to reach partial solutions and then chain partial solutions toward final novel solution. Read the following example (EX) and non-example (NE) of an unknown new rule (RU), one that the judges writing their opinions and orders have not expressly stated but that you must instead discern and record as your problem solution. Vocalize each mental operation taken toward a partial solution, until you reach and record the final novel rule. Check your answer against the model answer at the bottom of the next page.

EX   OPINION AND ORDER: In this legal malpractice case, plaintiff client alleges that she contacted defendant attorney by email supplying sufficient information for attorney to evaluate her employment-rights claim and that attorney replied indicating that attorney was reviewing the claim but that attorney did not further respond for a month after which the limitations period expired, causing plaintiff to lose a valuable claim. Defendant has moved to dismiss, arguing that defendant owed plaintiff no duty. The Court denies defendant's motion, setting plaintiff's claim for jury trial.

NE   OPINION AND ORDER: In this medical malpractice case, plaintiff patient alleges that she twice telephoned defendant physician's office within one week, leaving sufficient information for physician to evaluate her cardiac symptoms, but that defendant did not return her calls, following which plaintiff had a massive heart attack that prompt return calls and treatment would have avoided. Defendant through counsel assigned by defendant's insurer has moved to dismiss, arguing that defendant owed plaintiff no duty. The Court grants defendant's motion, dismissing plaintiff's case with prejudice.

RU   _____

_____

_____

_____

_____

> ***Answer to problem on other side:*** Although a care provider ordinarily owes no duty to act reasonably to prevent another's suicide, such a duty may arise when the care provider takes custody of a suicidal person for that specific purpose.

152

Problem-Solving Exercise Week 10 (Problem 2)

Think-aloud problem solving (TAPS) is a proven method of using vocalization to become a more creative and better problem solver. Professionals are effective problem solvers when they speak aloud to another, speaking aloud to themselves, or let their mental operations taking the silent form of words, concepts, principles, and strategies to reach partial solutions and then chain partial solutions toward final novel solution. Read the following example (EX) and non-example (NE) of an unknown new rule (RU), one that the judges writing their opinions and orders have not expressly stated but that you must instead discern and record as your problem solution. Vocalize each mental operation taken toward a partial solution, until you reach and record the final novel rule. Check your answer against the model answer at the bottom of the next page.

EX OPINION AND ORDER: Plaintiff estate alleges that defendant psychiatrist committed professional malpractice when psychiatrist failed to change and increase medications, order continuous observation, and order provisional physical restraint, while decedent was on suicide watch on psychiatrist's hospital ward, resulting in decedent taking his own life. Defendant has moved to dismiss, arguing no duty. The Court denies defendant's motion, bringing this case on for jury trial as to defendant's negligence and the amount of resulting damages.

NE OPINION AND ORDER: Plaintiff estate alleges that defendant psychologist committed professional negligence when psychologist failed to seek order of commitment for suicide watch of decedent when decedent was under psychologist's consult care and had suicidal ideation but had declined voluntary commitment and psychiatric review. Defendant has moved to dismiss, arguing no duty. The Court grants defendant's motion and dismisses plaintiff's case with prejudice.

RU _____

_____

_____

_____

_____

Answer for problem on other side: Although a professional owes no duty to one other than a client or patient with whom the professional has formed a relationship, a relationship-based duty may arise when the professional knows that the client or patient is relying on the professional to perform.

Torts I Workbook

Drafting Exercise—Motion for Summary Disposition

A motion for summary disposition tests whether the other party has stated a legal claim and can produce evidence to support its claim. Defendants often file these motions after pleadings and discovery close, and before the time and expense of a trial. Fill in the blanks in the motion. The next page has an answer key at the bottom.

[Caption omitted.]

DEFENDANT'S MOTION FOR SUMMARY DISPOSITION, MEMORANDUM BRIEF, AND NOTICE OF HEARING

Motion

Defendant Medical Transport Inc. moves under MCR 2.116(C)(8) and (10) for summary disposition and dismissal of plaintiff Hubert Swann's complaint saying:

1. Mr. Swann alleges his serious injury when the Medical Transport van transporting him from dialysis back to his nursing home stopped suddenly, causing him to slide from his gurney to the van floor.

2. While Medical Transport disputes Mr. Swann's account of how the driver had secured him, how he fell, and how serious was his injury, this motion rests instead on other undisputed facts.

3. Mr. Swann alleges and admits that the van's driver stopped suddenly when lightning struck in the roadway just ahead.

4. As plaintiff, Mr. Swann must allege and produce evidence of duty, breach, [1]_____, including both [2]_____ and [3]_____, and damages.

5. Proximate cause requires Mr. Swann to allege and produce evidence that his injury was the [4]_____ of the van driver's negligence.

6. Moreover, to address intervening and [5]_____ causes, Mr. Swann must show that his injury was *not* the result of an [6]_____.

7. Here, the evidence is undisputed that the only cause of Mr. Swann's injury was the extraordinary and unforeseeable occurrence of a lightning strike immediately in front of the van.

8. Mr. Swann can produce no other evidence that his injury was due to a foreseeable, predictable, or natural event.

9. The lightning strike was such an extraordinary and unforeseeable event that it constitutes a [7]_____ interrupting any arguable chain of causation from the van driver's alleged actions to Mr. Swann's injury.

10. Mr. Swann therefore cannot satisfy the required element of [8]_____ in his negligence claim against Medical Transport.

11. Medical Transport is therefore entitled under MCR 2.116(C)(8) and (10) to judgment as a matter of law and summary disposition of Mr. Swann's complaint for failure to state a claim and raise genuine issues of material fact.

Affidavits, exhibits, and memorandum brief support this motion.

ON THESE GROUNDS, defendant Medical Transport Inc. prays under MCR 2.116(C)(8) and (10) that the Court grant it summary disposition and dismiss plaintiff Hubert Swann's complaint with prejudice, together with costs and attorney's fees most wrongfully sustained.

Memorandum Brief

[Omitted.]

Notice of Hearing

[Omitted.]
[Signature block omitted.]

Answer key: 1. causation 2. cause in fact 3. proximate or legal cause 4. natural, probable, and foreseeable consequence or result 5. superseding 6. extraordinary, remote, freakish, and unforeseeable event 7. superseding cause 8. proximate cause.

Week 11
Professional Negligence (Standard of Care, Causation, & Informed Consent)

Bullet Outline for Week 11:
Professional Negligence (continued)
- [89] professional's standard of care requires a similarly qualified expert's testimony
  - except in the rare case of obvious breach.
- [90] Professionals who breach the standard of care causing injury are liable in tort, not contract
  - unless guaranteeing the result
- [91] testifying expert must show knowledge of practice in the same or similar locale
  - except as to defendant specialists who have a national standard (national board exams)
- [92] causation in malpractice cases ordinarily requires expert testimony
  - must show what would have happened if the defendant had complied with the standard of care
  - [93] In lawyer malpractice (legal malpractice), plaintiff proves what would have happened in the underlying case if the defendant had not committed malpractice (suit within a suit)
- [94] Medical malpractice includes failure to obtain informed consent when
  - defendant did not disclose a risk that customary practice required disclosing,
  - about which a reasonable patient would have wanted to know, and
  - to which the plaintiff would not have consented
- [95] no consent at all may be battery in addition to malpractice
- [96] medical-care providers must disclose conflicts of interest when
  - may affect their judgment and
  - about which the patient would want to know

Paragraph Outline for Week 11:
Professional Negligence (continued)

[89] The professional's standard of care requires a similarly qualified expert's testimony except in the rare case of obvious breach. [90] Professionals who breach the standard of care causing injury are liable in tort, not contract, unless guaranteeing the result. [91] The law may require an expert testifying in a malpractice case to show knowledge of practice in the same or similar locale except as to defendant specialists who have a national standard. [92] Causation in malpractice cases ordinarily requires expert testimony as to what would have happened if the defendant had complied with the standard of care. [93] In lawyer malpractice, the plaintiff proves what would have happened in the underlying case if the defendant had not committed malpractice. [94] Medical malpractice includes failure to obtain informed consent to a risk that the custom required disclosing, about which a reasonable patient would have wanted to know, and to which the plaintiff would not have consented. [95] A medical-care provider's failure to obtain any consent at all may be battery in addition to malpractice. [96] Medical-care providers must disclose conflicts of interest that may affect their judgment and about which the patient would want to know.

Fluency Cards for Week 11

Cover and uncover the response to each prompt until you fluently recall the exact response.

Malpractice Proof

Requires similarly qualified expert's testimony except for rare obvious breach.

Expert Qualifications

May have to show knowledge of same or similar locale unless a national standard.

Informed Consent

When custom requires disclosure, reasonable patient would want to know, and plaintiff would not consent.

No consent

No consent is battery.

Definitions Worksheet for Week 11

1. What is the malpractice standard of care? How does it differ from the ordinary standard?

2. How must a party prove the standard of care? Does the law recognize any exceptions?

3. Can contract law provide an alternative theory of recovery?

4. What qualifies an expert to establish the standard of care?

5. How do parties prove causation in malpractice cases? Does lawyer malpractice differ?

6. How does law define a claim for failure to obtain informed consent to a procedure?

7. What claims arise if a medical-care provider gets no consent at all?

8. What claim may arise when a medical-care provider has an undisclosed special interest?

Answer Key for Definitions Worksheet

1. *What is the malpractice standard of care? How does it differ from the ordinary standard?* The professional's standard of care is not what reasonable care or the reasonably prudent person would do but instead what minimally competent professionals in the same field customarily do. Custom controls, not reasonableness.

2. *How must a party prove the standard of care? Does the law recognize any exceptions?* The professional's standard of care requires a similarly qualified expert's testimony except in the rare case of obvious breach.

3. *Can contract law provide an alternative theory of recovery?* Not generally. Professionals who breach the standard of care causing injury are liable in tort, not contract, unless guaranteeing the result.

4. *What qualifies an expert to establish the standard of care?* An expert witness must know the standard of care by education, training, and experience, and may have to possess the same licensure and engage in similar clinical practice. The law may require an expert testifying in a malpractice case to show knowledge of practice in the same or similar locale except as to defendant specialists who have a national standard.

5. *How do parties prove causation in malpractice cases? Does lawyer malpractice differ?* Causation in malpractice cases ordinarily requires expert testimony as to what would have happened if the defendant had complied with the standard of care. In lawyer malpractice, the plaintiff proves what would have happened in the underlying case if the defendant had not breached the standard.

6. *How does law define a claim for failure to obtain informed consent to a procedure?* Medical malpractice includes failure to obtain informed consent to a risk that the custom required disclosing, about which a reasonable patient would have wanted to know, and to which the plaintiff would not have consented.

7. *What claims arise if a medical-care provider gets no consent at all?* A medical-care provider's failure to obtain any consent at all may be battery in addition to malpractice.

8. *What claim may arise when a medical-care provider has an undisclosed special interest?* Medical-care providers must also disclose conflicts of interest that may affect their judgment and about which a reasonable patient would want to know.

TORTS I WORKBOOK

Issue-Spotting Worksheet for Week 11

State the law each scenario raises. No analysis. Just spot the issue and state the law.

1. Your senior law partner hands you a medical-malpractice file, asking you to draft the complaint. Your file review indicates a bad result from a broken arm that the defendant physician treated in only a sling. Your drafting goes fine until you get to the standard of care.

_____

_____

2. Later that day, the partner pokes her head in your office, asking if you'd found an expert for the medical-malpractice case yet. You shake your head, forcing a smile because the partner hadn't asked you about finding an expert.

_____

_____

3. When you plop the draft complaint on the partner's desk at the end of the day, the partner flips through it, saying only, "No breach-of-contract count?"

_____

_____

4. In your search for a med-mal expert, you find a website that lists the qualifications of dozens of available experts, leaving you unsure of where to start.

_____

_____

5. At a scheduling conference in the med-mal case a couple of months later, the trial judge asks if you will be having any other experts other than the standard-of-care expert whom you found.

_____

_____

6. The trial judge notes that you pled only one count in the case, simply for medical malpractice. The trial judge grants you two weeks to amend the complaint when in-chambers discussion confirms that your client claims that she didn't know that defendant physician's treatment might produce a bad result.

_____

7. You learn at the pretrial conference that the defendant physician owned the physical-therapy clinic to which he sent your client instead of performing an alternative surgery.

_____

Answer Key for Issue-Spotting Worksheet

1. ***This scenario implicates the professional's standard of care.*** The professional's standard of care is not what reasonable care or the reasonably prudent person would do but instead what minimally competent professionals in the same field customarily do. Custom controls, not reasonableness.

2. ***This scenario implicates how one proves a professional's standard of care.*** The professional's standard of care requires a similarly qualified expert's testimony except in the rare case of obvious breach.

3. ***This scenario implicates whether contract law provides an alternative remedy.*** Professionals who breach the standard of care causing injury are liable in tort, not contract, unless guaranteeing the result.

4. ***This scenario implicates a malpractice expert's qualifications.*** An expert witness must know the standard of care and may have to possess the same licensure and engage in similar clinical practice. The law may require an expert testifying in a malpractice case to show knowledge of practice in the same or similar locale except as to defendant specialists who have a national standard.

5. ***This scenario implicates how a party proves malpractice causation.*** Causation in malpractice cases ordinarily requires expert testimony as to what would have happened if the defendant had complied with the standard of care. In lawyer malpractice, the plaintiff proves what would have happened in the underlying case if the defendant had not breached the standard.

6. ***This scenario implicates the theory of lack of informed consent.*** Medical malpractice includes failure to obtain informed consent to a risk that the custom required disclosing, about which a reasonable patient would have wanted to know, and to which the plaintiff would not have consented. A medical-care provider's failure to obtain any consent at all may be battery in addition to malpractice.

7. ***This scenario implicates claims over undisclosed interests.*** Medical-care providers must disclose conflicts of interest that may affect their judgment and about which a reasonable patient would want to know.

COMPREHENSIVENESS EXERCISE FOR WEEK 11

Insert words at the ^ mark that would make for a more-accurate or more-detailed law statement. Follow the italicized hints for help. Suggested answers are on the next page.

1. The professional's standard of care is what ^ professionals in the same field ^ do ^. *[Any professionals? And do how? And do when?]*

2. The professional's standard of care requires an ^ expert's testimony ^. *[Any expert? And always required?]*

3. Professionals who breach the standard of care ^ are liable in tort, not contract ^. *[Every breach creates liability? And never in contract?]*

4. An expert witness must know the standard of care and may have to ^ know the standard in the same ^ locale ^. *[Don't some states require more than knowing the standard? And does an expert have to know that exact locale? And does law always require some locale?]*

5. Causation in malpractice cases ordinarily requires expert testimony ^. *[Expert testimony about what?]*

6. Medical malpractice includes failure to obtain informed consent to a risk ^ to which the plaintiff would not have consented. *[Missing a couple of other conditions.]*

7. Medical-care providers must disclose conflicts of interest ^^. *[Every conflict of any kind? Missing something else.]*

ANSWERS FOR COMPREHENSIVENESS EXERCISE

1. The professional's standard of care is what *minimally competent* professionals in the same field *customarily* do *under the same circumstances*.

2. The professional's standard of care requires a *similarly qualified* expert's testimony *except in the rare case of obvious breach*.

3. Professionals who breach the standard of care *causing injury* are liable in tort, not contract, *unless guaranteeing the result*.

4. An expert witness must know the standard of care and may have to *possess the same license, engage in similar clinical practice, and* know the standard in the same *or similar* locale *except as to defendant specialists who have a national standard*.

5. Causation in malpractice cases ordinarily requires expert testimony *as to what would have happened if the defendant had complied with the standard of care*.

6. Medical malpractice includes failure to obtain informed consent to a risk *that the custom required disclosing, about which a reasonable patient would have wanted to know, and* to which the plaintiff would not have consented.

7. Medical-care providers must disclose conflicts of interest *that may affect their judgment and about which a reasonable patient would want to know*.

EXAMPLE/NON-EXAMPLE EXERCISE FOR WEEK 11

Identify whether each fact pattern is an example (E) or non-example (NE) of the **highlighted concept**. Answers follow. In the blanks, generate an additional example and non-example.

1. The professional's standard of care is not reasonable care or what the reasonably prudent person would do but instead what minimally competent professionals in the same field ***customarily do. Custom controls***.

   ___ The expert told counsel that plaintiff had a good case because cardiologists never do what defendant did.
   ___ The expert testified she always did the procedure just like defendant did but didn't know what others do.
   ___ The treatise listed five alternative treatment methods without indicating which, if any, were preferred.

   E: _____

   N: _____

2. The professional's standard of care requires a similarly qualified expert's testimony ***except in the rare case of obvious breach***.

   ___ Unfortunately, the orthopedist elected to immobilize the fracture site rather than use internal fixation.
   ___ Radiographs later showed that the neurosurgeon had mistakenly left a metal clip in the surgical site.
   ___ The patient was outraged to learn that the podiatrist had operated on her left rather than right foot.

   E: _____

   N: _____

3. Professionals who breach the standard of care causing injury are liable in tort, not contract, ***unless guaranteeing the result***.

   ___ The urologist said he'd never had an incontinent patient after the surgery, which was only a tiny risk.
   ___ The cosmetic surgeon's advertisement offered the patient's money back if not pleased with the result.
   ___ The oncologist recommended chemotherapy over radiation treatment because of the better outcomes.

   E: _____

   N: _____

4. The law may require an expert testifying in a malpractice case to show knowledge of practice in the same or similar locale ***except as to defendant specialists who have a national standard***.

   ___ The defendant board-certified internist testified that she had followed the local practice that she learned.
   ___ The rural general practitioner made frequent house calls like the one resulting in the patient's injury.
   ___ The defendant emergency-room physician, nearing retirement, hadn't kept up his continuing education.

   E: _____

   N: _____

Torts I Workbook

5. ***Causation in malpractice cases ordinarily requires expert testimony*** as to what would have happened if the defendant had complied with the standard of care.
    ___ Counsel couldn't tell what, if anything, the surgeon may have done wrong and so consulted an expert.
    ___ Medical records showed the ER nurse had delayed twenty minutes in administering the nitroglycerin.
    ___ The defendant pediatrician had clearly missed signs of the child's advanced-stage lymphoma.

E: _____

N: _____

6. In lawyer malpractice, the plaintiff must prove ***what would have happened in the underlying case*** if the defendant had not breached the standard.
    ___ The lawyer neglected to raise the Holmes Act, so the judge had no option to impose suspended sentence.
    ___ The plaintiff's lawyer blew the statute of limitations while waiting for medical records to review.
    ___ The lawyer forgot to disclose and call the second expert, but the jury still returned a favorable verdict.

E: _____

N: _____

7. Medical malpractice includes ***failure to obtain informed consent*** to a risk custom required disclosing, that a reasonable patient would have wanted to know, and to which the plaintiff would not have consented.
    ___ The patient had no idea that his stomach might stretch again so that the procedure lost its effect.
    ___ The form had listed that he might suffer knee stiffness, but he had hoped it wouldn't be *that* bad.
    ___ She liked the new appearance of her nose but was shocked that she couldn't breathe through one nostril.

E: _____

N: _____

8. A medical-care provider's ***failure to obtain any consent at all may be battery*** in addition to malpractice.
    ___ The consent form had not listed an allergic reaction as one of the possible medication side effects.
    ___ The doctor had indeed neglected to mention the possibility of a shed virus from the live vaccine.
    ___ The specialist had gone ahead with implants in *both* ears, although the parents had approved only one.

E: _____

N: _____

9. Medical-care providers must disclose ***conflicts of interest*** that may affect their judgment and about which a reasonable patient would want to know.
    ___ The specialist was earning hundreds of thousands of dollars in surgical fees from doing the procedures.
    ___ The doctor hadn't told the patient that he was harvesting a cell line from the patient's marrow.
    ___ The internist owned the clinic to which he was sending patients for the experimental therapy.

E: _____

N: _____

Answers: 1 ENN; 2 NEE; 3 NEN; 4 ENE; 5 NEE; 6 EEN; 7 ENE; 8 NNE; 9 NEE

Review Exercise for Week 11
Match these facts with the law on the next page that they trigger.

He figured that he had only himself to blame. ____ 1. First, after that little accident, he had swept up and discarded the debris and scuffed over the skid marks before anyone could get a good look at it. ____ 2. But was it really his fault that the stack of old tires on his back forty caught fire, spreading thick smoke across the neighbor's pool area? ____ 3. And so what if he let his kid use his old shotgun, when he had no idea that the kid would accidentally shoot the neighbor's dog? ____ 4. He was just angry when his homeowner's insurer refused to pay for the loss because what good is insurance if it doesn't pay? ____ 5. And then, when he had that little fender bender rear ending that already-disabled older woman, he had no idea that she'd be in such bad shape from a little bump that she could no longer get out of bed! ____ 6. And then when he whacked his neighbor with the baseball bat over that little argument, he never thought that the neighbor's wife who saw it would be so upset because he didn't mean to knock out the neighbor and break his jaw. ____ 7. Then again, he did know that she'd been depressed and he sort of wanted to make her more depressed—shame on him, he thought! ____ 8. But he'd only been trying to get back the hunting knife that he'd lent his neighbor the prior fall, when he saw his neighbor sharpening it in his garage, and he tried to grab it from him. ____ 9. Maybe he should have helped his neighbor after he knocked him out and his wife ran inside, and his neighbor was bleeding badly from the mouth, but hey, he had it coming to him! Or maybe, he thought, this stuff wasn't just bad luck but bad living.

Review Exercise for Week 11
Match this law with the facts on the prior page that the facts trigger.

___A. Tort practice seldom involves intentional torts because insurance does not ordinarily cover purposeful wrongs.[Week 1]

___B. IIED's outrageous conduct must be outrageous to the reasonable person, but knowledge the victim is susceptible may make conduct outrageous.[Week 2]

___C. Nuisance addresses interference with use and enjoyment (noise, smoke, light, smell) rather than exclusive possession.[Week 3]

___D. Law allows repossession from the land of another only without force and only by agreement or summary proceedings.[Week 4]

___E. Children owe care expected of reasonable children of like age, except that children engaged in adult activities owe adult duties.[Week 5]

___F. Absent special relationship, tort law imposes no duty to aid another unless one created the need, assumes a duty, or controls the instrumentality.[Week 6]

___G. Pure-emotional-distress claims arise for manifestly severely distressed family members contemporaneously witnessing physical injury.[Week 7]

___H. Prove breach, meaning failing to use reasonable care, by direct or circumstantial evidence and presumptions from spoliation of evidence.[Week 8]

___I. The eggshell-skull rule requires defendant to pay for all foreseeable and unforeseeable harm if at least some harm was direct and foreseeable.[Week 9]

Answer key: 1H, 2C, 3E, 4A, 5I, 6G, 7B, 8D, 9F

Drafting Exercise (Cross-Examination) for Week 11

Outline the cross-examination on deposition of the defendant surgeon in this malpractice case. A deposition is sworn testimony before a court report in an office, conducted as if in court, with the lawyer questioning and the witness answering. The deposition of a defendant, rather than a non-party witness, is especially important because the defendant's answers are party admissions. And because the witness is adverse, you may ask leading questions. Here, the plaintiff patient's complaint alleges that the defendant surgeon mistakenly cut the patient's bile duct during a laproscopic hysterectomy. The patient's abdomen slowly filled with bile over the next few days, undetected until the patient had suffered severe internal scarring that permanently disabled the patient from work. The complaint alleges that customary practice required the surgeon to identify, segregate, and avoid the bile duct, confirm after surgery that it remained intact, and monitor for signs that the surgery severed the duct, all of which the surgeon allegedly breached. Dictate and outline the questions that you would ask the surgeon on deposition, and topics you would address, to confirm your client patient's theory of the case.

DRAFT QUESTIONS AND TOPICS:

Model answer (condensed format): Did you sever your patient's bile duct in the surgery, as the medical records reflect? In doing so, did you depart from a hysterectomy patient's customary care? Customary care required that you identify the bile duct, didn't it? And yet you failed to do so, didn't you? Customary care required that you segregate the bile duct, didn't it? And yet you failed to do so, didn't you? Customary care required that you avoid cutting the bile duct, didn't it? And yet you failed to do so, didn't you? Customary care required that you confirm after the hysterectomy that the bile duct was intact, didn't it? And yet you failed to do so, didn't you? Customary care required that you monitor for signs of a severed duct, didn't it? And yet you failed to do so, didn't you? You are familiar with the customary care owed during a hysterectomy, aren't you? Your medical training taught you what surgeons customarily do when performing a hysterectomy, didn't it? And certainly, severing the bile duct is not part of that customary care, is it? How badly did the severing of your patient's bile duct harm your patient? Why did you sever her bile duct? Why did you not discover, when completing the hysterectomy, that your surgery had severed her bile duct? Why did you not discover, for days following the surgery, that your surgery had severed her bile duct? Hysterectomies are not to sever bile ducts, are they? The bile duct carries an essential function, doesn't it? And that function is to carry bile away from the gall bladder, into the stomach and intestines, and out of the body, isn't that correct? When you severed your patient's bile duct, her bile poured into her abdomen, isn't that correct? What is the effect of bile free-floating in the abdomen? A person would not long survive without an intact bile duct, would one? During a hysterectomy, the surgeon is in charge, isn't that correct? You don't blame the severing of your patient's bile duct on anyone else, do you? Did anyone, whether surgical nurse, operating room director, or anyone else, interfere with your ability to identify and avoid the bile duct? Did any equipment fail to function in the manner it should have functioned, contributing to the severing of your patient's bile duct? Did the hospital or its personnel play any role in the severing of your patient's bile duct?

Problem-Solving Exercise Week 11

Think-aloud problem solving (TAPS) is a proven method of using vocalization to become a more creative and better problem solver. Professionals are effective problem solvers when they speak aloud to another, speaking aloud to themselves, or let their mental operations taking the silent form of words, concepts, principles, and strategies to reach partial solutions and then chain partial solutions toward final novel solution. Read the following example (EX) and non-example (NE) of an unknown new rule (RU), one that the judges writing their opinions and orders have not expressly stated but that you must instead discern and record as your problem solution. Vocalize each mental operation taken toward a partial solution, until you reach and record the final novel rule. Check your answer against the model answer at the bottom of the next page.

EX   OPINION AND ORDER: In this legal-malpractice case, the plaintiff client alleges and has shown evidence that the defendant attorney violated a rule of professional conduct regarding confidentiality, causing plaintiff damage. Evidence shows that the attorney consulted an expert about plaintiff's case when, unknown to attorney, the other side had already retained the expert. Plaintiff's expert witness will testify to defendant's conduct-rule violation. Defendant through counsel has moved to dismiss, arguing that plaintiff has not produced and cannot produce evidence of a breach of customary care. The Court grants defendant's motion, dismissing plaintiff's case with prejudice.

NE   OPINION AND ORDER: In this legal-malpractice case, the plaintiff client alleges and has shown evidence that the defendant attorney disclosed a confidence about plaintiff to an investigator witness, causing plaintiff damage. Evidence shows that the attorney met and spoke with the investigator when the other side had already retained the investigator in the same matter. Plaintiff's expert witness will testify that other lawyers in the same field would not have made the disclosure. Defendant through counsel has moved to dismiss, arguing that plaintiff has not produced and cannot produce evidence of a breach of customary care. The Court denies defendant's motion, setting plaintiff's claim for jury trial.

RU   _____

_____

_____

_____

> ***Answer:*** A lawyer violating a conduct rule does not necessarily breach a standard of care. To support a legal-malpractice claim, a plaintiff must have other evidence of the customary practice and its breach, beyond the lawyer's violating a conduct rule.

Week 12
Premises Liability

Bullet Outline for Week 12:
Premises Liability
[97]in most states requires classifying the plaintiff as an invitee, licensee, or trespasser
- [101]status can change depending on activities, purpose, and scope or duration of permission
- some states require reasonable care as to all, abolishing classifications
- [98]landowners may have statutory immunity as to individuals using the land for recreational purposes
- [99]tenants controlling the premises owes the duties,
    - so do landlords who retain control, contract to repair, repair negligently, fail to disclose defects

[100]Invitees = those who enter for pecuniary purposes or accompany others who do = reasonable care
- [102]reasonable care may include the duty to
    - design,
    - construct,
    - maintain,
    - repair,
    - warn, and
    - protect against unreasonably dangerous conditions on the premises
        - [103]landowners may advertise and assume duties to protect against the criminal acts
        - or owe those duties by special knowledge or relationship

[104]Licensees = non-pecuniary purposes (social guests) = warn of known hidden dangers of unreasonable risk

[105]Trespassers = no duty except as to
- children,
    - [106]but may owe children of tender years duty to protect against an attractive nuisance
        - modern formulations assess landowner's and child's relative knowledge of risk
- active operations,
- tolerated intruders,
- concealed artificial conditions, and
- discovered peril

[107]Landowners may owe limited duties to protect neighboring landowners and passersby
- from artificial or unreasonable dangers on the premises (encroaching structures, blocked vision, etc.)

Paragraph Outline for Week 12:
Premises Liability

[97]Premises liability in most states requires classifying the plaintiff as an invitee, licensee, or trespasser, although some states require reasonable care as to all. [98]Landowners may have limited statutory immunity from negligence claims by individuals using the land for recreational purposes. [99]A tenant controlling the premises owes the duties, but so do landlords who retain control, contract to repair, repair negligently, and fail to disclose defects. [100]Landowners owe reasonable care to invitees, meaning those who enter for pecuniary purposes or accompany others who do so. [101]A person's status can change from invitee to licensee to trespasser, depending on their activities and purpose, and scope of permission. [102]Reasonable care may include the duty to design, construct, maintain, repair, warn, and protect against unreasonably dangerous conditions on the premises. [103]Landowners may advertise and assume duties to protect against the criminal acts of others, or owe those duties by special knowledge or relationship. [104]Landowners owe licensees, meaning those who enter for their own non-pecuniary purposes, like social guests and law officers, a duty to warn of known hidden dangers creating unreasonable risk. [105]Landowners owe trespassers no duty except as to children, active operations, tolerated intruders, concealed artificial conditions, and discovered peril. [106]Landowners traditionally owed children of tender years a duty to protect against an attractive nuisance, but modern formulations assess the landowner's knowledge of the risk and child's ability to recognize it. [107]Landowners may owe limited duties to protect neighboring landowners and passersby from artificial or unreasonable dangers on the premises.

Fluency Cards for Week 12

Cover and uncover the response to each prompt until you fluently recall the exact response.

Premises Liability

Classify as invitee, licensee, or trespasser. A few states require reasonable care for all.

Renters

Tenants controlling the condition owe the duty.

Owners

Duty only with retained control, contract to repair, negligent repair, or failure to disclose hidden defects.

Invitees

Reasonable care for those entering for pecuniary purposes.

Licensees

Warn of known hidden dangers for those who enter for their own purposes.

Trespassers

No duty except for active operations, tolerated intruders, and children attracted to nuisances.

Definitions Worksheet for Week 12

1. What is *premises liability*?

2. How does premises liability differ from other negligence actions?

3. Who owes the premises-liability duty when tenants have rented the land?

4. What duty does a landowner owe to prevent crime from harming a visitor?

5. What duty does a landowner owe an invitee? How does law define an *invitee*?

6. What duty does a landowner owe a licensee? How does the law define a *licensee*?

7. What duty does a landowner owe a trespasser? What exceptions does law recognize?

Answer Key for Definitions Worksheet

1. *What is **premises liability**?* Premises liability is a form of negligence action against the person who or entity that owns and controls the conditions on land where the plaintiff suffered injury.

2. *How does premises liability differ from other negligence actions?* Premises liability differs primarily in the duty that the landowner owes the person injured on the land. Premises liability typically requires classifying the plaintiff as invitee, licensee, or trespasser, although a few states require reasonable care as to all.

3. *Who owes the premises-liability duty when tenants have rented the land?* Tenants controlling the premises owe the duties, but landlords who retain control, contract to repair, repair negligently, or fail to disclose known defects may also owe the duty.

4. *What duty does a landowner owe to prevent crime from harming a visitor?* Landowners generally owe no duty to prevent crime but may advertise and assume duties to protect against crime or owe those duties by special knowledge or relationship.

5. *What duty does a landowner owe an invitee? How does law define an **invitee**?* Landowners owe reasonable care to invitees, who enter for pecuniary purposes or accompany others who do so. Status can change depending on the visitor's activities and purpose, and the scope or duration of permission.

6. *What duty does a landowner owe a licensee? How does the law define a **licensee**?* Landowners owe licensees, defined as ones who enter for their own purposes like social guests and law officers, a duty to warn of known hidden dangers creating unreasonable risk.

7. *What duty does a landowner owe a trespasser? What exceptions does law recognize?* Landowners owe trespassers no duty except as to active operations, tolerated intruders, concealed artificial conditions, discovered peril, and children attracted to nuisances.

TORTS I WORKBOOK

Issue-Spotting Worksheet for Week 12
State the law each scenario raises. No analysis. Just spot the issue and state the law.

1. A new client meeting you in your office tells you that she suffered a serious injury at a retailer's location in a nearby mall. She knows that lawyers sue for motor-vehicle accidents but wonders if you handle this kind of a case and if so what this kind of a case is called because she hadn't seen it in online lawyer advertisements.

---

2. After confirming that indeed you *do* handle this kind of case, and after answering the client's question about what type of case it is, the client asks how this kind of case differs from a routine motor-vehicle-accident case. Appreciating how thoughtful and articulate the client is, you answer her question just as thoughtfully and articulately.

---

3. The client next explains that she was hurt right at the retailer's entrance from the commons part of the mall just off the food court. She wonders who would be responsible.

---

4. After giving the client a brief answer, you ask her what happened. The client finally explains that a hooded youth, presumably a shoplifter or robber, had knocked her over while rushing past out of the store, causing her to break her elbow and strike the back of her head on the floor.

---

5. The client gives you a funny look when you ask why she was in the mall, but she answers that she was making a return at the store.

---

6. The client further explains that she had already made the return when she decided to go back in and ask if they had any extra boxes for her to use at home to pack and move.

---

7. The client laughs at your parsing of the law, asking what if she had been a trespasser?

Answer Key for Issue-Spotting Worksheet

1. ***This scenario implicates the definition of premises liability.*** Premises liability is a form of negligence action against the person who or entity that owns and controls the conditions on land where the plaintiff suffered injury.

2. ***This scenario implicates the difference between an ordinary negligence action and the premises-liability form of negligence.*** Premises liability differs primarily in the duty that the landowner owes the person injured on the land. Premises liability typically requires classifying the plaintiff as invitee, licensee, or trespasser, although a few states require reasonable care as to all.

3. ***This scenario implicates who owes premises-liability duties, tenant or landowner.*** Tenants controlling the premises owe the duties, but landlords who retain control, contract to repair, repair negligently, or fail to disclose known defects may also owe the duty.

4. ***This scenario implicates when a landowner owes a duty to prevent crime.*** Landowners generally owe no duty to prevent crime but may advertise and assume duties to protect against crime or owe those duties by special knowledge or relationship.

5. ***This scenario implicates the definition of an invitee and the duty owed invitees.*** Landowners owe reasonable care to invitees, who enter for pecuniary purposes or accompany others who do so. Status can change depending on the visitor's activities and purpose, and the scope or duration of permission.

6. ***This scenario implicates the definition of a licensee and the duty owed licensees.*** Landowners owe licensees, defined as ones who enter for their own purposes like social guests and law officers, a duty to warn of known hidden dangers creating unreasonable risk.

7. ***This scenario implicates the duty owed trespassers.*** Landowners owe trespassers no duty except as to active operations, tolerated intruders, concealed artificial conditions, discovered peril, and children attracted to nuisances.

Sameness Exercise for Week 12

Sort the fact patterns into the correct premises-liability form: invitee (I); licensee (L), or trespasser (T).

____: A shopper entered a store to buy a loaf of bread but slipped and fell on a banana peel in the produce section.

____: A thief fell through a skylight to his death after having climbed on a bank's roof trying to find a way to break in.

____: A hunter had a rotten tree trunk fall on him while traversing a woodlot his buddy owned, on the way to a blind that they shared.

____: A man who accompanied his wife into a department store cut his hand badly on a clothing rack while his wife shopped for a dress.

____: A hiker suffered a back injury falling in a ditch after climbing a fence into a construction site to take a shortcut toward a trail.

____: A fisherman drowned when his friend's dock collapsed, trapping him under it, after his friend had said he could fish.

____: A swimmer suffered severe hypothermia when swimming in an old gravel pit that the county had closed to all.

____: A diner tripped and fell over an unlit, unmarked step in the middle of a restaurant's dining room.

____: A woodsman broke an ankle sneaking his three-wheeler across a neighbor's tree farm, when striking a chain across the entrance gate.

____: A niece visiting her aunt for a game of gin rummy slipped and fell in her aunt's bathroom because of a loose rug.

____: A lawyer broke her wrist picking up her dry cleaning when the cleaner's waiting-area bench collapsed under the lawyer.

____: A woman using her friend's woodshop to make some shutters suffered a head injury when a ceiling tile fell on her.

____: A shopper suffered a head laceration on a falling mirror in the employee restroom into which she had snuck.

____: A homemaker suffered severe neck injury when her hairdresser tipped the homemaker back too far while doing a wash and rinse.

____: A man slipped and fell on black ice after returning to his buddy's house in the middle of the night to retrieve his wallet.

____: A man suffered a knee injury on a hidden pipe, when getting old boxes in which to pack, from behind a big-box retailer.

Answers are on the next page.

Answer Key for Sameness Exercise

Applicable Law: While some states may abandon the traditional classifications and require reasonable care as to all entrants, traditionally, premises liability requires classifying the plaintiff as an invitee, licensee, or trespasser. Landowners owe reasonable care to invitees, who enter for pecuniary purposes or accompany others who do so. Landowners owe licensees, defined as ones who enter for their own purposes like social guests and law officers, a duty to warn of known hidden dangers creating unreasonable risk. Landowners owe trespassers, who enter without permission, no duty, except as to active operations, tolerated intruders, concealed artificial conditions, discovered peril, and children attracted to nuisances. Status can change depending on the visitor's activities and purpose, and the scope or duration of permission.

I: A shopper entered a store to buy a loaf of bread but slipped and fell on a banana peel in the produce section. *Key trigger words: "shopper" and "to buy," together indicating business.*

T: A thief fell through a skylight to his death after having climbed on a bank's roof trying to find a way to break in. *"A thief" and "to find a way to break in" trigger to trespasser status.*

L: A hunter had a rotten tree trunk fall on him while traversing a woodlot his buddy owned, on the way to a blind that they shared. *"His buddy owned" and "they shared" suggests permission.*

I: A man who accompanied his wife into a department store cut his hand badly on a clothing rack while his wife shopped for a dress. *"Accompanied" and "while his wife shopped" implicates rule that those accompanying shoppers are also invitees.*

T: A hiker suffered a back injury falling in a ditch after climbing a fence into a construction site to take a shortcut toward a trail. *"After climbing a fence" and "to take a shortcut" suggest trespass.*

L: A fisherman drowned when his friend's dock collapsed, trapping him under it, after his friend had said he could fish. *"Had said he cold fish" suggest permission for recreational purposes.*

T: A swimmer suffered severe hypothermia when swimming in an old gravel pit that the county had closed to all. *"Had closed to all" indicates trespasser status.*

I: A diner tripped and fell over an unlit, unmarked step in the middle of a restaurant's dining room. *The "diner" status in "a restaurant" shows commercial status.*

T: A woodsman broke an ankle sneaking his three-wheeler across a neighbor's tree farm, when striking a chain across the entrance gate. *"Sneaking" implicates trespass.*

L: A niece visiting her aunt for a game of gin rummy slipped and fell in her aunt's bathroom because of a loose rug. *"For a game" suggests social status.*

I: A lawyer broke her wrist picking up her dry cleaning when the cleaner's waiting-area bench collapsed under the lawyer. *"Picking up her dry cleaning" shows commercial purpose.*

L: A woman using her friend's woodshop to make some shutters suffered a head injury when a ceiling tile fell on her. *"Using her friend's woodshop" suggests personal purpose.*

T: A shopper suffered a head laceration on a falling mirror in the employee restroom into which she had snuck. *"Snuck" is the key trigger suggesting trespass.*

I: A homemaker suffered severe neck injury when her hairdresser tipped the homemaker back too far while doing a wash and rinse. *"Hairdresser" suggests the business purpose.*

T: A man slipped and fell on black ice after returning to his buddy's house in the middle of the night to retrieve his wallet. *"In the middle of the night" suggests trespass.*

L: A man suffered a knee injury on a hidden pipe, when getting old boxes in which to pack, from behind a big-box retailer. *The "getting old boxes in which to pack" language shows personal purpose.*

Examples/Non-Examples Exercise for Week 12

Identify whether each fact pattern is an example (E) or non-example (N) of the **highlighted concept**. Answers are at the end. In the blanks, generate an additional example and non-example.

1. Landowners may have **limited statutory immunity** from negligence claims by individuals using the land *for recreational purposes*.
   ___ The hunter didn't see the farmer's broken-down old wire fence buried in leaves and tore his knee in it.
   ___ The shopper slipped and fell on cooking oil seeping down the shelf from where the store clerk put it.
   ___ The birder hadn't expected the sanctuary's old wooden bridge to give way under her, breaking her leg.
   E: _____
   N: _____

2. A tenant controlling the premises owes the duties, but so do landlords who **retain control**, contract to repair, repair negligently, and fail to disclose defects.
   ___ The apartment guest tripped and fell on the broom handle that the tenant had left in her bedroom hallway.
   ___ The tenant fell on ice that had accumulated in front of the rental unit's dumpster from sun melting snow.
   ___ The delivery person cut her hand badly on the broken door handle at the multi-unit's common entrance.
   E: _____
   N: _____

3. A person's **status can change** from invitee to licensee to trespasser, depending on their activities and purpose, and scope of permission.
   ___ The shopper hadn't asked to use the employee restroom in back where she fell but had just had to go.
   ___ The rancher hadn't given the hiker permission but, after he caught her, told to just go on ahead through.
   ___ The guest asked if her host was interested in seeing some jewelry to maybe buy, but the host said no.
   E: _____
   N: _____

4. **Reasonable care standards** for landowners caring for invitees may include to reasonably design, construct, maintain, repair, warn, and protect against unreasonably dangerous conditions on the premises.
   ___ The hotel hadn't thought that a pool guest might run into the unmarked glass door, thinking it was open.
   ___ The linoleum floor met every code and standard, so that no one knew why the shopper slipped.
   ___ The lodge owner would have discovered the loose railing on any simple, routine inspection of the cabin.
   E: _____
   N: _____

5. Landowners may advertise and assume **duties to protect against criminal acts** of others or owe those duties by special knowledge or relationship.
   ___ The clothing store never had any robberies or assaults in its upscale district until the customer got hurt.
   ___ The motel manager knew that drug dealers were renting rooms to deal drugs but liked the extra business.

_____ The fast-food joint had signs saying that it patrolled the premises for security during open hours at night.

E: _____

N: _____

6. Landowners traditionally owe children of tender years a duty to protect against an *attractive nuisance*, but modern formulations assess the landowner's knowledge of the risk and child's ability to recognize it.
   _____ Neighborhood kids loved to play on the broken-down old tractor until its axle collapsed on one's leg.
   _____ The owner's kids had grown, leaving the old trampoline used only by other kids sneaking in.
   _____ The woods made a good hiding place for the boys, until an old tree trunk fell over where they'd dug.

E: _____

N: _____

7. Landowners may owe limited duties to *protect neighboring landowners and passersby* from artificial or unreasonable dangers on the premises.
   _____ The landowner liked the rosebush he'd planted at his property's corner even though motorists complained.
   _____ The naturally wooded land had a lot of trees right up to the roadside, one of which blew over in a storm.
   _____ The golf driving range had a fence along the road that wasn't quite high enough for big, wild hitters.

E: _____

N: _____

8. Landowners owe licensees, meaning those who enter for their own non-pecuniary purposes, like social guests and law officers, a duty to *warn of known hidden dangers* creating unreasonable risk.
   _____ The host forgot to tell her visitor of the loose step and weak handrail on the way down to the beach.
   _____ She invited the neighbors over for cards, forgetting to shovel the snow from the front walk.
   _____ The homeowner invited the solicitor in for coffee on the bitter cold day, ignoring the hot wood burner.

E: _____

N: _____

9. Landowners owe trespassers no duty except as to children, active operations, *tolerated intruders*, concealed artificial conditions, and discovered peril.
   _____ The city manager knew that kids were swinging on the rope tied to the pole at the private police dock.
   _____ The railroad engineers had seen prospectors digging along the exposed sides of the deep railway cuts.
   _____ The mine owner had chased vandals off the property many times but couldn't always catch them at work.

E: _____

N: _____

Answers: 1 ENE; 2 NEE; 3 EEN; 4 ENE; 5 NEE; 6 EEN; 7 ENE; 8 ENE; 9 NEE

Review Exercise for Week 12
Match these facts with the law on the next page that they trigger.

What a month it had been. ____ 1. First, she had carelessly left the hose running one night with no idea that it would flood an old drain pipe into the library basement next door causing catastrophic loss. ____ 2. Then, animal-control officers had stolen her dog—well, not *stolen* it but impounded it, but they wouldn't give it back! ____ 3. Then she'd found out she was pregnant even though she'd had her tubes tied two years ago! ____ 4. Her boyfriend was so upset that he went ballistic and almost punched a delivery boy who gave him a hard time over not tipping him. You should've seen that boy run! ____ 5. Then her mom called saying that her doctor had operated on her wrong leg when she'd gone in for her knee replacement. ____ 6. As if that was not enough, her mom got an infection from the surgery and no one at the hospital would tell her how. ____ 7. When she came home late one night from the coffee shop where she'd been talking it out with her girlfriend, she'd found her now-ex boyfriend asleep on her couch—the rat! How'd he get in?! ____ 8. Later, she'd asked her little sister to help her move her boyfriend's equipment out of the garage, and she'd accidentally knocked his motorcycle over on her sister's leg and wasn't strong enough to get it off! ____ 9. Finally, she'd been driving to work one morning, going just a *little* over the speed limit, when some jerk ahead of her on the freeway had jammed on his brakes, and she'd not been able to stop in time, crumpling the rear of his vehicle and sending him off to the hospital in an ambulance. With her life spinning out of control, she hoped next month would bring some peace.

Review Exercise for Week 12
Match this law with the facts on the reverse side that the facts trigger.

___A. Assault is the reasonable apprehension of an imminent battery with the apparent present ability to carry it out.^{Week 2}

___B. Where no actual damage occurs from trespass, the law awards nominal and in egregious cases punitive damages.^{Week 3}

___C. Authority of law, discipline, and justification are defenses, where law authorizes or circumstances warrant the action.^{Week 4}

___D. The reasonably prudent person assumes the actor's physical, not mental, characteristics, except those with superior knowledge must use it.^{Week 5}

___E. Law may allow claim for wrongful conception (limit to cost of pregnancy/ delivery) and wrongful birth (negligent failure to inform to abort).^{Week 7}

___F. Violating statute is negligence per se or a presumption or inference of negligence, where statute protects plaintiff's class against injury risk.^{Week 8}

___G. Cause in fact on medical, legal, technical, and scientific matters may require expert testimony based on valid and reliable scientific methods.^{Week 9}

___H. Proximate cause, a judge than jury question, asks whether the breach led in direct sequence to harm or risk of harm was reasonably foreseeable.^{Week 10}

___I. A professional's standard of care requires a similarly qualified expert's testimony except in the rare case of obvious breach.^{Week 11}

Answer key: 1H, 2C, 3E, 4A, 5I, 6G, 7B, 8D, 9F

Week 12 Role Play—Opening Statement Outline

Draft an outline for your opening statement in the trial of a premises-liability case in which your client suffered a broken hip when slipping and falling on cooking oil that had leaked from a gallon plastic container with a split seam, on the shelf of the defendant grocery store. Your client will testify that as he lay in the oil after falling, he noticed that it has appeared to dry around the edges and was sticky even in the center. Your client was not shopping but was accompanying his wife who was shopping for dinner supplies. The jurisdiction follows the traditional law of premises liability. An example opening statement follows on the next page.

Model answer (condensed format): Jury members, you can see that my client Mr. Baxter remains wheelchair bound from fracturing his hip in a slip and fall on leaked cooking oil at the defendant Big Grocer. No witness will dispute that account. Mr. Baxter's own testimony, and that of his wife Mrs. Baxter and other witnesses, will further show you that Big Grocer left the cooking oil, which had leaked from a split tub of oil on the shelf, for so long that the oil had dried up around the edges and was sticky in the center. You'll need to know that Mr. Baxter's legal claim is for Big Grocer's negligence. At the case's conclusion, Judge Ward will instruct you in the law that Big Grocer owed its business visitors Mr. and Mrs. Baxter a duty of reasonable care, just as any of us owe one another such a duty. The witnesses' testimony will confirm for you that Big Grocer breached that duty when its stocker put the split tub of oil up on the shelf to leak to the floor and when its staff didn't clean up the oil for, from the looks of it, hours as it dried on the floor. The testimony will be, and we ask that you accordingly decide, that such sloppiness is not what the community expects. Big Grocer will not even dispute that Mr. Baxter's medical expense from his fractured hip has been in the tens of thousands of dollars, but we'll have Mr. Baxter's doctor tell you more about what Mr. Baxter had to go through because of this difficult event. And so, Mr. and Mrs. Baxter will ask that you have Big Grocer pay those expenses and provide other compensation as the law requires under these circumstances. Thank you in advance for serving, and please listen closely to these proofs. This matter is important to Mr. and Mrs. Baxter, just as it would be to you.

Week 13

Negligence Defenses (Comparative Negligence & Assumption of the Risk)

Bullet Outline for Week 13:

Negligence—Defenses

[108]Contributory negligence = bars claims by the plaintiff at fault in any part for the plaintiff's own harm
- last-clear-chance and other doctrines soften the all-or-nothing contributory-negligence defense
- contributory negligence old, disfavored defense, replaced in 46 states by comparative negligence

[109]Comparative negligence = reduces plaintiff's damages by plaintiff's percentage fault
- pure form from 1 to 99%
- modified forms up to 49% or 50% then barring plaintiff's claim if plaintiff is equally or more at fault
- [110]statutes may further alter comparative negligence rules
  - such as by limiting the plaintiff's failure to wear a seatbelt to 5% comparative negligence (MI)
- [111]states adopting comparative negligence may abolish
  - last-clear-chance doctrine,
  - joint-and-several liability,
  - defendants' rights of contribution
- [112]some states (MI) allow factfinder to allocate fault to non-parties
  - reduces the plaintiff's damages accordingly
  - uncollectible portions plaintiff loses or some states (MI) shift in part to collectible defendants

[113]Assumption of risk bars plaintiff's claim if plaintiff voluntarily encountered known risk
- [114]express assumption of risk = statements or writings accepting a disclosed risk
  - unless adhesion contracts (unequal power or public policy prohibits)
- [115]implied assumption of risk = circumstances showing voluntary acceptance of known risk
  - some states abolish the defense with comparative negligence's adoption

Paragraph Outline for Week 13:

Negligence—Defenses

[108]Contributory negligence barred claims by the plaintiff at fault in part in the plaintiff's own harm, while the last-clear-chance and other doctrines softened the all-or-nothing defense. [109]Comparative negligence reduces plaintiff's damages by plaintiff's percentage fault, the pure form from 1 to 99% but modified forms up to 50% then barring the claim. [110]Statutes may further alter comparative negligence rules, such as by limiting the plaintiff's failure to wear a seatbelt to 5% comparative negligence. [111]States adopting comparative negligence may abolish the last-clear-chance doctrine, joint-and-several liability, defendants' rights of contribution, and

related doctrines. [112]Some states allow the factfinder to allocate fault to non-parties, reducing the plaintiff's damages accordingly. [113]Assumption of risk bars plaintiff's claim if plaintiff voluntarily encountered and accepted hazards of a known risk. [114]Express assumption of risk involves statements or writings accepting a disclosed risk unless barred as adhesion contracts, by unequal power, or by public policy. [115]The law may also imply assumption of risk from circumstances showing the plaintiff's voluntary acceptance of a known risk, although some states abolished the defense with comparative negligence's adoption.

Fluency Cards for Week 13

Cover and uncover the response to each prompt until you fluently recall the exact response.

Contributory Negligence

Bars claims where plaintiff has any fault.

Comparative Negligence

Reduces damages by the percentage of plaintiffs' fault.

Comparative Forms

Pure form from 1 to 99% but modified not greater than to 50% or less than to 49%.

Assumption of Risk

Bars claims by plaintiffs who voluntarily encounter known risks.

Assumption Forms

Express assumption involves words, while implied assumption involves circumstances.

Definitions Worksheet for Week 13

1. What are the two different forms of the negligence defense addressing plaintiff's fault?

2. How does contributory negligence operate? How do courts address its harshness?

3. How does comparative negligence operate? What modified forms may law recognize?

4. How may comparative negligence change other negligence rules?

5. What is the assumption-of-risk defense?

6. What two forms does assumption of risk take? Define each form.

Answer Key for Definitions Worksheet

1. *What are the two different forms of the negligence defense addressing plaintiff's fault?* Contributory negligence and comparative negligence are alternative forms of the negligence defense addressing the plaintiff's own fault. Most negligence cases will involve some allegation that the plaintiff was at least in part to blame for the plaintiff's injury or loss.

2. *How does contributory negligence operate? How do courts address its harshness?* Contributory negligence bars claims by the plaintiff who is at fault in any part for the plaintiff's own harm. The vast majority of states have replaced contributory negligence with comparative negligence. Those four states that still follow contributory negligence may use the last-clear-chance doctrine to soften the all-or-nothing defense.

3. *How does comparative negligence operate? What modified forms may law recognize?* Comparative negligence reduces plaintiff's damages by plaintiff's percentage fault, the pure form from 1 to 99%. Some states adopt modified not-greater-than or less-than forms that bar claims where the plaintiff is 51% or 50% or more at fault.

4. *How may comparative negligence change other negligence rules?* States adopting comparative negligence may abolish the last-clear-chance doctrine, joint-and-several liability, and defendants' rights of contribution, and related doctrines. Some states allow the factfinder to allocate fault to non-parties, reducing the plaintiff's damages accordingly. Statutes may further alter comparative negligence rules, such as by limiting the plaintiff's failure to wear a seatbelt to 5% comparative negligence.

5. *What is the assumption-of-risk defense?* Assumption of risk bars plaintiff's claim if plaintiff voluntarily encountered and accepted hazards of a known risk.

6. *What two forms does assumption of risk take? Define each form.* Express assumption of risk involves statements or writings accepting a disclosed risk unless barred as adhesion contracts, by unequal power, or by public policy. Implied assumption of risk arises when circumstances show plaintiff's voluntary acceptance of a known risk. Some states abolished the defense with comparative negligence's adoption.

Issue-Spotting Worksheet for Week 13

State the law each scenario raises. No analysis. Just spot the issue and state the law.

1. A new client meets you in your office, describing how she drove her motor vehicle out from a stop sign right into another vehicle's path, causing a major collision in which she suffered serious injury. The accident didn't hurt the other driver. She wants to know if she can sue the other driver for her injuries even though she probably wasn't looking when she should have done so.

2. In response to your explanation, the client discloses further that the other driver appeared to be texting or doing something else within the vehicle rather than watching the road and may also have been speeding. She wants to know if those observations would make any difference in the outcome.

3. The two of you agree that you will obtain the police report and do a little other investigation before making a recommendation to the client. Pleased with your acumen, the client asks you about another matter in which her husband injured himself bungee jumping. She first just asks if you've ever heard of a bungee-jumping claim.

4. The client then pulls a paper from her handbag saying that it was what the bungee-jumping company made her husband sign before he jumped. She wonders what difference the paper might make.

Answer Key for Issue-Spotting Worksheet

1. ***This scenario implicates the two forms of the defense having to do with the plaintiff's own fault.*** Contributory negligence and comparative negligence are alternative forms of the negligence defense addressing the plaintiff's own fault. Most negligence cases will involve some allegation that the plaintiff was at least in part to blame for the plaintiff's injury or loss.

2. ***This scenario implicates the rules for comparative negligence.*** Comparative negligence reduces plaintiff's damages by plaintiff's percentage fault, the pure form from 1 to 99%. Some states adopt modified not-greater-than or less-than forms that bar claims where the plaintiff is 51% or 50% or more at fault.

3. ***This scenario implicates the assumption-of-risk defense.*** Assumption of risk bars plaintiff's claim if plaintiff voluntarily encountered and accepted hazards of a known risk.

4. ***This scenario implicates the two forms of assumption of risk.*** Express assumption of risk involves statements or writings accepting a disclosed risk unless barred as adhesion contracts, by unequal power, or by public policy. Implied assumption of risk arises when circumstances show plaintiff's voluntary acceptance of a known risk. Some states abolished the defense with comparative negligence's adoption.

TORTS I WORKBOOK

Discrimination Exercise for Week 13

Indicate whether each statement *overgeneralizes*, *undergeneralizes*, or *misconceives* the rule, explaining why. *Overgeneralizing* states the rule too broadly, capturing circumstances to which it does not apply. *Undergeneralizing* states the rule too narrowly, omitting circumstances to which it applies. *Misconceiving* states the rule incorrectly. Answers are on the next page.

1. Contributory negligence and comparative negligence are two negligence defenses addressing the plaintiff's own fault.
____OVER/____UNDER/____MISS/ Why? _____
_____

2. Contributory negligence reduces a negligence claim by a plaintiff who has the most fault for the plaintiff's own harm.
____OVER/____UNDER/____MISS/ Why? _____
_____

3. Comparative negligence reduces plaintiff's damages by plaintiff's percentage fault, if defendant's fault is greater than plaintiff's fault.
____OVER/____UNDER/____MISS/ Why? _____
_____

4. States adopting comparative negligence must retain the last-clear-chance doctrine, joint-and-several liability, and defendants' rights of contribution.
____OVER/____UNDER/____MISS/ Why? _____
_____

5. Assumption of risk is a negligence defense that bars plaintiff's claim if plaintiff encountered hazards of a risk.
____OVER/____UNDER/____MISS/ Why? _____
_____

6. Express assumption of risk is a negligence defense that involves plaintiff's statements or writings accepting a disclosed risk.
____OVER/____UNDER/____MISS/ Why? _____
_____

7. Implied assumption of risk is a negligence defense that arises when plaintiff voluntarily expresses acceptance of a known risk.
____OVER/____UNDER/____MISS/ Why? _____
_____

Answer Key for Discrimination Exercise

1. The statement **OVERgeneralizes** the rule. Contributory negligence and comparative negligence are *alternative forms* of the negligence defense addressing the plaintiff's own fault. *A state will recognize only one of the two forms*. Most negligence cases will involve some allegation that the plaintiff was at least in part to blame for the plaintiff's injury or loss. *Defendant will plead whichever form of the defense the jurisdiction recognizes*.

2. The statement **UNDERgeneralizes** the rule. Contributory negligence *entirely bars* a negligence claim by a plaintiff who is at fault *in any part* for the plaintiff's own harm. The vast majority of states have replaced contributory negligence with comparative negligence. The four states that still follow contributory negligence may use the last-clear-chance doctrine to soften the all-or-nothing contributory-negligence defense.

3. The statement **UNDERgeneralizes** the rule. Comparative negligence reduces plaintiff's damages by plaintiff's percentage fault, *the pure form from 1 to 99%*. Some states adopt modified not-greater-than or less-than forms that bar claims where the plaintiff is 51% or 50% or more at fault.

4. The statement **MISconceives** the rule. States adopting comparative negligence *often abolish* the last-clear-chance doctrine, joint-and-several liability, and defendants' rights of contribution. Some states allow the factfinder to allocate fault to non-parties, reducing the plaintiff's damages accordingly.

5. The statement **OVERgeneralizes** the rule. Assumption of risk bars plaintiff's claim if plaintiff *voluntarily* encountered *and knowingly accepted* hazards of a *known* risk.

6. The statement **OVERgeneralizes** the rule. Express assumption of risk involves statements or writings accepting a disclosed risk *unless barred as adhesion contracts, by unequal power, or by public policy* such as for emergency medical care or public education. Some service and facility providers, including lawyers, must not require those with whom they deal to waive negligence risks.

7. The statement **MISconceives** the rule. Implied assumption of risk arises *when circumstances show* plaintiff's voluntary acceptance of a known risk. The law implies the waiver from circumstances showing plaintiff knew and accepted the injury-causing risk, *not from plaintiff's express statements*.

Sameness Exercise for Week 13

Contributory or comparative negligence is a defense that examines whether the plaintiff was at fault for the plaintiff's own injury or loss, in whole or in part. The few states still following contributory negligence (CN) bar plaintiff's claim for any fault on plaintiff's part. The modern pure comparative negligence (PCM) assigns percentage fault to plaintiff in any amount. The modified not-greater-than form of comparative negligence (NGTCM) assigns plaintiff fault up to fifty percent but bars plaintiff's claim if plaintiff's fault is more than defendant's fault (more than half of total fault). The modified less-than form of comparative negligence (LTCM) assigns plaintiff fault up to forty-nine percent but bars plaintiff's claim if plaintiff's fault is half or more of the total one-hundred percent fault. Working with a seatmate, *sort the following fact patterns into the suggested form*. Answers are on the back.

_____ : The jury found defendant at fault and plaintiff at fault, and so the judge entered a judgment of no cause for action.

_____ : The jury found defendant 25% at fault and plaintiff 75% at fault, and so the judge entered a judgment for plaintiff for 25% of the plaintiff's damages.

_____ : The jury found defendant and plaintiff equally at fault, and so the judge entered a judgment for plaintiff for one half of plaintiff's damages.

_____ : The jury found both defendants 25% at fault and plaintiff 50% at fault, and so the judge entered a judgment of no cause for action.

_____ : The jury awarded plaintiff $100,000 in damages, but the judge adjusted the verdict to $50,000 based on the jury's finding of fault.

_____ : The jury awarded plaintiff $200,000 in damages, but the judge adjusted the verdict to $50,000 based on the jury's finding of fault.

_____ : The jury awarded plaintiff $250,000 in damages, but the judge adjusted the verdict to $0 based on the jury's finding plaintiff had a little fault.

_____ : The jury awarded plaintiff $100,000 in damages, but the judge adjusted the verdict to $0 based on the jury's finding of equal fault.

_____ : Plaintiff's counsel strongly recommended settling because plaintiff was going just five over the speed limit, but the jury was sure to find a little fault.

_____ : Plaintiff's counsel recommended rejecting the modest settlement offer because although plaintiff had a lot of fault, damages were catastrophic.

_____ : Plaintiff's counsel recommended rejecting the modest settlement offer because plaintiff and defendant both did the same thing wrong and were equally at fault.

_____ : Plaintiff's counsel strongly recommended settling for the modest offer because plaintiff and defendant both did the same thing wrong and were equally at fault.

TORTS I WORKBOOK

Answer Key for Sameness Exercise

Contributory or comparative negligence is a defense that examines whether the plaintiff was at fault for the plaintiff's own injury or loss, in whole or in part. The few states still following contributory negligence (CN) bar plaintiff's claim for any fault on plaintiff's part. The modern pure comparative negligence (PCM) assigns percentage fault to plaintiff in any amount. The modified not-greater-than form of comparative negligence (NGTCM) assigns plaintiff fault up to fifty percent but bars plaintiff's claim if plaintiff's fault is more than defendant's fault (more than half of total fault). The modified less-than form of comparative negligence (LTCM) assigns plaintiff fault up to forty-nine percent but bars plaintiff's claim if plaintiff's fault is half or more of the total one-hundred percent fault.

CN: The jury found defendant at fault and plaintiff at fault, and so the judge entered a judgment of no cause for action. *With both at fault but no-cause entered, contributory negligence is the rule.*

PCM: The jury found defendant 25% at fault and plaintiff 75% at fault, and so the judge entered a judgment for plaintiff for 25% of the plaintiff's damages. *Only pure comparative would allow the plaintiff to get just 25% of damages.*

NGTCM: The jury found defendant and plaintiff equally at fault, and so the judge entered a judgment for plaintiff for one half of plaintiff's damages. *The not-greater-than form of comparative would just work here, although so would pure comparative.*

LTCM: The jury found both defendants 25% at fault and plaintiff 50% at fault, and so the judge entered a judgment of no cause for action. *Only the less-than form of comparative would bar any damage with plaintiff 50% at fault. So would contributory negligence, except the judge wouldn't request an allocation, just whether the plaintiff had any fault.*

NGTCM: The jury awarded plaintiff $100,000 in damages, but the judge adjusted the verdict to $50,000 based on the jury's finding of fault. *This award suggests a finding of 50% at fault, which the not-greater-than form would support, as would pure comparative.*

PCM: The jury awarded plaintiff $200,000 in damages, but the judge adjusted the verdict to $50,000 based on the jury's finding of fault. *Only pure comparative would work here. Any other form would bar plaintiff's recovery of just 25%.*

CN: The jury awarded plaintiff $250,000 in damages, but the judge adjusted the verdict to $0 based on the jury's finding plaintiff had a little fault. *Only contributory negligence would bar based on a little fault.*

LTCM: The jury awarded plaintiff $100,000 in damages, but the judge adjusted the verdict to $0 based on the jury's finding of equal fault. *Only less-than would bar based on plaintiff's equal (50%) fault, or contributory, but the judge wouldn't ask for an allocation if in a contributory state.*

CN: Plaintiff's counsel strongly recommended settling because plaintiff was going just five over the speed limit, but the jury was sure to find a little fault. *Only contributory negligence would bar for a little fault, and so only a contributory state would warrant strong settlement recommendation based on small fault.*

PCM: Plaintiff's counsel recommended rejecting the modest settlement offer because although plaintiff had a lot of fault, damages were catastrophic. *Only pure would allow plaintiff to recover with a lot of fault on plaintiff's part, and so rejecting a modest offer would only make sense in a pure-comparative state.*

NGTCM: Plaintiff's counsel recommended rejecting the modest settlement offer because plaintiff and defendant both did the same thing wrong and were equally at fault. *Only not-greater-than or pure comparative would make sense here.*

LTCM: Plaintiff's counsel strongly recommended settling for the modest offer because plaintiff and defendant both did the same thing wrong and were equally at fault. *Only less than would make sense here, or contributory, but if in a contributory state, the defendant wouldn't likely make a modest offer.*

Week 13 Drafting Exercise—Defenses

Draft the affirmative defenses at the end of this answer in a motor-vehicle negligence case in which the plaintiff Mrs. Bertrand alleges that your client defendant Jonathan Carter struck her vehicle at an intersection, causing her serious injuries. A model answer follows, but complete the defenses working on your own with a seatmate first.

[Caption omitted.]

Answer

Defendant Jonathan Q. Carter answers the complaint of plaintiffs Pamela S. Bertrand and Johnnie P. Bertrand by like headings and numbered paragraphs as follows:

PARTIES, JURISDICTION, AND VENUE

1. No contest as to Mrs. Bertrand's residence.
2. No contest as to Mr. Bertrand's residence.
3. No knowledge as to the marital status of Mrs. Bertrand and Mr. Bertrand, leaving them to their proofs.
4. Admitted as to Mr. Carter's residence in Wayfair, Glen County, Michigan.
5. No contest that the complaint alleges a case within this Court's jurisdictional minimum, but Mr. Carter denies that he is liable to Mrs. and Mr. Bertrand in any amount.
6. No contest as to the location of the vehicle collision for purposes of establishing venue in this Court, but Mr. Carter denies that Mrs. and Mr. Bertrand have this cause of action against him.
7. No contest as to this Court's jurisdiction over the parties in this case.
8. No contest that this Court is a proper and convenient venue for this case.

FACT ALLEGATIONS

9. Admitted that the motor-vehicle collision occurred, but denied as untrue that the collision occurred as the Bertrand complaint alleges. Mr. Carter denies that he was negligent and affirmatively avers that Mrs. Bertrand was negligent and the sole cause of any injury or damage.
10. Admitted that the collision occurred at the intersection of Wagner and Fruitdale Roads, but denied as untrue that the collision occurred as the Bertrand complaint alleges. Mr. Carter denies that he was negligent and affirmatively avers that Mrs. Bertrand was negligent and the sole cause of any injury or damage.
11. No contest as to the time and date of the collision at or about 8:26 a.m. on April 14, 2016.
12. No contest that Mrs. Bertrand was driving a 2011 Subaru Forester motor vehicle, but no knowledge at this time whether she was wearing her seatbelt, leaving Mrs. and Mr. Bertrand to their proofs.
13. Admitted that Mr. Carter was driving his 2008 Jeep Wrangler motor vehicle.
14. Admitted that Mrs. Bertrand's vehicle was eastbound on Wagner Road, but denied as untrue that it was a "through intersection" under the circumstances. Mr. Carter affirmatively avers that he entered the intersection prudently and lawfully before sight of Mrs. Bertrand's vehicle, which approached and came into the intersection at an excessive rate of speed.
15. Admitted that Mr. Carter's vehicle was northbound on Fruitdale Road, but denied as untrue that it was a "stop intersection" under the circumstances. Mr. Carter affirmatively avers that he entered the intersection prudently and lawfully before sight of Mrs. Bertrand's vehicle, which approached and came into the intersection at an excessive rate of speed.
16. Denied as untrue that Mr. Carter pulled his vehicle out from the stop sign into Mrs. Bertrand's vehicle. Mr. Carter affirmatively avers that he entered the intersection prudently and lawfully before sight of Mrs. Bertrand's vehicle, which approached and came into the intersection at an excessive rate of speed.
17. Denied as untrue in the manner and form alleged that Mr. Carter received and acknowledged traffic citations for causing the collision. Citations are inadmissible as evidence of fault. While Mr. Carter received unwarranted citation, he did not acknowledge and instead denied and disputed that any violation occurred.
18. Admitted only that the collision damaged both vehicles and temporarily disabled Mr. Carter's vehicle. Mr. Carter denies any further allegation in this paragraph, leaving Mrs. and Mr. Bertrand to their proofs.
19. No knowledge as to the full and detailed extent of Mrs. Bertrand's injuries, leaving Mrs. and Mr. Bertrand to their proofs, but Mr. Carter affirmatively avers that he was not at fault and is not liable for any of Mrs. Bertrand's injury, loss, or damage.

20. Admitted that emergency technicians backboarded and removed Mrs. Bertrand by ambulance, but Mr. Carter affirmatively avers that he was not at fault and is not liable for any of Mrs. Bertrand's injury, loss, or damage.

21. No knowledge of the destination of the ambulance that removed Mrs. Bertrand, leaving Mrs. and Mr. Bertrand to their proofs, but Mr. Carter affirmatively avers that he was not at fault and is not liable for any of Mrs. Bertrand's injury, loss, or damage.

22. No knowledge as to the full and detailed extent of Mrs. Bertrand's injuries, leaving Mrs. and Mr. Bertrand to their proofs, but Mr. Carter affirmatively avers that he was not at fault and is not liable for any of Mrs. Bertrand's injury, loss, or damage.

23. No knowledge as to the full and detailed extent of Mrs. Bertrand's injuries, leaving Mrs. and Mr. Bertrand to their proofs, but Mr. Carter affirmatively avers that he was not at fault and is not liable for any of Mrs. Bertrand's injury, loss, or damage.

24. No knowledge as to Mrs. Bertrand's work history and alleged disability, leaving Mrs. and Mr. Bertrand to their proofs, but Mr. Carter affirmatively avers that he was not at fault and is not liable for any of Mrs. Bertrand's injury, loss, or damage.

25. No knowledge as to the full and detailed extent of Mr. Bertrand's losses, leaving Mrs. and Mr. Bertrand to their proofs, but Mr. Carter affirmatively avers that he was not at fault and is not liable for any of Mr. Bertrand's losses.

COUNT I: MOTOR-VEHICLE NEGLIGENCE, MCL §500.3135

[Answers omitted.]

COUNT II: LOSS OF CONSORTIUM

[Answers omitted.

Affirmative Defenses

For his affirmative defenses, defendant Jonathan Q. Carter states as follows:

A. _____

B. _____

C. _____

D. _____

E. _____

F. _____

G. _____

ON THESE DEFENSES, defendant Jonathan Q. Carter prays for judgment in his favor and that the Court dismiss the complaint of plaintiffs Pamela S. Bertrand and Johnnie P. Bertrand with prejudice, together with costs and attorney's fees most wrongfully sustained.

[Signature block omitted.]

Model answer: A. Plaintiffs Mrs. and Mr. Bertrand have failed to state a claim against Mr. Carter in that Mr. Carter was not negligent and did not cause any injury to Mrs. Bertrand. B. Mrs. Bertrand was negligent and comparatively negligent, and her negligence and comparative negligence were greater than any negligence on the part of Mr. Carter (of which there was none), such that the applicable law bars her damages in whole, in that she drove her vehicle at an excessive speed, failed to keep a lookout for Mr. Carter's vehicle, entered the intersection when Mr. Carter's vehicle was already in the intersection, and failed to slow, brake, and take prompt evasive action. C. Mrs. Bertrand's negligence and comparative negligence were the sole factual and legal or proximate cause of her injuries. D. Mr. Carter leaves to the Court whether Mrs. Bertrand's alleged injuries meet Michigan's statutory tort threshold of serious impairment of body function with respect to No-Fault Act immunity. MCL §500.3135. E. Mrs. Bertrand has received and is entitled to receive No-Fault Act work-loss, allowable-expense, and replacement-service-expense benefits, such that the No-Fault Act bars her claim for economic loss other than excess economic loss. MCL §500.3135. F. If the proofs show that Mrs. Bertrand failed to mitigate her damages, then the applicable law will bar those damages in whole or in part. G. Mr. Carter reserves defenses pending discovery.

Practice Assessments

WEEK 1

TORT-LAW POLICY
1. A patient sued a family physician for medical malpractice. The physician had allegedly failed to order a critical test that was part of the standard protocol. The test would almost certainly have revealed her patient's serious disease. The test results would also very probably have led to immediate treatment that would have prevented the patient's crippling injury. Another family physician was a professional acquaintance of the first family physician. Like the first physician, the second physician often disregarded the standard protocol. After hearing that the first physician's insurer had paid the first physician's patient $100,000, the second physician began routinely ordering the critical test but complained to his lawyer about wasteful testing. What tort-law policy does the second physician's decision reflect?

A. The payment of $100,000 to someone suffering a crippling injury can have a positive effect on that person's health and life, compensation being a tort-law policy.
B. The influence of the first physician's liability on the actions of the second physician represents a reasonable deterrent effect on future wrongdoing, deterrence being a tort-law policy.
C. The payment of $100,000 by an insurer on behalf of an alleged wrongdoer who was nonetheless attempting to practice a healing art is a reasonable loss-spreading device.
D. The payment of $100,000 is an excessive amount that places an unreasonable burden on the liberty of physicians to practice their calling, tort law being bad policy.

Correct answer: B. In general, tort law's twin policies are to deter and compensate. Here, the second physician decided to follow the protocol because of the tort liability of another physician. Option B reflects that deterrent effect of tort liability. Option A is incorrect because although compensation can have a positive effect on the injured and is a tort law policy, the deterrent prospect of liability is what influenced the physician. Option C is incorrect because although the distribution of loss so as not to unduly burden or destroy the productive capabilities of those whose rare careless acts unintentionally cause serious injury is another tort law policy, that policy did not influence the physician. Option D is incorrect because the call of the question asks for a justifying tort-law policy, not criticism of tort law, and there is no basis on which to conclude from these facts that $100,000 is excessive for a crippling injury.

TORTS CLASSIFIED BY INTENT
2. A man was walking along a dirt road with his dog when he happened upon a truck driver who was inspecting a leaking valve on her truck parked alongside the road. Unknown to the man, the driver's truck hauled toxic waste from a nearby leather-treating plant. The driver explained to the man that she had probably driven too fast across a series of washboard potholes in the dirt road, causing the valve to leak. The man did not notice that his dog was licking the leaking chemical. When the driver finally pointed it out to the man and said, "That's a toxic chemical," the man instantly shooed the dog away and cussed at the driver for not having warned him or said something sooner. The driver shoved the man in retaliation. The man's dog later died. How might tort law classify the various forms of intent the driver exhibited with respect to the leaking chemical, shoving the man, and death of the man's dog?

A. The driver's actions were intentional and would be classified as such by tort law for purposes of any resulting tort actions.
B. The driver's actions were negligent, meaning lacking in ordinary and reasonable care, and would be classified as such by tort law for purposes of any resulting tort actions.
C. The driver's actions were innocent and would be classified as such by tort law, meaning that there would be no tort actions.

D. The driver may have committed a tort of strict liability for transport of a dangerous chemical, an intentional tort (battery) for shoving the man, and a tort of negligence for her too-fast driving and failing to warn the man of the poisoning of his dog.

Correct answer: D. Torts are classified by intent as intentional torts, negligence, or strict liability. Option D is correct because transport of dangerous chemicals may be so hazardous as to warrant strict liability for resulting damage even if all care is exercised, shoving someone is an intentional act, and driving too fast and failing to warn of dangers may be negligence. Option A is incorrect because the driver presumably did not intend the leaking chemical or death of the man's dog. Option B is incorrect because the driver's shoving the man was intentional, not negligent. Option C is incorrect because the driver's actions were not innocent but were intentional (shoving the man) and careless (driving too fast and, arguably, failing to warn the man of the dangerous chemical).

INTENTIONAL TORTS—INSURANCE
3. A man was an intimate acquaintance of a woman until the man decided to start seeing other women. The woman found out about the man's unilateral decision through a mutual acquaintance who was shocked that the man had not told the woman and embarrassed that the woman had only found out by chance. The woman, who was enraged at the man both for his decision and for not telling the woman, went over to the man's trailer with a baseball bat and broke his leg with it. The local prosecutor charged the woman with assault and battery. The woman had no job or money and was on Social Security disability. The public defender was unable to prevent the woman's conviction. The woman was sent to prison. The man consulted you for advice on whether he should sue the woman in tort for his medical expenses, wage loss, and pain and suffering. After your wise advice, the man probably decided which of the following?

A. There was little or no sense in suing the woman, who was without assets and whose actions would not be covered by liability insurance.
B. There was little or no sense in suing the woman, whose criminal conviction took care of everything for the man.
C. There was good reason to proceed with a tort lawsuit against the woman, because if the woman did not pay the tort judgment, then the state would do so for her as a social-welfare benefit.
D. There was good reason to proceed with a tort lawsuit against the woman, because there would likely be some liability insurance to cover the woman's actions.

Correct answer: A. Tested concept: Intentional torts are peripheral to tort practice because insurance does not ordinarily cover them. The facts state that the woman had no job or money, was disabled, and was sent to prison, meaning that she would have no apparent way of paying a judgment if the man were to obtain one against her. Option B is incorrect because criminal proceedings do not ordinarily provide for the full compensation available through a civil (tort) proceeding. Option C is incorrect because the state does not pay individual tort judgments when they go unpaid by destitute individuals. Option D is incorrect because liability insurance ordinarily does not cover intentional torts like the woman's assault and battery of the man.

INTENTIONAL TORTS—TRADITIONAL AND NEW
4. In retaliation for his firing, a man entered his employer's plant, spray-painted profanities and destroyed computers in the offices, and tried to sneak back out with some tools but was caught by a security guard. The man knocked down the security guard inside the building, frightened the guard with threats of murder, and then barred the door so that the guard was temporarily trapped inside. The man was apprehended by police two days later. Police later recovered a few of the tools that the man had stolen in the escapade. During the criminal proceeding against him, when the prosecutor was offering a plea deal, the man asked his lawyer about his potential civil liability. The lawyer might reasonably advise the man:

TORTS I WORKBOOK

A. Not to worry because the criminal prosecution would resolve everything including any potential civil claims the employer and security guard might bring against the man.
B. Not to worry because fired employees are almost never sued civilly by their former employers, who prefer to let matters alone rather than stir up litigation.
C. That the man's actions probably gave rise to several intentional-tort claims for assault, battery, false imprisonment, trespass to land and chattels, IIED, and conversion, for which the man might be held liable.
D. That the man's actions probably gave rise only to property-damage torts like trespass because the personal injuries to the guard would be addressed by the prosecution.

Correct answer: C. Tested concept: The seven intentional torts are assault, battery, false imprisonment, trespass to land and chattels, IIED, and conversion, the first five of which are traditional and the last two new. The man's actions could arguably satisfy the elements of most or all of those intentional torts involving both personal injury and property loss and damage. Option A is incorrect because criminal proceedings are ordinarily distinct from and do not bar civil proceedings. Option B is incorrect because employers will sometimes pursue former employees for the vindication of various rights including tort claims, and the guard would also have claims. Option D is incorrect because although there are property-damage torts that the man committed, he also committed personal-injury torts against the guard, which would not be resolved by the criminal prosecution.

INTENTIONAL TORTS—INTENT—DESIRE TO HARM
5. A homeowner and a gardener with whom the homeowner contracted had an argument over payment. The gardener was angry enough at the homeowner that the gardener warned the homeowner to "watch his step." Later that day, the gardener dropped a hanging basket on the homeowner as the homeowner stood beneath the gardener's ladder, seriously injuring the homeowner's neck. The homeowner retained a lawyer to file suit against the gardener for battery. At a mediation of the claim, opposing counsel argued that the gardener had simply accidentally let the basket slip. How should the lawyer respond to opposing counsel?

A. The lawyer should use the gardener's anger and threats against the homeowner as evidence that he intended the homeowner's offense or injury.
B. The lawyer should use the gardener's anger and threats against the homeowner as evidence that he was upset enough to have let the basket accidentally slip.
C. The lawyer should use the gardener's skill and experience as evidence that the gardener could not have accidentally let the basket slip.
D. The lawyer should use the gardener's knowledge that the homeowner was beneath the ladder as evidence that the gardener intended the homeowner's injury.

Correct answer: A. The specific purpose or desire to harm is the first of three forms of intent. The purpose to offend or injure the homeowner might well be drawn from the gardener's anger and warning. Option B is incorrect because the homeowner's claim is for battery, which is an intentional tort. Letting the basket slip accidentally does not support an intentional-tort claim. Option C is incorrect because there is no given evidence of the gardener's skill and experience (the gardener might have been unskilled and inexperienced), which might not prevent an accident in any case. Option D is incorrect because the gardener's anger and warning are much stronger evidence of ill will and the desire to offend or injure than the mere fact that the homeowner was under the ladder.

INTENTIONAL TORTS—INTENT—SUBSTANTIAL CERTAINTY
6. A robber called a pizza place requesting that a pizza be delivered to an apartment complex. The robber waited in a dark spot in the apartment hallway to rob the delivery person. The robber wanted the delivery person's money. When the delivery person hesitated to give the robber the money, the robber grew excited demanding the money and then finally shot the delivery person once to finally induce the delivery person to hand over the money. When the delivery person's lawyer sued the robber for battery,

the robber, who was unrepresented, filed a summary-judgment motion arguing that the robber did not intend to hurt the delivery person but only wanted the delivery person's money. What argument should the lawyer make to survive the summary-judgment motion?

A. Although the robber only wanted the money, the robber knew to a substantial certainty that the delivery person would be harmed by the gunshot.
B. Although the robber only wanted the money, the robber was reckless in his discharge of the firearm.
C. The robber wanted to hurt the delivery person more than the robber wanted the delivery person's money.
D. The robber wanted to hurt the delivery person along with wanting to take the delivery person's money.

Correct answer: A. The general knowledge of substantial certainty of harm is a second form of intent. If the robber knew to a substantial certainty that the delivery person would be harmed, then the robber will be taken to have intended the harm. Option B is incorrect because recklessness does not establish intent (except as to IIED). Options C and D are incorrect because there is no evidence that the robber wanted to hurt the delivery person. The facts state the opposite.

INTENTIONAL TORTS—INTENT—TRANSFERRED INTENT

7. An archer walked reserve lands looking for a place from which to hunt. While resting in a hidden location, the archer shot a hiker in the leg with an arrow. Which of the following additional facts would be most helpful in establishing that the archer committed battery on the hiker?

A. The archer saw the hiker climb in over a fence surrounding the reserve and thus reasonably believed that the hiker was a trespasser.
B. The archer did not want the hiker disturbing game in the area and thus had a motive to shoot at the hiker.
C. The archer meant only to scare the hiker with the arrow and thus reasonably believed that the hiker would not be hit by the arrow when he shot it at him.
D. The archer was unlawfully on the lands, without the owner's permission, and thus never should have been in a position to shoot at the hiker.

Correct answer: C. Transferred intent is a third form of intent, along with the purpose (desire) to harm and the knowledge of substantial certainty of harm. The archer's intent to scare (an assault) would transfer to satisfy the archer's intent to injure (a battery). Option A is incorrect because the hiker's status is irrelevant to whether the archer committed an assault or battery. Option B is incorrect because motive, although potentially probative of intent, does not satisfy that or any other element of assault or battery. Option D is incorrect because the archer's status is irrelevant to whether the archer had the intent to scare or injure the hiker. Whether the archer's intent to trespass would transfer to satisfy the intent to injure the hiker is open to question.

INTENTIONAL TORTS—INTENT—CHILDREN AND DISABLED

8. A four-year-old girl accompanied her father on a visit to the neighbors. The four-year-old girl wandered off to play with the neighbors' baby who was in an outdoor playpen. There were some loose bricks near the playpen. The girl laughed at the baby's reactions as the girl dropped bricks one by one on the baby. The baby was seriously injured. The baby's parents consulted a lawyer regarding the baby's potential claim against the four-year-old girl. What accurate statement of law could the lawyer tell the baby's parents about the baby's claim?

A. Young children can be held liable for intentional torts, so long as there is an adult around who should have been watching.

B. Young children can be held liable for intentional torts, so long as their actions are voluntary and they know the nature of the act.

C. Young children cannot be held liable for intentional torts, because they have inadequate appreciation for what others expect of them.

D. Young children cannot be held liable for intentional torts, because they have no assets and there would be no point.

Correct answer: B. Children and the mentally ill can be held liable for intentional torts, so long as their actions are voluntary and they know the nature of the act. The four-year-old girl has committed a battery and perhaps also an assault on the baby, notwithstanding that the girl may not have appreciated the seriousness of the baby's harm. The girl was acting voluntarily and understood the basic nature of her act, even if not its wrongfulness. Option A is incorrect because adult supervision, although appropriate, has no bearing on whether a young child has committed an intentional tort. Option C is incorrect because young children can be held liable for intentional torts, even if they do not always appreciate community standards. Community standards may establish the basis for a negligence claim but not for intentional torts, which instead depend on the actor's intent. Option D is incorrect because some young children do have assets, and the presence or absence of assets is irrelevant as to whether the cause of action exists (although it may be important on the question of whether to maintain the cause).

INTENTIONAL TORTS—INTENT—MISTAKE NOT NEGATING

9. A farmer owned a woodlot bordering on his fields. The farmer determined to reduce the size of the wood lot in order to have more acreage to plant. He cut the trees from five acres that he reasonably believed were on his own woodlot property. The farmer was shocked to discover that the many of the trees he had cut down were on his neighbor's property. The neighbor consulted a lawyer over whether the neighbor would have a claim regarding the farmer cutting trees from woodlot property that the farmer reasonably believed to be his own property, when it in fact was the neighbor's property. What advice would the lawyer best offer to the neighbor?

A. The neighbor does not have an intentional-tort claim against the farmer because honest mistake, whether or not reasonable, negates intent.

B. The neighbor does not have an intentional-tort claim against the farmer because mistake, as long as reasonable, negates intent.

C. The neighbor has an intentional-tort claim against the farmer because mistake, even if reasonable, does not negate intent.

D. The neighbor has an intentional-tort claim against the farmer only if the value of the land as woodlot was more than the value as field.

Correct answer: C. Mistake does not negate intent, whether or not the mistake is reasonable. The farmer committed a trespass to land, which is an intentional tort dependent on the actor having intended to enter the land, whether or not the actor knew the land was someone else's. Option A is incorrect because the subjective belief of an actor that the land was his does not give the actor a defense to trespass. Option B is incorrect because even a reasonable belief is not sufficient to negate intent. Option D is incorrect because comparative values before and after a trespass may be relevant to damages, but nominal damages would be available even if there was no difference or if the trespass resulted in an increase in value.

INTENTIONAL TORTS—NOMINAL DAMAGES PRESUMED

10. An elderly woman was on an airplane flight to visit her adult children. The flight was held on the runway for a long period after landing. The elderly woman several times firmly but politely told a flight attendant that she urgently needed to use the restroom. The attendant grew irate, twice raised his hand as if to slap the woman, and then purposefully bumped and blocked the elderly woman in her seat with a drink cart. Afterward, the elderly woman was adamant that she receive some compensation or that suit be filed over the attendant's frightening actions. The airline's claim representative correctly maintained that

the elderly woman had no physical injury or actual loss to prove. How should the elderly woman's lawyer respond as to the law?

A. That damages are presumed for intentional torts like assault, battery, and false imprisonment, even without actual loss or physical injury.
B. That damages are presumed for intentional torts like assault, battery, and false imprisonment, if the elderly woman can prove that the reasonable person would have sued.
C. That claim representatives should not be arguing about the law because they lack the legal knowledge, understanding, and training.
D. That claim representatives are not supposed to have confidential medical information about claimants and that there might be an injury to prove.

Correct answer: A. Nominal damages are presumed for assault, battery, false imprisonment, and trespass to land, and defendants are liable for other damages as to which their conduct was a substantial factor in causing. Option B is incorrect because there is no reasonable-person standard for whether a claimant is entitled to sue. Suit may be filed whenever there the claim is supported by fact and law, and not frivolous. Option C is incorrect because claim representatives are employed, trained, and entitled to discuss facts and law with claimants and their lawyer representatives. Option D is incorrect because with claimant authorization, claim representatives routinely do obtain confidential medical information and because when (as stated in the facts here) there is no injury, a lawyer must not suggest otherwise.

INTENTIONAL TORTS—BATTERY—ELEMENTS
11. A server served a customer several alcoholic drinks at the customer's order. The customer grew louder and ruder with each successive drink. The customer complained to the server about the taste of the last drink. The customer also called the server by a sexual slur and in other ways offended her. The server told the customer that she would bring him another drink. The server purposefully poured a toxic powder into the customer's drink and served it to him, knowing it would make him deathly ill, which it did. What tort, if any, has the server committed?

A. Assault.
B. Battery.
C. Intentional infliction of emotional distress.
D. Misrepresentation.

Correct answer: B. Battery is an intentional harmful or offensive contact. The waitress purposefully brought a toxic powder into contact with the customer intending that he be harmed by that contact, when he in fact was. Option A is incorrect because there is no indication that the customer apprehended an imminent battery. Option C is incorrect because there is no indication of the degree to which the customer was emotionally distressed, when the IIED tort requires evidence of severe distress. Option D is incorrect because the waitress made no representation with the intent that the customer rely on it. Option E is incorrect because the waitress committed a battery.

INTENTIONAL TORTS—BATTERY—BENEFICIAL EFFECT
12. A female passenger attempted to board a departing train. A conductor on the train platform tried to help the female passenger aboard the train but in doing so inappropriately touched the female passenger. The female passenger was furious at and deeply embarrassed by the conductor's touching. The female passenger sued the conductor for battery. The female passenger's lawyer brought the case before a panel of three case evaluators. What question should the case evaluators ask the female passenger's lawyer to determine whether the female passenger has a battery claim?

A. Whether the conductor only meant to help the female passenger get on the train.
B. Whether the conductor actually did help the female passenger get on the train.
C. Whether the conductor's action would have been offensive to the reasonable passenger.

D. Whether the conductor had touched other female passengers inappropriately.

Correct answer: C. To be actionable in battery, the touching must be offensive to the reasonable person. Options A and B are incorrect because good motive and beneficial effect do not excuse a battery. Option D is incorrect because other torts or wrongs by the conductor would not determine whether or not this tort claimant, the female passenger, has a battery claim.

INTENTIONAL TORTS—BATTERY—CONTACT INCLUDES
13. A student and teaching assistant were having a heated conversation at the head of the stairwell after the student had disrupted the assistant's class. The student grew disgusted with the conversation and turned around to walk down the stairs. The assistant gave a sharp pull on the student's backpack cord, causing the student to spin around and fall down the stairs. The student, who was seriously injured in the fall, sued the assistant for battery. The assistant's lawyer filed a motion to dismiss the student's battery claim because the assistant had not in fact touched the student. What rule should the judge who decides whether to dismiss the student's battery claim apply?

A. Contact with anything within a few feet of the person satisfies the contact element of a battery claim.
B. Contact with anything intimately associated with the person's body satisfies the contact element of a battery claim.
C. Contact must be with the person's own body or with reasonably tight-fitting clothing worn by the person.
D. Contact must be with the person's own body and not with things that the person wears or carries.

Correct answer: B. Contact with anything closely connected with the person satisfies the contact element of battery. Option A is incorrect because contacting things within a few feet of the person may not bring about any harmful or offensive contact. Option C is incorrect because although contact with the person's body or clothing would satisfy the contact element of battery, so would contact with something the person held or wore other than clothing. Option D is incorrect because contact with clothing and things carried can satisfy the contact element of a battery claim.

Intentional Torts—Intent: A crazed stranger attacked and beat a hotel guest in his room, after the hotel clerk carelessly gave the stranger a programmed key card to the guest's room. Distinguish and explain for the guest whether his claims against the stranger and hotel are for intentional or unintentional torts, and identify the probable procedural and substantive effects of that determination. *Model Answer:*

The hotel guest needs to know whether his claims against the crazed stranger and hotel are for intentional or unintentional torts and what would be the procedural and substantive effects of that determination.

An intentional tort is one in which the wrongdoer acts with purpose to bring about the harm or knowing to a substantial certainty that harm will result. Transferred intent is a third form of intent in which the wrongdoer's intent to commit one traditional intentional tort (assault, battery, false imprisonment, or trespass to land or chattels) transfers to satisfy the intent element for another traditional intentional tort or transfers from intended victim to actual victim. An unintentional tort is one in which the wrongdoer does not desire or know of the harm but acts carelessly with respect to the harm nonetheless.

The guest would have intentional-tort claims against the crazed stranger who apparently either desired the guest's harm or at least knew to a substantial certainty that harm would result from the stranger's deliberate attack on and beating of the guest. An attack and beating is clearly a purposeful act either intending the harm or knowing that harm would result. The stranger did not stumble into the guest but instead beat the guest, implying purpose. On the other hand, the guest would have unintentional-tort claims against the hotel. The hotel did not wish harm to its guest. The hotel clerk was only careless in giving the stranger the key card to the guest's room. Carelessness is not the same as intent. Carelessness involves unreasonable thoughtless action, not the desire to harm. The clerk did not wish to see the guest harmed but was only thoughtless in giving the key card to the stranger, as the facts appear.

Intentional torts may have different limitation periods from unintentional torts. Insurance is likely available for the unintentional tort but not for the intentional tort, whose wrongdoer may not have insurance or be collectible. Vicarious liability may be available for the unintentional tort but not the intentional tort. Damages may also be somewhat different particularly for the additional distress that one would suffer from an intentional tort and the punitive damages that may be available to punish the intentional wrongdoer. These are the major procedural and substantive differences.

The guest may thus have to sue the stranger sooner than the hotel under the applicable limitations periods. The guest may get larger damages from the stranger due to the exemplary and punitive damages but may not be able to collect those damages because no insurance would be available and the stranger may not have income or assets. The hotel would not have vicarious liability for the stranger's intentional harm but would for the clerk's carelessness. The hotel would also likely to have insurance to cover the guest's harm.

To conclude, the guest's recourse against the stranger would be for an intentional tort and against the hotel for an unintentional tort, those claims having different time periods, damages, and prospects for insurance and collectability. These distinctions would be quite important to achieving the guest's lawful objectives.

Battery: A tenant rents an apartment. The property owner employs a maintenance person, giving him a master key to all apartments. The maintenance person supplements his income by stealing from tenants, using the master key. The maintenance person believed that the tenant was away one evening. He entered her apartment using the master key, with the intent to steal. Leaving the lights off, he edged his way into the apartment's bedroom, stumbling against the tenant's bed and mistakenly putting his hand on the sleeping tenant's leg. The tenant awoke and screamed, causing the maintenance person to flee. Authorities arrested the maintenance person and convicted him of attempted theft. Analyze whether the tenant has a battery claim against the maintenance person. *Model Answer:*

This case requires analysis of whether a maintenance person breaking into an apartment to steal has committed a battery when stumbling into the sleeping tenant whom the maintenance person did not believe was home.

A battery claim requires the claimant to prove that the respondent committed an intentional harmful or offensive contact. Intent generally means either the desire to harm or knowledge of substantial certainty of harm but can include transferred intent from traditional intentional tort to traditional intentional tort (assault, battery, false imprisonment, and trespass to chattel or lands) and from intended victim to actual victim.

The maintenance person intended to use the master key to enter the apartment to steal. That entry would be trespass (intentional unauthorized interference with exclusive possession). The maintenance person did touch the tenant, putting his hand on her leg as she slept. The touch awoke the tenant, who screamed. The tenant thus appears to have felt the contact and taken appropriate offense, satisfying the offensive contact element. The tenant may have reasonably feared sexual assault or other injury, a point we may need to confirm as to the cause for her scream but a natural inference from the given facts. While the maintenance person believed the tenant to be away and only stumbled against the bed and mistakenly put his hand on the tenant, the maintenance person's intent to trespass would transfer to satisfy the intent element as to the tenant's battery claim against the maintenance person.

In sum, the tenant has an unusual but clear battery claim against the maintenance person with transferred intent from the trespass satisfying the intent element as to the touch on the leg, which would be offensive. While the tenant could maintain a battery claim against the maintenance person, the lack of insurance and collectability may make a negligence claim (negligent hiring and supervision) against the apartment complex a better claim to investigate and make.

WEEK 2

INTENTIONAL TORTS—ASSAULT—ELEMENTS

14. A landowner was clearing small trees from his land using an axe. A government forester entered the land to inspect the landowner's work. When the forester approached the landowner interrupting the work, the landowner told the forester to get off the land. The forester just began to recite the government authority on which the forester was acting, when the landowner suddenly raised the axe and swung it down toward the feet of the forester. The forester jumped back at the landowner's swing with the axe and fainted, even as the landowner laughed. Which is the best evaluation of the forester's assault claim?

A. The landowner has probably not committed an assault on the forester because the forester should not have fainted under circumstances where the landowner only had cause to laugh.
B. The landowner has probably not committed an assault on the forester because the forester should not have jumped back and instead should have stood his ground on the government authority on which he acted.
C. The landowner has likely committed an assault on the forester because the landowner intentionally created the forester's imminent apprehension of a harmful contact while having the apparent present ability to carry it out.
D. The landowner has likely committed an assault on the forester because the landowner intended or knew to a substantial certainty that the forester would faint, coming into contact with the land.

Correct answer: C. An assault is the reasonable apprehension of an imminent harmful or offensive contact (an imminent battery) with the actor's apparent present ability to carry it out. The landowner's actions probably satisfy each of those elements. Option A is incorrect because an assault likely was committed and because the forester's fainting was not determinative. The forester's jumping back apparently in fear of the axe swing would have been enough to show the apprehension of an imminent battery. Option B is incorrect because an assault likely was committed and because there is no tort-law requirement that individuals submit to assault and battery. Option D is incorrect because there is no requirement that the forester faint and come into contact with the land. Apprehension of an imminent battery would have been enough without the fainting and fall.

INTENTIONAL TORTS—DISTINGUISH ASSAULT AND BATTERY

15. A jogger was making his way across rough terrain. A team of competitive runners approached the jogger from behind just as the jogger stopped at a particularly steep and gravelly point along the trail. The jogger looked back, saw the runners coming, and then looked forward again to see if the jogger could either negotiate the trail or step out of the runners' way. But before the jogger could decide, the first runner in the pack abruptly shoved the jogger out of the way. The jogger pitched forward when shoved from behind, his head snapping back as he was completely unprepared for it, and fell down the steep trail. Which claim or claims could the jogger properly plead against the runner on this evidence?

A. Assault.
B. Battery.
C. Assault and battery.
D. Battery and intentional infliction of emotional distress.

Correct answer: B. Battery is intentional harmful or offensive contact. One may have a battery with or without an assault and an assault with or without a battery. Options A and C are incorrect because an assault is the apprehension of an imminent battery, but here, the jogger did not apprehend the approaching battery, so there was no assault. Option A is also incorrect because it does not include the battery tort that the runner committed. Option D is incorrect because IIED requires outrageous conduct causing severe distress. The runner's shove was probably not outrageous (beyond all bounds of decency), and there is no evidence of the jogger's severe distress.

INTENTIONAL TORTS—ASSAULT—THREATS

16. A student came into an empty classroom while the other students were outside at play. The student grew bored and began to rummage through some materials for something to do. A teacher walked by, saw the student, and stopped to see what the student was doing. The student, who had not been misbehaving, was nevertheless too nervous to answer. The teacher mistook the student's silence for insolence and guilt, and grew angry. The teacher's evident anger made the student decide to run. "You'd better watch yourself next time you're around here," the teacher hollered to the student, causing the student to blanch in fear. When the student refused to return to school and her parents learned about the incident, the parents consulted a lawyer. What is the best evaluation of whether the teacher committed a tort?

A. The teacher probably committed an assault when hollering at the student in a manner that created an apprehension or fear within the student.
B. The teacher probably committed an assault when hollering at the student but only if the student's apprehension or fear was reasonable.
C. The teacher committed no tort because no reasonable student would have fled in fear or apprehension under those circumstances.
D. The teacher committed no tort because words alone are generally not enough for an assault unless combined with an overt act suggesting imminent harmful contact.

Correct answer: D. Words (threats) alone are generally not enough for an assault unless combined with an overt act suggesting imminent harmful contact. Option A is incorrect because no assault was committed without a reasonable apprehension of an imminent harmful or offensive contact. The student might have been fearful, but if so, it should not reasonably have been of an imminent battery. Option B is incorrect because the teacher did not indicate that the teacher was about to commit a battery. The words warned of future events. Option C is incorrect because it is uncertain on these facts whether the student's response was reasonable or unreasonable, and even if reasonable, there was no threat of an imminent battery.

INTENTIONAL TORTS—ASSAULT—APPREHENSION

17. A speaker took the podium to address a crowd in a small auditorium. The speaker addressed a controversial subject that had raised protests when advertised. A custodian watched the speech from the wings of the stage on which the podium was located. Suddenly, the speaker heard shouts of alarm and saw the crowd disperse for the exits. The speaker was perplexed, wondering what the speaker had said or what had happened to cause the crowd's alarm and the crowd to suddenly disperse. The speaker later learned that the custodian had been pointed a gun at the back of the speaker's head as everyone scattered. What analytic problem does the speaker face in obtaining tort relief for the custodian's actions?

A. The speaker cannot satisfy the apprehension element of an assault claim.
B. The speaker cannot satisfy the imminence element of an assault claim.
C. The speaker cannot satisfy the apparent present ability element of an assault claim.
D. The speaker cannot show the reasonableness of the anticipation of harm.

Correct answer: A. Learning about an imminent contact after the contact occurs is not enough. The victim must apprehend the assault when it occurs. Option B is incorrect because harm would have appeared imminent to the speaker, as it did to the crowd, if the speaker had apprehended (seen) the custodian. Option C is incorrect because the custodian did have an apparent present ability to harm, as the crowd's reaction showed. The speaker just did not apprehend it. Option D is incorrect because the crowd's reaction also shows the reasonableness of the anticipation of harm.

INTENTIONAL TORTS—FALSE IMPRISONMENT—ELEMENTS

18. A carpenter was installing doors in a project with the help of an apprentice. The carpenter decided to play a prank on the apprentice. The carpenter sent the apprentice into an outbuilding on which the carpenter had just installed a door that did not yet have a handle. A plank was on the ground outside the door. The carpenter jammed the plank against the door, trapping the shouting apprentice in the outbuilding, and marched happily away, intending to leave the apprentice in the outbuilding for a little while. The apprentice suffered an attack of claustrophobia and injured himself attempting to batter open the door. Which tort claim or claims do these facts support for the apprentice against the carpenter?

A. Assault, battery, and intentional infliction of emotional distress.
B. Assault and battery.
C. Battery and false imprisonment.
D. False imprisonment.

Correct answer: D. False imprisonment is intentional unauthorized restraint against will. The carpenter intended that the apprentice be restrained within the outbuilding against the apprentice's will. Option A, B, and C are incorrect because there was no battery. The carpenter did not intentionally bring about a harmful or offensive contact with the apprentice. Options A and B are also incorrect because there was no assault. The carpenter did not intend to bring about the apprentice's apprehension of an imminent battery. Option A is also incorrect because the carpenter did not intend the apprentice's severe distress nor know to a substantial certainty that it would occur.

INTENTIONAL TORTS—FALSE IMPRISONMENT—RESTRAINT
19. A woman was a passenger on a snowmobile ride with several others after a New Year's party. The temperature was below zero with strong winds making it seem much colder. The snowmobile riders stopped at a hut that had a wood stove in which they built a fire. The others then took out some illicit drugs to use for their unlawful recreation. When the woman refused to participate, the others left the woman in the hut and rode away on the snowmobiles. The woman could either risk freezing to death hiking back from the hut where the others had dumped her, or just stay put, hoping for rescue. The woman remained in the hut overnight, comfortable and secure, until rescued by another snowmobile rider the following morning. She retained a lawyer to evaluate a claim for false imprisonment against the group of snowmobile riders. How should the lawyer advise the woman on the restraint element of her false-imprisonment theory?

A. The snowmobile riders effectively restrained the woman because her only means of escape from the restraint presented unreasonable dangers.
B. The snowmobile riders effectively restrained the woman because no one should have to hike when they could have ridden.
C. The snowmobile riders did not restrain the woman because she was free to move about the hut while secure and comfortable.
D. The snowmobile riders did not restrain the woman because she was free to leave the hut at any time.

Correct answer: A. The restraint element of false imprisonment is ordinarily satisfied by forceful restraint but may also be satisfied by subjecting the victim to unreasonable danger on escape or risking loss of significant property. The woman risked death if she left the hut and so was clearly restrained by avoiding that unreasonable danger. Option B is incorrect because if hiking had offered a reasonably safe means of escape, then the woman would not have been restrained. Option C is incorrect because restraint can include being confined to a room or hut. Option D is incorrect because although the woman could leave the hut, she could only do so by risking freezing to death.

INTENTIONAL TORTS—FALSE IMPRISONMENT—ESCAPE
20. A resident had a disagreement with an aide at a nursing home. The aide felt that the resident had been unkind, unappreciative, and verbally abusive. So as the aide left the resident's first-floor room, the

aide slammed and locked the door in a manner that would prevent the resident from being able to open it. When the door slammed, the resident just smiled. If the resident sued the aide for false imprisonment, what information would a defense lawyer seeking to challenge the claim most want to know?

A. That the aide only intended that the resident be locked in her room long enough not to be verbally abusive.
B. That the resident hated being locked in her room but was glad to have irritated the aide enough to make the aide slam the door.
C. That the resident did not mind so much being locked in against her will because she knew at least that she could sue for false imprisonment.
D. That the resident knew she could step safely out through the first-floor window, as she had secretly done on many prior occasions.

Correct answer: D. A known, reasonably safe means of escape means that there is no false imprisonment. If the resident knew she could step safely out and had done so in the past, then there would be no false imprisonment. Option A is incorrect because even a short false imprisonment, to induce behavioral change or for other reasons, would still be actionable. Option B is incorrect because the resident's pleasure at having irritated the aide would not offset or defeat the resident's false-imprisonment claim. It might somewhat reduce the resident's damages but not bar a false-imprisonment action. Option C is incorrect because the fact that the resident was less upset at being locked up would only reduce damages, not eliminate the cause of action.

INTENTIONAL TORTS—FALSE IMPRISONMENT—KNOWLEDGE

21. A sorority member imbibed heavily at a sorority event that stretched late into the night. The member finally passed out drunk on the couch of the sorority's parlor. Other members decided to bar the sorority member in the parlor so that she could not get out later that night and get more to drink or to get drugs. Another member who was not involved returned to the sorority early the next morning and, seeing the parlor barred for a reason she did not know, unbarred the parlor and left its doors open. When the drunken sorority member awoke later that morning, the parlor doors were wide open. The drunken sorority member later sued the other sorority member on several claims, one of which was for false imprisonment related to this incident. On deposition of the drunken sorority member in her false-imprisonment claim against the other sorority members for this incident, what would defense counsel best seek to establish?

A. The drunken sorority member had a serious problem with drug and alcohol abuse especially at sorority parties.
B. The drunken sorority member knew that the other sorority members had locked her in the parlor for her own good even if she disagreed with it.
C. The drunken sorority member only learned later that she had been locked in the parlor overnight and was not conscious of it at the time because she remained passed out until morning.
D. The drunken sorority member knew that she was locked in the room at the time the incident happened but had enough to drink within the confines of the parlor.

Correct answer: C. The victim must know of the restraint for it to be false imprisonment. If the drunken sorority member was not conscious of the restraint at the time it existed, then there would be no false imprisonment. Options A and B are incorrect because the other sorority members' motive to help the drunken sorority member would not defeat their intent to restrain her. Restraint against will remains an offense to personal autonomy notwithstanding the good intent of the one doing the restraining. Option D is incorrect because having certain comforts or advantages while restrained would not defeat a false-imprisonment action.

INTENTIONAL TORTS—IIED—OUTRAGE

22. A decorator completed a challenging job and rendered her bill to the client. The client was extremely upset by the bill and not very pleased with the job. The client's displeasure manifested in personal and professional accusations toward the decorator. The dispute escalated to the point that the client obtained the carcass of a dead cat, wrapped it inside a package that also contained a check for the decorator's bill, and left it at the decorator's office with a note that stating the check and a token were inside. The decorator almost fainted when she opened the package, seeing the dead cat inside, and suffered an anxiety attack requiring brief hospitalization. The decorator's lawyer may properly plead what tort or torts against the decorator's client?

A. Assault with an offensive item.
B. The intrusion form of invasion of privacy.
C. Outrage, also known as intentional infliction of emotional distress.
D. Defamation for injury to business reputation.

Correct answer: C. Intentional infliction of emotional distress, also known as the outrage tort, involves the intentional infliction of severe distress by outrageous conduct. Giving someone a dead cat in a box under pretense of payment is beyond all bounds of decency. Option A is incorrect because the client did not intentionally create the decorator's apprehension of an imminent battery. Option B is incorrect because the client did not cause an intrusion into the decorator's seclusion, which would form the basis for that form of invasion of privacy. Option D is incorrect because the facts do not show that the client published to a third party false words of and concerning the decorator, injuring the decorator's business reputation.

INTENTIONAL TORTS—IIED—OUTRAGEOUS DEFINED
23. Two dancers had a bitter personal dispute just before a major performance. To utterly embarrass the other dancer in an attempt to ruin the other dancer's career, the first dancer ripped a significant part of the second dancer's costume off during the performance, indecently exposing the second dancer. The first dancer's indecent exposure of the second dancer was seen by the entire shocked audience. As expected, the second dancer rushed in embarrassment from the stage, withdrew from the dance scene, and fell into deep distress and depression. Eventually, as a step toward recovery, the second dancer filed suit for intentional infliction of emotional distress against the first dancer. The first dancer's lawyer moved to dismiss the lawsuit, arguing that the conduct was not outrageous. How should the court rule on the motion to dismiss?

A. Deny the motion because outrageous conduct is that which severely distresses the target of the conduct.
B. Deny the motion because outrageous conduct is that which is beyond all bounds of decency in a civil society.
C. Deny the motion because outrageous conduct is that which no one in their right mind would engage in.
D. Grant the motion because outrageous conduct is that which no one has ever heard of before, and this scenario is familiar.

Correct answer: B. For IIED, outrageous conduct is that which is beyond all bounds of decency. This conduct calculated to embarrass and destroy a career by extraordinary means readily qualifies as outrageous. Option A is incorrect because a distressed reaction is not a definition of the conduct that causes and does not qualify the conduct. Individuals can react in a distressed manner to even ordinary conduct. Option C is incorrect because people not in their right mind engage in other conduct that is yet not outrageous, and people in their right mind engage in outrageous conduct. It is the conduct that matters, not the mind. Option D is incorrect because the motion should be denied and the familiarity of the conduct is not a determinant of its outrageousness.

INTENTIONAL TORTS—IIED—INTENT

24. A case worker was following the care for a child whose mother was under a court-ordered reunification plan. The case worker did not want to see the mother and child reunited. So the case worker determined to sabotage the mother's efforts at caring for her child. When the mother had the child at an unsupervised visit at the mall for a brief period and looked away, the case worker hid the child, hoping that the mother would be frantic over the child's loss, be severely distressed over the incident, and lose her parental rights. The case worker's secret plan worked, except that police located a witness. What witness testimony would be most helpful to an intentional infliction of emotional distress claim by the mother against the case worker?

A. That the case worker was seen following mother and child and grabbing the child in the store where the mother lost her and moving swiftly out of the mall with the child.
B. That the case worker was seen walking and talking with mother and child and later walking the mall with the child looking for and asking the whereabouts of the mother.
C. That the case worker seemed obsessed over this file and spending an inordinate amount of time on it compared to the case worker's other files.
D. That the child was located six stores away from where the mother lost the child and the case worker called to pick up the child from police who had identified the court file.

Correct answer: A. The conduct for IIED must be intentional (including recklessness), meaning that it must be directed to cause the plaintiff severe distress. Intent is often determined from circumstantial evidence. Testimony that the worker was seen acting furtively with respect to the mother's loss of the child would strongly tend to establish the worker's intent to create the incident bringing about the harm. Options B and D are incorrect because they tend to establish the case worker's ordinary innocence. Option C is incorrect because although unusual, it does not point to the case worker's particular intent and may be explained by other reasons including job diligence.

INTENTIONAL TORTS—IIED—OUTRAGEOUSNESS FACTORS
25. A journalist was having a hard time with writer's block and was in jeopardy of losing her job. Everyone in the bureau knew it, and most of the other employees were highly supportive. But a proofreader wanted to see the journalist's job given to an acquaintance. So the proofreader began mercilessly teasing the journalist every time it looked like the journalist was having a problem. The journalist probably could have taken it once, but by the tenth time, she just mentally cracked, left the bureau, and was hospitalized. An associate writing a memorandum evaluating the strength of the journalist's intentional-infliction-of-emotional-distress claim for a partner should stress what factor?

A. The repetitive nature of the proofreader's misconduct.
B. The special relationship of the journalist and proofreader.
C. The authority of the proofreader over the journalist.
D. The proofreader's bad motive.

Correct answer: A. Repetition may make the conduct more outrageous, as may the conduct's location and duration. The proofreader's repeating of the conduct brought about the journalist's severe distress. Option B is incorrect because although special relationship is generally a factor, here there was no special relationship between the journalist and proofreader. Option C is incorrect because although the authority of the perpetrator over the victim is generally a factor, here the proofreader had no evident authority over the journalist. Option D is incorrect because motive, although sometimes helpful as circumstantial evidence on an element, is not itself an element, and the motive to get an acquaintance a job is not an obviously or outrageously bad motive.

INTENTIONAL TORTS—IIED—UNUSUAL SUSCEPTIBILITY
26. A cashier was having a hard time with family matters at home. The cashier shared his family problems with a supervisor, admitting to her that the cashier had grown suicidal. The supervisor wanted to be rid of the cashier and his problems. So the supervisor began making things harder for the cashier at

work, especially with derogatory jokes and quips calling attention to the poor mental health of the cashier. The cashier's condition quickly grew worse to the point that he attempted suicide. What should a lawyer argue when presenting the cashier's claim for intentional infliction of emotional distress against the supervisor?

A. That the reasonable person would not have been upset by the supervisor's joke and quips about mental health problems.
B. That the supervisor had a job to accomplish in ensuring that the cashier's job was done properly.
C. That the cashier had voluntarily disclosed to the supervisor a mental health problem that the cashier could have kept confidential.
D. That the supervisor knew that the cashier had already been suicidal but figured she could take advantage of that in making him quit.

Correct answer: D. The conduct must be outrageous to the reasonable person, but the actor's knowledge that the victim is unusually susceptible may make the conduct more outrageous. The supervisor was picking on the cashier whom the supervisor knew to be susceptible. Option A is incorrect because the fact that reasonable persons would not have been upset would tend to help the supervisor, not the cashier. Option B is incorrect because the fact that the supervisor had a job to do would help the supervisor, not the cashier. Option C is incorrect because the fact that the cashier could have kept it confidential tends to help the supervisor, not the cashier.

Assault: A man wanted a woman never to forget that he was the toughest man in town. Dressed in hunting gear, he walked up to the counter in the store where she was working, pulled his knife from his boot, raised it shoulder high, and swung it down hard toward her, stabbing its tip in the counter right in front of her. She jumped back and passed out. Analyze whether these facts satisfy the elements of an assault. *Model Answer:*

The case requires analysis of whether a man committed an assault on a woman store clerk when he walked up to her counter, pulled out a knife, and stabbed it into the counter in front of her, causing her to jump back and pass out.
An assault involves the victim's apprehension of an imminent battery, meaning an imminent intentional harmful or offensive contact, when the wrongdoer has the apparent present ability to carry out the battery. Imminence means immediate rather than delayed. The wrongdoer's ability must be apparent to the victim, and the victim's apprehension must be reasonable rather than distorted (paranoid). The law presumes damages for this traditional intentional tort.
Here, the woman clearly apprehended something when she jumped back and passed out. Although we may need more information from her, probably her jumping back and passing out had to do with some anticipation that the man might be in the action of stabbing her when he raised his knife shoulder high and swung it down hard toward her, even though he only stabbed the counter with it. If indeed she apprehended his actions as his intent to bring the knife in contact with her, which seems quite reasonable, then the facts satisfy the imminent (immediate) battery element. The man would also have clearly had the ability to carry out the battery as he swung the knife toward her. The facts give no indication that the counter was too tall for him to reach her, for instance. Her jumping back gives further indication that his ability was apparent to the victim. The man might argue that she knew or should have known that he was only going to stab the counter, but that argument seems weak under the circumstances, which a reasonable person could easily construe as frightening and threatening. Note that the facts say he swung the knife "toward her."
To conclude, the woman has a strong assault claim for the man's swinging the knife down hard toward her, stabbing the counter immediately in front of her and causing her to jump back and pass out. While the woman need not show damages, she may be able to show substantial mental distress, fear, fright, and shock, and may also have suffered physical injury after passing out, another point to investigate.

False Imprisonment: At a sorority-house party, a man drugged a young woman who fell unconscious under the drug's influence on a sitting room couch. The young man then locked and barricaded the unconscious woman in the sitting room as a prank. Early the next morning, another young woman noticed the barricaded door, removed the barricade and unlocked it, and found the young woman still unconscious inside. Analyze whether these facts satisfy the elements of a false-imprisonment claim against the young man. *Model Answer:*

The case involves analyzing whether a man's drugging a young woman asleep and then locking and barricading her in the room constitutes false imprisonment, when another woman later removed the barricade and undid the lock, finding the woman inside still asleep.

False imprisonment involves an intentional unauthorized restraint against will. The victim must be aware of the restraint for the wrongdoer's actions to constitute false imprisonment.

Here, the man drugged the young woman asleep. That action in itself could constitute false imprisonment. The man apparently did not have the woman's permission to do so. The drugging restrained the woman in causing her to fall asleep. It is difficult to say whether she would have been aware of that restraint in that she simply fell asleep and remained unconscious, so we have some question over that aspect of her claim. As to the man locking and barricading her in the room, she was already asleep and thus apparently not aware. The other woman removed the barricade and unlocked the door before the woman awoke. The facts say the woman was *still unconscious*, although query whether the woman might have awoken during the night and discovered herself locked in. If she had, then she would be able to establish her knowledge of the restraint. The facts do not suggest this possibility, but it would be something to investigate.

In sum, the woman would likely not have a false-imprisonment claim as to the man locking her in the room unless the drugging itself constitutes a sufficient restraint, which it may well depending on how one interprets the *awareness* aspect. As to the locked door, the woman can satisfy the unlawful restraint elements but not that she was aware of the restraint, even if it would have been against her will. She may have other torts claims against the man possibly including battery.

Intentional Infliction of Emotional Distress: Two young men were rivals at work, fishing, hunting, and sports. One young man went to the other's home when the other and his parents were away, and spray painted profanities on the garage door that (translated politely) meant that the other was in an incestuous relationship. The offended young man grew depressed as a result of the incident, the public attention it drew to him, and the embarrassment and hectoring it caused him. A counselor recorded his sleep disruption, moderate anxiety disorder, and moderate weight gain from the stress surrounding the matter. Analyze whether these facts satisfy the elements of an intentional infliction of emotional distress claim. *Model Answer:*

The case requires analysis of whether a young man whose rival spray painted profanities on his parents' garage door has a claim for intentional infliction of emotional distress against the rival, after the young man's counselor recorded his sleep disruption, anxiety disorder, and weight gain from the incident's stress.

In those jurisdictions recognizing intentional infliction of emotional distress as a tort claim, the claimant must prove that the wrongdoer's intentional outrageous conduct caused the claimant severe distress. To qualify as outrageous, the conduct must be beyond all bounds of decency in civil society. To qualify as sufficiently severe, the distress may have to cause physical manifestations, which is a way that some states control for exaggerated claims. The intent may take the form of recklessness defined as knowledge of a high probability of harm (rather than substantial certainty of harm).

Here, rival clearly acted with intent to distress the young man when spray painting profanities suggesting incest. From the reprehensibility of the conduct alone, the rival must have desired the young man's distress or at least been reckless as to it, knowing a high probability of harm. The rival's conduct was outrageous in all likelihood. Trespassing on real property to vandalize a garage door with embarrassing spray-painted profanities, while prankish in nature, would in most communities be a rare, extraordinary, and criminal act well beyond any bound of decency in civil society. The young man saw a counselor, suggesting relatively severe distress, with the counselor documenting what would constitute physical manifestations at least in the weight gain and probably also in the sleep disruption and maybe even the anxiety disorder. The fact call the disorder *moderate*, which might work against it being *severe* in the way that the law requires, but that judgment would probably present a fact issue for the jury. The claim would likely survive summary judgment and be a reasonably compelling case before a jury.

In sum, the case presents a reasonably strong claim for intentional infliction of emotional distress. The young man's challenge might be in proving the distress sufficiently severe, but depending on that additional investigation, the case looks like one that would make it to the jury with a good probability of the young man prevailing against his rival.

WEEK 3

INTENTIONAL TORTS—TRESPASS TO LAND—ELEMENTS
27. A dog walker had certain routes he liked to take for different dogs for which he was hired to care. One route took him across an old man's back yard. The dog walker especially liked cutting across the old man's back yard, knowing that it irritated the old man. The old man did several things to try to discourage the dog walker but was unsuccessful. So he consulted a lawyer. What advice should the lawyer give the old man regarding the dog walker?

A. That the old man should ignore the dog walker who is doing no harm.
B. That the old man should keep trying to discourage the dog walker.
C. That the old man could sue the dog walker to stop the trespass to land.
D. That the old man could sue the dog walker to stop the trespass to chattels.

Correct answer: C. Trespass to land is the intentional interference with the exclusive possession of land or the intentional unauthorized physical entry onto land of another. The dog walker was clearly trespassing. Option A is incorrect because the old man sought counsel about his legal rights after having been irritated by their violation. Option B is incorrect because the old man had already tried unsuccessfully to put a stop to them and was seeking counsel about legal rights. Option D is incorrect because trespass to chattels involves interference with personal property, not real property.

INTENTIONAL TORTS—TRESPASS TO LAND—MISTAKE
28. A homeowner constructed a wood deck attached to his home along the boundary between his property and the neighbor's property. Later, the neighbor notified the homeowner that much of the deck was on the neighbor's property and that it should be removed. When the homeowner protested, the neighbor commissioned a survey that confirmed that the homeowner had constructed a substantial part of his deck on the neighbor's land. The neighbor repeated his demand that the deck be removed. The homeowner, who could not believe the survey results, consulted a lawyer. What evaluation should the lawyer make of the homeowner's conduct?

A. The homeowner's construction of the deck does not constitute a trespass to the neighbor's land because it was innocently constructed by the homeowner.
B. The homeowner's construction of the deck constitutes a trespass to the neighbor's land because the homeowner's mistaken understanding is of no consequence to the fact of the entry.
C. The homeowner's construction of the deck constitutes a trespass to the neighbor's land because the homeowner should have known he was building on the neighbor's land.
D. The homeowner's construction of the deck may constitute a trespass to the neighbor's land but is not so substantial that the homeowner should worry.

Correct answer: B. Mistaken entries are still trespass so long as they are intentional, even if the boundaries are not known and are mistakenly assumed. Option A is incorrect because the knowledge or innocence of the homeowner is irrelevant. An intentional entry is sufficient, and the homeowner intended to construct the deck. Option C is incorrect because it is not established that the homeowner should have known, and whether or not the homeowner should have known is not a determinative factor as to the intentional entry. Option D is incorrect because the substantiality of the construction is not established and is not a determinative factor. Damages are presumed, and the deck's construction precludes the neighbor's alternative use of his land and may be a substantial interference.

INTENTIONAL TORTS—TRESPASS TO LAND—DAMAGES
29. A woman owned a residence with a backyard that included a clothesline on which to hang laundry. A company constructed a processing plant next door that operated round the clock. Noise and bright lights from the processing plant irritated the woman when she tried to relax in her backyard, but it was only when soot from the processing ruined her hanging laundry and siding that she called a lawyer. What should be the lawyer's advice as to whether the woman has tort claims?

A. The woman may have a claim of nuisance for the noise, bright lights, and soot that ruined her laundry.
B. The woman may have a claim of trespass to land for the noise, bright lights, and soot that ruined her laundry.
C. The woman may have a claim of nuisance for the noise and lights but trespass to land for the soot that ruined her laundry.
D. The woman may have a claim of trespass to land for the noise and lights but nuisance for the soot that ruined her laundry.

Correct answer: C. Trespass damages are presumed from the interference with exclusive possession except when the entry is intangible (environmental), in which case damages must be shown. The ruin of the woman's laundry may constitute a trespass to land. Interference with use and enjoyment rather than exclusive possession may give rise to a claim for nuisance. The noise and bright lights interfered with use and enjoyment and so may have been a nuisance. Options A and D are incorrect because the soot may have given rise to trespass to land rather than or in addition to nuisance. Options B and D are incorrect because the noise and lights are probably only nuisances at best and not trespass to land, without evident damage.

INTENTIONAL TORTS—TRESPASS TO LAND—NUISANCE
30. A resident lived in a posh development with the houses crowded closely together. A neighbor with teenage children moved in next door. The neighbor's teenagers frequently played amplified guitars, drums, and other rock-band instruments late into the night in the neighbor's garage. The resident called the police over the noise, who confirmed that the noise probably violated local ordinance but who also indicated that nothing would be done about it. The resident was fed up calling the police over the neighboring garage band's noise-ordinance violations. Wondering whether there was anything else he could do to put a stop to the sleep-shattering racket, the resident consulted an attorney. What would be proper legal advice?

A. The resident may be able to pursue a nuisance action to stop the ordinance violations.
B. The resident may be able to pursue a trespass action to stop the ordinance violations.
C. The resident may be able to pursue invasion of privacy claims to stop the teenagers.
D. The resident has no tort remedy and can only hope the city enforces the ordinance.

Correct answer: A. Intangible entries (noise, smell, light, etc.) may be addressed through the tort of nuisance, which involves unreasonable interference with use and enjoyment rather than exclusive possession. The violation of law may provide a stronger basis on which to maintain that the noise was unreasonable. Option B is incorrect because there was no interference with exclusive possession (no entry). Option C is incorrect because there was no invasion of privacy (no exploitation, intrusion, false light, or public disclosure). Option D is incorrect because there may be a nuisance remedy.

INTENTIONAL TORTS—NUISANCE—PUBLIC/PRIVATE

31. A farmer periodically watered his truck garden by opening and closing sluice gates to briefly flood the garden fields. Often, the sluicing of the fields would result in a pond forming across a public bike path and road running alongside the truck garden. The pond that formed across the bike path and road when the farmer sluiced his truck garden received more and more complaints from passersby using the bike path and road. The board of a nearby homeowner's association asked its legal counsel for an opinion on what could be done to correct the pond problem so that it no longer interfered with homeowner use of the bike path and road. What tort rights should counsel address in the opinion?

A. The pond problem is just something to live with because the truck garden is productive.
B. The pond problem may constitute a trespass to land to abate by damages action.
C. The pond problem may constitute a private nuisance to discourage by damages action.
D. The pond problem may constitute a public nuisance that could be abated by injunction.

Correct answer: D. A public nuisance is one that interferes with public enjoyment, while a private nuisance is one that substantially affects the use and enjoyment of private lands. Here, the pond may have interfered substantially enough with the use of the road and bike path so as to warrant a court action to abate the problem by injunction. Option A is incorrect because there may be a public-nuisance remedy. Option B is incorrect because no private land has been identified onto which the pond encroached as an entry. Option C is incorrect because there was no private nuisance, and no single individual would be likely to be able to prove sufficient damages to discourage the problem.

INTENTIONAL TORTS—TRESPASS TO LAND—PUNITIVES

32. A woman had a condition that required her to make frequent visits to a doctor. A truck driver who lived nearby occasionally parked his rig in the woman's driveway. The woman had once consented to his doing so. But after the truck driver's rig blocked the woman from getting her car out to go to the doctor, she told the truck driver not to again do so because she needed to get to the doctor. The truck driver did so anyway on another occasion, causing the woman the inconvenience of calling a friend to drive her to the doctor. The woman was livid that the contractor had gone ahead and parked his rig in her drive yet again, after she had expressly warned him not to. What dollar figure could a case-evaluation panel assign the woman's trespass claim against the truck driver?

A. $1 as nominal damages and $250 as compensatory damages.
B. $1 as nominal damages and $250 as punitive damages.
C. $1 as nominal damages only.
D. Nothing because the woman had no loss.

Correct answer: B. Where there is no actual damage from a trespass to land, nominal damages may be awarded and, in egregious cases, punitive damages. Because the truck driver was specifically told not to park in the woman's drive and also a medical reason not to do so, the truck driver's conduct was probably egregious enough for punitive damages. Option A is incorrect because there is no evidence of compensatory damages, only small inconvenience. Option C is incorrect because punitive damages are arguably awardable. Option D is incorrect because the woman could receive nominal and punitive damages.

INTENTIONAL TORTS—TRESPASS—EXCEEDING SCOPE

33. A shopper in a clothing store asked a clerk if the store had a rest room. The clerk explained that there was an employees-only restroom in the store's back room but that the shopper could use it. The shopper used the restroom but then figured he would just have a little extra look around in the store's back room, when no one was looking. The shopper moved from the restroom to an employee-break room where there were employee lockers. The shopper opened a locker and looked through the clerk's personal belongings. The shopper then left the store through the back delivery door marked as private on the outside of the door. At what point did the shopper first trespass?

A. When entering the back room to use the restroom.
B. When entering the employee-break room.
C. When opening the employee locker and looking through personal belongings.
D. When leaving the store through the back delivery door.

Correct answer: B. Trespass to land may be established by exceeding the scope or duration of consent to entry on the land. The shopper exceeded the scope of consent when leaving the restroom and entering the employee-break room. Option A is incorrect because the shopper had the clerk's consent to use the restroom. Option C is incorrect because although opening the locker was also a trespass, entering the employee-break room occurred earlier. Option D is incorrect, because leaving the private part of the store would not constitute a trespass. It might have been a trespass if the shopper had first entered through the private back door.

INTENTIONAL TORTS—TRESPASS TO CHATTELS—ELEMENTS
34. A college student located a schoolroom in which to study. There was a laptop computer in a backpack belonging to a staff member, on a table in the room. With no one in sight, the student removed the computer, opened it, altered the background and screensaver, and randomly deleted some files. The student snuck the laptop computer back into the backpack, having thoroughly enjoyed messing with the computer's background, screensaver, and files. The staff member entered the room and saw the student just as the student was setting down the backpack. Does the staff member have a tort claim against the student?

A. Yes so long as the student's actions interfered with the staff member's use of the computer.
B. Yes even if the student's actions did not interfere with the staff member's use of the computer.
C. No even if the student's actions interfered with the staff member's use of the computer.
D. No unless the student's actions deprived the staff member of the computer's use.

Correct answer: A. Trespass to chattels is the intentional interference with the exclusive possession of another's personal property, compensated by lost-use value. Probably, the deleting of the files and perhaps even if the changing of the background and screen interfered with the staff member's use of the computer, even if the staff member was not deprived of its use for any period. Interference could also come from alteration or damage rather than solely deprivation of use. Option B is incorrect because there must be some interference. A de minimis handling of another's personal property would ordinarily not constitute interference. Option C is incorrect because interference with the computer's use would constitute trespass to chattels. Option D is incorrect because alteration or damage could also constitute interference.

INTENTIONAL TORTS—CONVERSION—ELEMENTS
35. A mountain-bike rider asked her acquaintance if the rider could borrow her acquaintance's road bike for a few days. The acquaintance agreed to the loan of his road bike to the mountain-bike rider, whom he knew to be an extraordinary mountain-bike rider. The road bike had narrow tires on lightweight rims with composite spokes. It also had a lightweight titanium frame, handlebars, and seat post. The mountain-bike rider rode the road bike off the road on a mountain trail. The mountain trail blew out one of the tires, bent the lightweight rims, damaged the composite spokes, and scratched and badly damaged the titanium frame, handlebars, and seat post. Is the mountain-bike rider liable for the road bike's conversion?

A. No, so long as the mountain-bike rider was an experienced rider doing her best to make the bike last as long as possible.
B. No, so long as the mountain bike had at least nominal remaining value after its substantial destruction.

C. Yes, if the mountain-bike rider knew she was ruining the road bike's substantial value by riding the bike on the mountain trail.
D. Yes, if the mountain-bike rider should have known she was ruining the road bike by riding the bike on the mountain trail.

Correct answer: C. Conversion is the intentional dominion over another's tangible personal property substantially or totally interfering with the other's control, compensated by the value at conversion. If the rider intended or knew to a substantial certainty that the bike would be ruined on the mountain trail, and its substantial value was destroyed, then the rider is liable for conversion. Option A is incorrect because the rider's effort to make the bike last would not preclude her knowledge that its substantial value would soon be destroyed. Option B is incorrect because destruction of the substantial value of the bike would be enough for conversion. It need not be completely destroyed. Option D is incorrect because a "should have known" standard is a negligence standard and does not establish intent.

INTENTIONAL TORTS—CONVERSION/TRESPASS TO CHATTELS
36. A mechanic kept an old truck behind his junkyard shop to transport car parts around the junkyard. Some teens climbed over the junkyard fence to vandalize the junkyard. They drove the old truck around the junkyard, crashing it into various obstacles. In the process, they ground the gears of its standard transmission, burned its tires up spinning them in the loose gravel, cracked the windshield, and broke off the mirrors. When the mechanic discovered the truck the next morning halfway into the pond at the back of the junkyard, the mechanic could not tell whether the old truck the teens had vandalized could be fixed for anything less than its whole value. What torts have the teens committed with respect to the truck?

A. Conversion or trespass to chattels, depending on the cost and sense of fixing the truck or simply junking it for spare parts of nominal value.
B. Conversion or trespass to land, depending on the cost and sense of fixing the truck or simply junking it for spare parts of nominal value.
C. Trespass to chattels or trespass to land, depending on whether the teens had any authority to have entered the junkyard.
D. Trespass to chattels only, because the truck was not stolen but was found halfway in the pond at the back of the junkyard.

Correct answer: A. Conversion involves the total or substantial deprivation or destruction of the property, whereas trespass to chattels is only a temporary deprivation or partial destruction or diminution in value. In this instance, where the remaining value of the truck is undetermined, the teens may have committed either tort. Options B and C are incorrect because the teens' damage to the truck was damage to personal, rather than real, property, and trespass to land has to do with entry onto real property. The teens committed a trespass to land, but the question asks about torts with respect to the truck. Option C is also incorrect because the facts plainly state that the teens climbed into the junkyard to vandalize, for which they would not have had authority. Option D is incorrect because complete deprivation of the personal property is not necessary for conversion, only its substantial destruction.

INTENTIONAL TORTS—CONVERSION—SUBSEQUENT
37. A young woman had a wide circle of friends who often bartered goods and services. An acquaintance of one of the young woman's friends offered to sell a high-quality leather designer purse to the young woman at a small fraction of the purse's retail value. The man explained that the purse was part of an over-shipment of new goods to a store that went out of business. The young woman gladly bought the purse from the man for his asking price. The young woman later found a card in a pocket of the purse identifying another woman. Now suspicious of the man's story as to the origins of the purse, the young woman gave the card to a police officer, explaining her story. The officer later contacted the woman saying that the purse had been stolen from the woman identified on the card. The young woman, who said she had paid the man "good money" for the purse, was pretty upset to learn that the man had stolen it. Who would be liable to the purse's original owner for the purse's value?

A. The man who sold it to the young woman.
B. The man who sold it to the young woman and the young woman.
C. The young woman.
D. Only the person who first stole it from the woman identified on the card as its owner.

Correct answer: B. The owner or holder of converted property may pursue a conversion claim against the original converter or subsequent holders, even those who take in good faith. Option A is incorrect because the young woman is also liable. Option C is incorrect because the man who sold it to the young woman is also liable. Option D is incorrect because the man who sold it and the young woman who bought it are both also liable.

Trespass to Land and Nuisance: A car hit a patch of black ice and spun into a yard in the middle of the night. The inebriated driver decided to sleep it off in a barn in the yard. Early the next morning, he called a friend asking that the friend use his four-wheel-drive truck to drag the car out of the yard. The friend did so, leaving deep ruts in the yard. Recall and apply the elements of trespass to determine whether and for what actions the property owner has trespass claims against the inebriated driver and friend. *Model Answer:*

The case requires analysis of whether the property owner has trespass claims against an inebriated driver whose car slid into the owner's yard, after which the driver slept in the owner's barn until a friend dragged the driver's car out of the yard the next morning.

Trespass to land is intentional interference with exclusive possession of another, or put another way, intentional unauthorized entry on land. The entry must be intentional, not accidental, although mistake as to the right to enter is no defense when the entry is intentional. An entry that is initially authorized or accidental can become unauthorized, intentional, and actionable in trespass if the person overstays any welcome. The law presumes damages in trespass.

In this case, the inebriated driver's initial entry was accidental, indicated by his car sliding on a patch of ice and spinning into the owner's yard. The driver did not intend to end up in the yard. To that point, the owner would not have a trespass claim because intent was lacking, even though the driver and car were clearly entries interfering with the owner's exclusive possession of the land. Yet the driver also clearly overstayed his temporary unintentional entry when he decided, quite intentionally, to sleep it off in the owner's barn. The driver also induced another intentional entry when calling his friend to use a four-wheel-drive truck to pull the car from the yard. The friend may have thought that he had permission to be on the land but did not have the *owner's* permission, only the drunken driver's request. Thus even if the friend was mistaken as to permission, the friend also trespassed, having made an intentional unauthorized entry onto the owner's land in the form of the truck. While the fact that they left ruts in the yard would add to the owner's damages, the owner need not prove any damages, which the law would instead presume simply from their entry.

In sum, the owner has trespass claims against both the driver and friend, although not for the initial slide off, only for the subsequent sleeping in the barn and towing from the yard. Damages, while presumed from the entries alone, would be greater for the ruts in the yard.

Trespass to Chattels: In the previous case study, the inebriated driver also found a pair of shears in the barn when he woke early the next morning and for a prank cut the long tails off two draft horses stalled in the barn. Recall and apply the elements of the trespass to chattels tort to determine whether the horses' owner has a claim against the inebriated driver. *Model Answer:*

The case requires analysis of whether the owner of two draft horses stalled in a barn would have a claim for trespass to chattels when an inebriated driver cut off the horses' tails.

Trespass to chattels is an intentional tort requiring proof of the impairment of personal property. Impairment could be any temporary deprivation resulting in the loss of use or partial destruction diminishing the personal property's value. The law does not presume damages for trespass to chattels. The claimant must prove some loss of use or diminution in value.

In this instance, the two draft horses qualify as personal property. The owner of those two horses would be an appropriate claimant in a trespass-to-chattels case. The driver's act of cutting of the horses' tails with shears was intentional, not accidental. The driver had no cause to do so other than as a prank, which would clearly indicate both intent and the absence of any consent. While cutting off a horse's tail would not deprive the owner of the horse's use, the act could diminish the horse's value, a horse's tail being both useful for swatting away flies and also aesthetic for activities like showing. It might be difficult or impossible to show the horses without a tail or to protect them from biting insects. Growing back the tail hair could take years but would not be a permanent deprivation, thus qualifying for the trespass-to-chattels tort rather than permanent deprivation or total destruction, which would involve the conversion tort.

To conclude, the horses' owner would have a strong claim against the inebriated driver for trespass to chattels when the driver cut off the tails of both horses as a prank. While the law does not presume damages for trespass to chattels, the horses' owner could prove some diminution in current use and value.

Conversion: A woman lent her pearl necklace to a friend for the friend's job interview. The friend did not return the necklace but instead gave the necklace to her boyfriend to get money to buy crack cocaine. The boyfriend took the necklace to a barber who gave the boyfriend money and marked the necklace for sale in his barbershop. The necklace's owner learned these facts when authorities arrested the boyfriend on drug charges. Recall and apply the elements of conversion to determine whether the necklace's owner has that claim against her friend, the boyfriend, and the barber. *Model Answer:*

The case requires analysis of conversion claims by the owner of a necklace against the friend to whom she loaned the necklace, the boyfriend to whom the friend gave it to get money to buy crack cocaine, and the barber who bought it from the boyfriend to put in his shop for sale.

Conversion is an intentional tort requiring that the claimant prove permanent deprivation or substantial destruction of personal property. The classic conversion case is one involving criminal theft, conversion being the equivalent civil claim for damages. The original owner retains conversion claims against subsequent purchasers of the personal property including those giving value in good faith. The claimant must prove damages.

In this case, while the friend's initial use of the necklace was by the owner's consent, the friend acted intentionally thereafter when giving the necklace to her boyfriend to get money to buy cocaine. The friend intended its sale, which would obviously permanently deprive the owner of the necklace for its future use. The owner would thus have satisfied the intent and deprivation elements as to the friend. The same would be true of the boyfriend, whom it sounds like was in on the whole thing. Even though if the boyfriend thought that the necklace belonged to his girlfriend, the owner would still have a claim because even those taking in good faith and for value remain liable for conversion. You must be careful from whom you buy or take. The same would also be true of the barber under the same rules. Even if he was not a knowing participant in the scheme (a fence), the barber would still be liable in conversion despite having given money for the necklace in good faith. Conversion does not require knowledge of ownership, only intentional deprivation. Again, be careful from whom you buy.

To conclude, the owner of the necklace has valid conversion claims against all three defendants the friend, her boyfriend, and the barber, despite that one or two of these defendants may not have known who truly owned the necklace. The owner should have the full value of the necklace back in damages from any or all of the three.

WEEK 4

INTENTIONAL TORTS—DEFENSES—CONSENT
38. A physical therapist had a thriving practice relating to sports medicine. The therapist was regularly providing shoulder and neck manipulation to a patient who was a world-class sprinter. The sprinter asked the therapist to stretch out the sprinter's hamstring with leg stretches and rubbing. The

therapist did so with the sprinter cooperative and not complaining. The therapist later heard from the sprinter's coach that the sprinter had complained to the coach that the therapist had injured the sprinter's hamstring and inappropriately touched the sprinter during the leg stretching. The therapist reported the complaint to his malpractice insurance carrier who assigned legal counsel to interview the therapist and sprinter in order to evaluate the sprinter's complaint for tort liability. Assuming that the interviews confirm the above information, what would be an appropriate evaluation?

A. There may well be a battery claim for the hamstring injury.
B. There may well be a battery claim for the inappropriate touching.
C. There may well be battery claims for the hamstring injury and inappropriate touching.
D. There should at least be no intentional-tort claims.

Correct answer: D. Consent is an agreement or permission defense to an intentional tort. The sprinter pretty clearly consented, both expressly and impliedly, to the leg stretching. Whether there is a professional negligence (malpractice) claim would depend on additional information on the standard of care and the therapist's compliance with it, but at least there should be no intentional-tort claims. Options A, B, and C are incorrect because the sprinter's request, compliance, and non-complaining indicates express and implied consent.

INTENTIONAL TORTS—DEFENSES—CONSENT—OBJECTIVE
39. A truck driver was hired to deliver bags of feed to a cattle feedlot. The truck driver drove his truck up to the gate of the feedlot. A gatekeeper came out of the feedlot office, looked over at the truck driver, shrugged, tipped his head toward the gate, and pushed a button to activate the gate to swing open. With the gatekeeper's shrug and tip of the head toward the gate, the truck driver stepped on the truck's gas pedal to get the truck moving through the gate just as the gate swung open. Just then, the truck driver noticed the gatekeeper waving frantically, yelling, and shaking his head no. But by then the truck was mired in deep mud just inside the feedlot gate. Cattle quickly escaped through the gate which was blocked open by the mired truck. The gatekeeper later explained that he had opened the gate only to slip through it himself in order to go get a tractor and wagon for the feed unloading. Does the feedlot have an intentional tort claim against the truck driver for the loss of the cattle?

A. Yes, because the truck driver intended to drive the truck through the gate.
B. Yes, because the gatekeeper did not intend that the truck driver drive through the gate.
C. No, because of the gatekeeper's shrug, tip of the head, and opening of the gate.
D. No, because of the deep mud which the feedlot should have cleared from the gate.

Correct answer: C. Consent is determined from an objective standpoint, what the words or actions would have conveyed to a reasonable observer. The gatekeeper's actions reasonably appeared to convey consent for the truck driver to drive through the gate. That the gatekeeper had something else in mind is of no consequence if his actions indicated consent. Options A and B are incorrect because there was consent. Option D is incorrect because the feedlot's mud would not have excused an intentional tort if one had been committed.

INTENTIONAL TORTS—DEFENSES—CONSENT—CAPACITY
40. Four participants joined a river guide on an inner-tube ride over huge boulders in a raging current down a turbulent river. Each of the four participants was a stranger to one another. All four participants agreed to the ride after the river guide explained that the ride was extremely bumpy and that there was some slight risk of capsize and injury, which made it fun and exciting. All four participants were shocked at how rough the ride turned out to be. Each participant also suffered some physical injury when the inner tube capsized in the middle. All four sued the river guide's company. A lawyer hired by the insurance carrier covering the river guide's company filed a motion to dismiss the actions. Which participant's action is the court most likely to dismiss?

A. A child participant too young to know what river-riding was like.
B. An adult participant of ordinary intelligence but no river-riding experience.
C. An adult participant on Social Security disability for low mental function.
D. An adult participant who did not understand the river-guide's language.

Correct answer: B. To give consent, a person must have enough mental capacity to understand the conduct and risks to which the person is consenting. An adult participant might have understood the risks sufficiently from the river-guide's explanation. Option A is incorrect because a child too young to understand the risks would not have been capable of consent. Option C is incorrect because a low-mental functioning adult may not have understood and appreciated the risks. Option D is incorrect because someone who does not understand the language would not have learned of the risks when explained in that language.

INTENTIONAL TORTS—DEFENSES—CONSENT—EMERGENCY
41. A patient arrived at a hospital unconscious from a serious car accident. The patient's airway was obstructed by accident injuries in a way that threatened the patient's life. A surgeon examining the patient immediately on the patient's arrival at the hospital determined that the patient needed an immediate tracheotomy in order to survive. The patient could not be identified. The surgeon promptly performed the tracheotomy, as a result of which the patient survived. It was later discovered that just before the accident, the patient had left a note clearly indicating that the patient had purposefully wrecked the car intent on killing himself. Has the surgeon committed a tort on the patient?

A. No.
B. No, so long as the patient is glad that he survived.
C. Yes, if the patient still wishes that he had died.
D. Yes.

Correct answer: A. A medical-care provider may, in an emergency, act without consent if it cannot be obtained, the reasonable person would have consented, and there is no indication that the patient would not have consented. The surgeon had no one from to obtain consent and was not aware, nor should the surgeon have been aware, that the patient wished to die. Consent is implied in the emergency. Options B and C are incorrect because the surgeon could not have known or predicted the patient's wishes post-treatment. Liability does not depend on whether a patient changes his or her mind. Option D is incorrect because the surgeon did not commit a tort, given the implied consent.

INTENTIONAL TORTS—DEFENSES—CONSENT—ILLEGAL ACT
42. A man dated a young woman. The dating led to intimacy. When a friend of the man found out about their relationship, the friend warned the man that the young woman was well under the age of lawful consent. The man was aghast to discover it, having reasonably believed that she was at least in her early twenties. The man was then alarmed to hear from a lawyer who represented the young woman's parents with regard to the young woman's welfare. The lawyer's correspondence warned against further contact between the man and the young woman and mentioned damages. The man consulted his own lawyer. What evaluation would most likely be appropriate?

A. The man is liable for a battery against the young woman.
B. The man is liable for intentional infliction of emotional distress as to the young woman.
C. The man is liable to the parents for alienating the affections of the young woman.
D. The man is not liable for any tort as to the young woman.

Correct answer: A. Consent to an illegal act is generally considered invalid, particularly if the statute making the act illegal was meant to protect the plaintiff's class against the defendant's act. Statutory rape provisions are meant to protect the underage from sexual relationships. The man committed a battery against the young woman. Option B is incorrect because the man did not intend to inflict severe distress and there is no mention in the facts of severe distress. Option C is incorrect because the parents have no cause of action and alienation of affections is not a recognized tort. Option D is incorrect because the man is liable for battery.

INTENTIONAL TORTS—DEFENSES—BURDEN OF PROOF
43.   A father had temporary custody of his child under court order. A case worker assigned to the custody file visited to interview the father and see father and child together. The case worker grew angry during the father's interview. When the case worker stepped forward in an effort to forcibly take the child from the father, the father reached out and shoved her backward. The case worker filed a civil suit against the father that included a claim for battery based on the father having shoved her backward. The father told his own lawyer that the case worker had made the first move and that he was only protecting his child. What advice can the father's lawyer give the father?

A.   The case worker must prove each element of her battery claim including that the father had no right to defend the child.
B.   The case worker must prove each element of her battery claim, but the father must prove defense of the child.
C.   The father must disprove each element of the battery claim including that the father had the right to defend the child.
D.   The father must disprove each element of the battery claim, but the case worker must prove that the father had no right to defend the child.

Correct answer: B. Plaintiffs have the burden of proof on the elements of their claims. Defendants have the burden of proof on each element of affirmative defenses. The case worker must prove her battery claim. The father must prove defense of the child. Options A and D are incorrect because the father, not the case worker, must prove defense of the child. Options C and D are incorrect because the case worker, not the father, must prove the elements of her battery claim.

INTENTIONAL TORTS—DEFENSES—SELF-DEFENSE
44.   A bank manager was closing up a bank branch office for the evening. Just as the manager walked to the front door to lock it, a man approached the door from the outside, took hold of the door handle, and pulled it open. The bank manager stopped the man, saying that the branch was closed for the evening. The man stood in the open door, arguing with the bank manager. The bank manager would not relent, insisting that the branch was closed. The man then pulled a knife from his pocket and brandished it at the bank manager. The bank manager shoved out the door the man who was brandishing the knife at him, and locked the door. The man fell heavily backward, severely cutting the back of his head. The man's lawyer made a demand for compensation from the bank manager for the man's injury. Which is the best response?

A.   To request proof of damages because the bank manager is liable.
B.   To request an explanation of the man's motive for brandishing the knife.
C.   To deny the demand because the bank manager is not liable.
D.   To apologize for the man's injury and hope that he does not sue.

Correct answer: C. One may use reasonable force in self-defense of physical injury. The bank manager, when confronted with a man brandishing a knife, could reasonably shove the man back and lock the door, even if it caused the man to cut his head. A brandished knife threatens death or serious injury. Option A is incorrect because the bank manager is not liable and a poor strategic move to encourage a frivolous claim. Option B is incorrect because motive is not an element and a poor strategic move to encourage a frivolous claim. Option C is incorrect because there is no reason to be concerned about suit and no real reason to apologize. The man should apologize to the bank manager, who gave the man what he had coming to him.

INTENTIONAL TORTS—DEFENSES—SELF-DEFENSE—RETREAT

45. A racer crashed her race vehicle because of the actions of another driver. The racer drove a golf cart to the pit area of the other driver to complain. A mechanic met and confronted her there. The mechanic had harassed the racer before and now resumed the harassment again. The mechanic stood face to face with the racer, hollering at her, invading her personal space, and physically intimidating though not threatening her. The racer could have gotten in the golf cart and driven away. Instead, she decided to put an end to the mechanic's harassment. She took a wrench from the golf cart and hit the mechanic on the head, seriously injuring him. What would be the best approach for the racer's defense of the mechanic's resulting tort claim against her?

A. To treat the mechanic's claim as frivolous because the racer is not liable.
B. To treat the mechanic's claim as tenable but weak because he started it.
C. To file a counterclaim to win more damages than the mechanic has against the racer.
D. To take it seriously because the racer is liable.

Correct answer: D. Retreat may be required before force likely to cause serious injury or death may be used in self defense. Retreat likely would be required in this instance. The racer was only intimidated, not threatened. She could have driven away and had no right to retaliate with force likely to cause serious injury. Option A is incorrect because the mechanic has a claim and the racer is liable. Option B is incorrect because the mechanic did not start it (the racer came to the mechanic's pit area), the mechanic may have been responding as is customary, and the mechanic, being seriously injured by the racer when the racer had no privilege to do so, is strong, not weak. Option C is incorrect because the racer may not have a counterclaim (depending on the nature of the harassment) and has no evident serious injury to win damages greater than the mechanic.

INTENTIONAL TORTS—DEFENSES—DEFENSE OF PROPERTY

46. A store owner suffered losses due to looting during local power outages over the course of one summer. The outages occurred during predictable peak demand times associated with hot weather and air-conditioner usage. The store owner was fed up with the looting. That winter, he purchased a gun with which to defend his store when the hot weather and power outages returned. But when he heard a warning from his trade association about store-owner liability, he decided to get a legal opinion. What would be the most appropriate counsel to the store owner about his civil liability for use of the gun to defend his store and its goods during looting?

A. To shoot in defense of the store and its goods whenever it appeared reasonable, even if mistaken.
B. To shoot in defense of the store and its goods only when genuinely necessary, understanding that there would be no excuse for mistakes whether or not reasonable.
C. Not to shoot in defense of the store and its goods unless the looters looked as if they were able to shoot back in their own defense.
D. Not to shoot in defense of the store and its goods.

Correct answer: D. One may use reasonable force to defend property, so long as the force is not likely to cause death or serious injury. Guns are likely to cause serious injury or death. A store owner risks civil (not to mention criminal) liability for injuring or killing others with a gun, even if those are others are looting the owner's store and goods. Options A and B are incorrect because there is no privilege to use deadly force to defend property and, as to Option A, certainly none when one is mistaken. Option C is incorrect because one is not entitled to shoot in defense of property even if those threatening the property can shoot in their own defense. One would only have a right to use deadly force on deadly threat to the person, not property.

INTENTIONAL TORTS—DEFENSES—DEFENSE OF PROPERTY—DEMAND

47. A rent-to-own store had DVD players available for rent as a popular item. A youth entered the store. The rental manager observed the youth looking at and handling a DVD player. The youth left the store with the DVD player without having rented or paid for it, and without other authorization. What additional facts would most help the rental manager avoid liability for non-serious injury of the youth when stopping the youth from stealing the DVD player?

A. The rental manager first made a demand to the youth to stop which the youth ignored.
B. The rental manager first waited one hour to see if the youth would return.
C. The rental manager first followed the youth home to see if the youth changed his mind.
D. The rental manager first fired shots over the youth's head before shooting at the feet.

Correct answer: A. One must make a demand before using reasonable force to recover property, unless a demand would be futile. A demand in this instance would increase the likelihood that the manager's use of non-deadly force was warranted. Options B and C are incorrect because use of force to recover property is warranted only in fresh pursuit on or about the premises. Option D is incorrect because use of deadly force is not permitted and its use here would increase, not decrease, the likelihood of the manager's liability.

INTENTIONAL TORTS—DEFENSES—RECOVERY OF PROPERTY--REPOSSESSION

48. A vehicle-finance company employed and trained a young man to repossess vehicles. The young man located a car that he had been assigned to repossess. The car was in the driveway of its owner's residence. The owner was not in sight of the young man. The young man hopped in the car, jimmied the ignition, and drove away, satisfied that he had once again earned his keep for the company. The vehicle-finance company promptly notified the owner that her vehicle had been repossessed. The finance agreement authorized the above actions. What legal advice can be given the owner of the vehicle with respect to any torts committed in the course of the young man's repossession of her car?

A. The young man committed a trespass to land when entering the driveway.
B. The young man committed a trespass to chattels when entering and moving the car.
C. The young man committed a conversion when taking the car for the finance company.
D. No torts were committed.

Correct answer: D. Property may be repossessed from the land of another if no force is necessary to do so and agreement so provides. The young man repossessed the woman's vehicle pursuant to the terms of the finance agreement, without committing a tort. Option A is incorrect because the finance agreement authorized the entry. Options B and C are incorrect because the woman had lost the right to the car, and thus the young man did not interfere, either in part or substantially, with an asset that she could claim to be her own chattel.

INTENTIONAL TORTS—DEFENSES—PUBLIC NECESSITY

49. A rancher maintained a large herd of cattle. Under federal regulations, the cattle were periodically tested for a rare disease. If uncontrolled, the disease could affect the beef supply in a way that would cripple the entire ranching industry. Three of the rancher's prize cows tested positive for the disease. Federal officials condemned the rancher's herd on the basis of the positive tests. The rancher was desolate that his entire herd would be lost simply because three of the cows had tested positive. He consulted a lawyer about legal rights and remedies for the condemnation of his herd. What is the most appropriate evaluation?

A. The rancher has a tort claim for conversion of the entire herd.
B. The rancher has a tort claim for conversion of the herd except the three infected cows.
C. The rancher has no tort claim because of public necessity.
D. The rancher has no tort claim because of private necessity.

Correct answer: C. Public necessity is a complete defense to property-damage torts, where the damage was reasonably necessary to protect a public interest. Destruction of a cattle herd because of a disease that threatens the entire beef industry is a public necessity. Options A and B are incorrect because of the public-necessity defense to a conversion action. Option D is incorrect because it was a public necessity (a broad public interest) rather than a private necessity (the specific interest of one or small number of individuals) that warranted the action.

INTENTIONAL TORTS—DEFENSES—AUTHORITY OF LAW
50. A police officer met a woman on the street. The officer had no probable cause to arrest the woman. The officer spoke with the woman for several minutes, asking her about suspicious behaviors he claimed to have witnessed. The woman grew irate by the officer's insinuations to the point that she moved to strike the officer with her fist. The officer grabbed the woman's arm as she tried to strike, spun the woman around, and put the cuffs on her. He then placed the woman in his police vehicle and transported her to the police station for booking before her release. The woman later sought counsel on whether she had a tort claim against the officer for abrasions she suffered to her wrist. What is the best evaluation?

A. The woman has no tort claim against the officer.
B. The woman will have a tort claim against the officer if she was charged.
C. The woman has a false imprisonment claim against the officer.
D. The woman has an assault and battery claim against the officer.

Correct answer: A. Authority of law is a defense to certain intentional torts, where the law authorized the action. Lawful arrest is an example of the authority-of-law defense to a claim for false arrest or false imprisonment. Here, the woman gave the officer cause for arrest when she attempted to strike him. There is no clear indication of excessive force or unlawful arrest or detention. Option B is incorrect because there was a ground on which to charge, and charging would tend to reduce the likelihood of a valid tort claim for false imprisonment, not increase it, especially if the charge results in conviction. Option C is incorrect because of the authority-of-law defense. Option D is incorrect because of the officer's right of self defense to stop the woman from striking him and authority of law to arrest.

Intentional Torts Defenses—Consent, Self-Defense, & Defense of Others: A patron stepped toward a bartender saying threatening words about what he was going to do to the bartender for having offended his girlfriend sitting next to him at the bar. The bartender picked up a beer bottle, gripping it by its neck and raising it to shoulder level in an offensive posture. The patron took another step toward the bartender. The bartender started to take a swing at the patron with the bottle. The girlfriend screamed. The patron managed to knock the bartender's arm aside and slug the bartender in the stomach. Analyze whether the defenses of consent, self-defense, or defense of others would apply in the patron's assault claim and bartender's battery counterclaim. *Model Answer:*

The case requires determining whether the defenses of consent, self-defense, or defense of others apply to an assault claim and battery counterclaim between a bartender and bar patron after the patron threatened the bartender for offending the patron's girlfriend, and the bartender raised a beer bottle in an offensive posture following which the patron knocked the beer bottle aside and slugged the bartender.

Consent is a permission defense under circumstances where the tort claimant had agreed to or reasonably appeared to invite the complained-of conduct. One evaluates consent from the standpoint of the reasonable observer, not what the claimant subjectively desired or intended. Self-defense and defense of others depend on proof that the defendant reasonably perceived an imminent battery and used only that force reasonably necessary to prevent the battery, in a force continuum. One must not use deadly force or force likely to cause serious injury unless the threat is deadly or likely to lead to serious injury. Words alone are generally not enough to warrant self-defense or defense of others unless combined with actions.

In this instance, the bartender's offense to the patron's girlfriend would not have warranted the patron's use of force in self-defense or defense of others. Words, even insults, alone are not generally enough, and that was all that the bartender had done to that point. One must not use force in retaliation, so the patron's stepping toward the bartender while threatening what he was going to do to the bartender was not self-defense or defense of others. Depending on the words and stepping action, the patron may have given the bartender reasonable cause to perceive an imminent battery. Hence, the bartender's raising a beer bottle to his shoulder offensively could arguably have been in preparation for self-defense, but only as a close call because the patron might argue the opposite that his stepping action and threats were harmless bravado in defense of his girlfriend. When the patron took another step toward the bartender, the bartender's swing could also have been in self-defense, again in a close call because the patron might argue again that his stepping actions were bravado and that the bartender's use of the beer bottle as a potentially deadly weapon or one that could seriously injure was excessive force. When the patron knocked the bartender's arm aside, the patron would argue self-defense at that point, which would be hard to rebut except that the bartender could argue that the swing was in defense of the patron stepping forward. When the patron slugged the bartender in the stomach, the patron could again argue self-defense from the bartender's bottle-swinging motion, while the bartender could argue that knocking his arm aside was the only necessary force and that the punch to the gut was excessive force and a battery.

In sum, both sides have arguments for self-defense in this case, which looks very much like the typically difficult-to-sort-out fight case. The outcome could go either way. Consent and defense of others (the girlfriend) do not appear to apply.

Intentional Torts Defenses—Defense & Recovery of Property: A private merchandise-security officer watched security-camera monitors for evidence of shoplifting by a lone customer wandering aimlessly about the store. Although the video images were not clear, the officer believed that she witnessed the customer attempt to pocket and conceal store items. The officer stepped in front of the customer at the front door as he prepared to leave without having gone through customer checkout. The officer reached into the customer's jacket pocket and pulled out its contents, which were nothing more than the customer's wallet. The shocked customer protested, reaching toward the officer to take back his wallet. The officer stepped back from the customer, accusing the customer of shoplifting and starting to thumb through the customer's wallet as other customers stared. The customer pulled out his cell phone, pretended to dial 911, and said loudly into the phone that someone was trying to steal his wallet, causing the officer to return the wallet. Discuss and evaluate whether privilege protects the officer's actions. *Model Answer:*

The case requires determining whether a security officer's reaching into a customer's pocket for suspected shoplifted items falls within a shopkeeper's privilege to defend and recover property.

Shopkeepers have limited rights to defend and recover property from shoplifting and theft. They must act only with reasonable suspicion, limit their attempts to recover property to on or about their own premises in fresh pursuit of the suspect, and act reasonably in their investigatory actions so as not to unduly imprison or embarrass the suspect. They must also not use excessive force, deadly force, or force likely to cause serious injury. Request for investigation should ordinarily precede any investigatory search or physical restraint.

In this case, the security officer had reasonable grounds to investigate based on the video surveillance showing the customer's aimless wandering and apparently putting things in his pocket before attempting to leave the premises. The officer's stepping in front of the customer at the doorway after the customer apparently passed the checkout and was walking out was very likely a reasonable investigatory action. The officer should then have quietly informed the customer of the officer's suspicion and politely requested that the customer accompany the officer to a private office or area. Instead, the officer reached into the customer's pocket, when the officer should have asked the customer to reveal the contents of the customer's pocket. That reaching action grabbing the wallet from the shocked customer's pocket was probably outside the scope of the privilege. The officer should have preceded the action by request and should have avoided the public area with other customers observing. The officer's public accusation may also have been unreasonable given that the officer had the wallet in hand and the customer stopped. Whether the officer had the privilege to thumb through the wallet is questionable unless the wallet could have concealed unpaid store items, which seems unlikely. While the officer did not physically restrain the customer, holding the customer's wallet could arguably be construed as restraint.

In sum, although with the wallet's return and customer's release from any momentary detention reduces damages in this case, the security officer probably exceeded the privilege to defend and recover property. While the officer had an initial ground to stop, the officer did not follow reasonable steps in completing the investigation.

Intentional Torts Defenses—Policy Defenses: A police department authorizes off-duty officers to take actions consistent with their training and law enforcement duties when they personally witness what they reasonably believe to be a violation of the law. While walking home from a movie late one night, an off-duty officer witnessed a man using a tool to try to unlock a car door. Assuming that the man was attempting to steal the vehicle (a felony), the officer asked what the man was doing. The man merely glared back at the officer while continuing to work with the tool. So the officer pulled the man's shoulder around toward him, intending to disclose his identity as a police officer and to question the man. When the man instead pulled away, the officer shoved the man over on the hood of the car. The man then truthfully told the officer that the man was simply trying to open his own car out of which he had mistakenly locked himself. Analyze whether the officer has defenses of necessity, authority of law, discipline, or justification. *Model Answer:*

The question requires analyzing the policy defenses of necessity, authority of law, discipline, and justification when an off-duty police officer physically turned around and restrained a motorist who was attempting to break in to the motorist's own locked car.

The defenses of public and private necessity involve reasonable actions taken to protect public or private property. An authority-of-law defense typically applies to law-enforcement actions but may also apply to teachers, regulators, mental-healthcare providers, and others. A discipline defense typically involves teacher or military-superior actions, often closely regulated by statute. The justification defense is a sort of catchall defense when strong public policies warrant actions. In each case, the actor must use only that amount of force that is reasonable under the circumstances.

In this case, the police officer could arguably have had a necessity defense in protecting private property of another. The officer's actions are better analyzed under an authority-of-law defense. The officer's department had authorized off-duty officers to take proper action when observing a suspected law violation. The facts make it appear that the officer may have acted reasonably when suspecting a vehicle theft, although more facts are necessary to determine reliably. The facts say that the officer *assumed* a theft, which might be reasonable from the late hour but might not be reasonable given other circumstances such as the public location or the motorist's indiscrete actions. Car thieves may act more furtively than car owners, but determination requires investigation on this point. The officer's request also seems reasonable, as does the officer turning the man when the man only glared, particularly if those actions are consistent with department training. Shoving the man over the car hood sounds a little aggressive, like it could be more than reasonable force, but it could also be within department training after the man pulled away, with investigation also required on this issue. The facts certainly give no indication of a discipline defense nor anything suggesting a general justification defense.

In sum, the officer may have the policy defense of authority of law particularly if investigation shows that his actions were consistent with department training. Shoving the motorist over the car hood sounds like a potentially excessive force but may have been warranted when the man pulled away without answering.

WEEK 5

NEGLIGENCE—ELEMENTS
51. An operator of mechanical equipment was working on a construction site. Children had been known to frequent the construction site. The operator had been trained to watch for children as a safety measure. He had also been instructed not to operate equipment if there were any children on the site, until the children were removed, to ensure their safety. The operator observed several children on the site but continued operating equipment. One child was nearly injured by the operator due to his failure to follow the training procedures and heed safety instructions. News of the near miss reached the child's

parents, who consulted a lawyer regarding a negligence claim against the operator. Which of the following is the best advice?

A. The child has a clear negligence claim on the stated facts.
B. There is a claim if the stated facts describe a breach of the standard of care.
C. There is no claim if the operator had a reason for being distracted.
D. The child likely has no negligence claim on the stated facts.

Correct answer: D. The elements of a negligence claim are duty, breach, causation, and damages. Damages are not presumed. In this instance, the facts do not describe any injury to the child, meaning that there is no evidence of damages on the stated facts. Without evidence of damages, the negligence claim fails. Option A is incorrect because of the lack of evidence of damages (injury to the child). Option B is incorrect because even if the stated facts describe a breach of the standard of care, that breach has not caused any injury and hence no damages. Option C is incorrect because duty and breach are determined by community standards, not subjective judgments. The operator's reason for being distracted might have been judged sufficient or insufficient.

NEGLIGENCE—DUTY
52. A company operated a fleet of fishing boats using practices hazardous to its fishing crews. The company's practices earned the crews substantial wages beyond those ordinarily earned by others in the same fishing industry. The crews, including those members who were injured by the practices, understood and accepted the risks. But competitor fleets and members of the local fishing community objected to the company's hazardous practices. They retained a lawyer who filed negligence claims on their behalf to stop the company's hazardous practices injuring the company's crew members. The company's lawyer filed a motion to dismiss the lawsuit. How should the court rule?

A. Deny the motion to dismiss.
B. Adjourn pending evidence of the public effect of the crews' injuries.
C. Under advisement pending research on competitive effects.
D. Grant the motion to dismiss.

Correct answer: D. A negligence claim requires proof of duty, breach, causation, and damages. The duty element of a negligence claim asks whether a person or entity should have been exercising ordinary or reasonable care toward another. The company owed no tort-based duty to competitors and members of the local community with respect to the safety of the company's own workers. The company's actions were not creating a risk of harm to competitors and members of the public. Option A is incorrect because the motion should be granted for lack of a duty. Option B is incorrect because some public effect from crew-member injuries would not give rise to a duty to competitors or the members of the public. It might be the cause for legislation or regulation but not a tort action. Option C is incorrect because competitive effects are irrelevant to duty. One company would not owe a duty in negligence to its competitors, with respect to the treatment of its own crew members.

NEGLIGENCE—DUTY—PROTECTION AGAINST CRIME
53. A hotel had front and side entrances that were secured by card-entry systems after nightfall. The card-entry systems discouraged anyone from entering the hotel after nightfall, other than hotel guests with key cards issued for that night. In the back of one wing, the hotel had a service door that was not secured by card-entry system. The night supervisors knew about the unsecured back door. No guest had yet been hurt until a senior guest was seriously injured in the back wing by an intruder. What additional fact would increase the senior guest's likelihood of prevailing in a negligence claim against the hotel for his injuries?

A. The identity of the intruder who injured the senior guest remains unknown.
B. The hotel recently suffered several break-ins into rooms in that same wing.

C. The hotel's advertising was of a general nature not asserting anything as to security.
D. The senior guest had stayed in the hotel before on several occasions.

Correct answer: B. The disputed duty to protect against crime may depend on several factors including the past experience of crime, offers of security, available means of protection, and foreseeability. That the hotel recently suffered several break-ins into rooms in that same wing increase the foreseeability of the senior guest's injury. Option A is incorrect because the intruder's identity is irrelevant to the hotel's negligence liability. Not knowing that identity does not make the hotel's liability any more or less likely. Option C is incorrect because general advertising without reference to security does not increase the likelihood of proving foreseeability. If the hotel had advertised security, then the guest's claim might have been stronger. Option D is incorrect because the senior guest's having stayed in the hotel on other occasions would not increase the hotel's foreseeability of the guest's injury.

NEGLIGENCE—DUTY—STANDARDS OF CARE—FACTORS—CUSTOM
54. A laborer was part of a crew contracted to mow, trim vegetation, and do other maintenance alongside a busy urban road. The work required the crew to frequently cross the road with maintenance equipment. The laborer was seriously injured by a driver who had not noticed the work until it was too late to avoid the laborer. The laborer hired a lawyer to investigate a claim against the company that was responsible for the work area and had contracted the crew. Which of the following would most help the lawyer establish a standard of care for an action against that company?

A. A national standard that warning signs should have been placed around the area.
B. The driver's admission that he was uninsured, unemployed, and unlicensed.
C. Evidence that there were several close calls involving other crew members.
D. The laborer was crossing the road with a cumbersome piece of maintenance equipment.

Correct answer: A. Standards of care may depend on a variety of particular factors including custom, published standards, experience, and the likelihood and foreseeability of injury. A national standard that warning signs should have been placed around the work area would tend to establish that the company should have done so in order to alert the inattentive driver to a potential hazard to the work crew. Option B is incorrect because it does not establish a standard of care for the company and tends only to implicate the driver rather than the company. Option C is incorrect because although several close calls involving other crew members might help prove that drivers were unaware of the work crew's activities, it does not indicate the conduct in which the company should have engaged to protect the workers. It is helpful evidence on causation, more so than on standard of care. Option D is incorrect because it does not identify conduct in which the company should have engaged.

NEGLIGENCE—DUTY—STANDARD OF CARE—EMERGENCIES
55. A vehicle skidded into a roadside creek. The vehicle's occupants were trapped inside the vehicle in imminent peril of drowning. A tow truck pulled the vehicle from the creek. The vehicle's occupants were saved, but one was injured when the vehicle toppled over as it was pulled from the creek. The vehicle would not have toppled over if the tow-truck operator had used the customary safety equipment. Which of the following additional facts would most help the tow operator in defense of the injured occupant's negligence action?

A. Law-enforcement personnel summoned the tow-truck operator to the scene.
B. The tow operator reasonably believed that he had no time to use the safety equipment.
C. None of the other vehicle occupants were injured when the vehicle toppled over.
D. The creek into which the vehicle skidded was overflowing in a 100-year flood.

Correct answer: B. Emergencies may alter the standard of care to that which was reasonable under the emergency, except as to the conduct of the one who created the emergency. A tow operator who is trying to save the lives of a vehicle's trapped occupants may depart from the customary safety procedures in order to do so, without being subject to a negligence action for harm resulting from reasonable departures. Option A is incorrect because the mere fact that law-enforcement personnel summoned the two truck operator to the scene would not grant that operator law-enforcement authority or immunity. Tow trucks are commonly called by law-enforcement personnel but must still exercise ordinary and reasonable care. Option C is incorrect because that others were not injured does not change that one occupant was. Non-injury of others is not a defense to injury of one. Option D is incorrect because the extraordinary nature of the creek hazard does not change the operator's standard of care. It is the emergency circumstance that alters the standard, not the extraordinary nature of the underlying event.

NEGLIGENCE—DUTY—STANDARD OF CARE—PHYSICAL CHARACTERISTICS

56. Through no fault of her own, a driver accidentally caused her vehicle to strike and knock over a road barrier. Road-construction crews had placed the barrier to keep vehicles from entering a construction area. The driver immediately realized that with the barrier down, other drivers would be at risk of injury from entering the construction area. The driver, a petite woman of unusually small size, did not have the strength to replace the barrier. The driver immediately called for help. Another driver was injured because of the missing barrier. That other driver sued the driver who had knocked over the barrier. Which of the following is the most accurate statement of the defendant driver's standard of care?

A. The actions of a reasonably prudent person of the defendant driver's knowledge, skill, and experience under the circumstances.
B. The actions of a reasonably prudent person of the defendant driver's physical characteristics under the circumstances.
C. The actions of a reasonably prudent person without respect to the defendant driver's physical or mental characteristics.
D. The actions of a reasonably prudent person of average height, weight, strength, knowledge, skill, and experience.

Correct answer: B. In determining the standard of conduct, the reasonably prudent person takes on the physical characteristics of the one whose conduct is in question. There is no expectation that a driver too small or weak to take an action should be liable for failing to do so. Option A is incorrect because the subjective knowledge and individual skill and experience of the defendant is not the standard. Standards are objective except with respect to physical characteristics. Option C is incorrect because the standard does account for physical characteristics. Option D is incorrect because the standard does not contemplate an average person, especially as to physical characteristics. The standard is the reasonably prudent person, not the average person, and the standard accounts for the defendant's physical characteristics.

NEGLIGENCE—DUTY—STANDARD OF CARE—ADULT ACTIVITY

57. A father mowed the fields around his home with a tractor. The father had a six-year-old boy who loved to watch from the porch of the home as his dad drove the tractor. The father stopped the tractor by the home and left for work, leaving fields unmown. Though only six years old, the boy decided to help his father finish the mowing using the tractor. The boy climbed onto the tractor seat and started the tractor. The boy managed to get the tractor into gear but could not work the brake pedal to stop it. The tractor ran into and damaged a car that a guest had parked in the home's driveway. The car's owner made a demand that a homeowner's insurer whose liability policy covered the boy pay for the vehicle damage. The insurer consulted a lawyer about whether to pay the demand. Which of the following is the best recommendation based on the standard of care applicable to the boy?

A. Deny the claim because children with good intentions make sympathetic defendants.
B. Deny the claim because children that age have no negligence liability.
C. Pay the claim because a child engaged in that activity has an adult's liability.
D. Pay the claim because a guest should not have to worry about vehicle damage.

Correct answer: C. A child who is engaged in an adult activity will be held to an adult's standard of care. Operating a tractor is an adult activity for which the law would hold a six-year-old boy to an adult standard. Option A is incorrect because although the boy may be a sympathetic defendant, sympathy does not determine the standard of care. Option B is incorrect because children performing adult activities owe adult duties. Option D is incorrect because the question asks for a recommendation based on the boy's standard of care, not the guest's interests.

NEGLIGENCE—DUTY—LEARNED HAND FORMULA
58. A company manufactured a window-washing rig for use on high-rise buildings. The company secured the rig's safety line by bolt and nut. During the rig's use, the nut came undone from the bolt, allowing the safety line to come free. The rig suddenly tipped as a result, causing a worker to fall from the rig. Workplace safety officials inspected the rig after the worker's injury. They determined that the company could have secured the nut to the bolt using a lock washer costing a few pennies. Which of the following is the best way to use this evidence to support that the company was negligent in securing the safety line?

A. The cost to the company of including a lock washer was so small that the company should have provided it no matter what difference it made in the probability or magnitude of loss.
B. If the cost to the company of including a lock washer was less than the probability times the magnitude of loss from the design without the lock washer, then the company should be liable.
C. If the lock washer would have secured the safety line, then the company should have provided it, and the company is liable for not having provided an available means to eliminate the risk.
D. If the safety line would have saved the worker from injury, then the company should have secured it in a fail-safe manner, whether by lock washer or other means, no matter the reduction in risk or loss.

Correct answer: B. Learned Hand's formula provides that liability exists when the burden of precautions is less than the probability of loss times the magnitude of loss. The formula requires one to compare the cost of the lock washer to the probability and magnitude of loss to determine whether the company should have provided the lock washer. Option A is incorrect because small cost alone does not require that the company provide the lock washer. One must connect the cost to a commensurate reduction in injury probability and value. Option C is incorrect because feasibility alone does not require that the company supply a design or measure. Option D is incorrect because it, too, adopts an absolute rather than reasonableness standard.

Negligence—Duty Generally: A contractor drove his pickup truck into an intersection colliding with a vehicle driven by a mother. The mother had her three-year-old daughter riding in her car without a child seat. The collision injured both mother and daughter. A subcontractor's compressor was stored loose in the back of the contractor's pickup truck. The collision damaged the compressor beyond repair. On her way to the scene, an emergency vehicle driver raced through an intersection causing a motorist to drive his vehicle hard up against a curb. Identify the facts supporting the elements of potential negligence claims as to each instance of personal injury or property damage. *Model Answer:*

The question requires identifying facts that support the elements of potential negligence claims involving a vehicle collision, injury to mother and daughter occupants, damage to a transported compressor, and damage to another vehicle avoiding emergency responder.

The elements of a negligence claim include duty, breach, causation, and damages. By duty, the law refers to that obligation of reasonable care that arises whenever one acts in ways that cause risks to person or property. Duty implies objective standards of care depending on the circumstances. Breach is the violation of duty, proven by direct or circumstantial evidence of the loss event. Causation is the connection between the breach and the loss. Damage can be to person or property.

Here, the contractor driving his pickup truck into an intersection colliding with another motorist's vehicle implies duty (that the contractor should have acted reasonably), breach (that the contractor failed to keep a lookout), causation (that the breach caused the collision with the other vehicle), and damage (injury to the mother and daughter occupants of the other vehicle). The same analysis would apply to any damage to either vehicle due to the collision. Query next whether the daughter might have a claim against her mother, who would have owed the daughter a duty (to use a car safety seat, likely required also by traffic-safety law) but breached that duty (not using the seat) contributing to the daughter's personal injury. In other words, both the contractor and mother may have liability to the daughter. The same analysis would also apply to the subcontractor's claim for destruction of the compressor in the back of the contractor's pickup truck. The contractor would have owed the subcontractor a duty (to transport the compressor with reasonable care including to secure it) but breached that duty (failing to secure the compressor and failing to keep a lookout when entering the intersection) causing the compressor's destruction. The other vehicle driver who hit the curb hard avoiding an emergency vehicle could potentially have a negligence claim for any vehicle damage based on the emergency driver's duty (to use reasonable care responding to the emergency), breach (perhaps failing to use emergency lights and siren, subject to investigation), causation (requiring the other driver to swerve), and damages (any vehicle damage from hitting the curb).

Each of these conclusions requires investigation and confirmation, but these facts could support negligence claims for the mother and daughter personal injuries, compressor destruction, and any damage to each involved vehicle.

WEEK 6

NEGLIGENCE—DUTY—CONTRACT MISFEASANCE
59. A contractor negotiated a snow-removal agreement with a retail store just as the snow season started. The contract began December 1st. It snowed on December 2nd. The contractor did not hire the personnel to perform the contract until December 3rd. A store customer slipped and fell on snow and ice on December 2nd, before the contractor had performed any aspect of the contract. The customer sued the contractor, whose lawyer moved to dismiss the lawsuit for no duty. How should the court rule?

A. Deny the motion.
B. Deny the motion if the contractor should have had the personnel in place already.
C. Grant the motion if the contractor is usually prudent in the performance of contracts.
D. Grant the motion.

Correct answer: D. Ordinarily, the promisor on a contract owes a tort-based duty to a third party only when the promisor has undertaken some act performing the contract (misfeasance, not nonfeasance). Here, the contractor had not yet performed. The contractor's only duty was therefore a contract duty owed the store, not a tort-based duty owed the customer. Option A is incorrect because the court should grant the motion for lack of a duty. Option B is incorrect because whether the contractor should have started sooner or not does not change the duty issue. The contract clearly indicated so, but it made no difference if the contractor had not performed some part of the contract. Option C is incorrect because whether the contractor is usually prudent or not does not affect whether there was a duty in this instance.

NEGLIGENCE—DUTY—ORDINARILY NO DUTY TO RESCUE
60. A farmer maintained her crops using a large tractor. The large tractor had the tires and engine power to enter the fields at all times of year including when they were flooded from heavy rains, melting snow, and runoff. A gardener who lived next door to the farmer maintained his gardens with a small garden tractor and several pieces of associated small equipment. The gardens flooded severely early one spring, endangering the gardener's equipment. The farmer could have saved the gardener's equipment using the farmer's large tractor. What additional facts would be necessary for the farmer to be liable to the gardener for the loss of the gardener's equipment?

A. No additional facts.

B. The gardener asked the farmer to save the equipment, but the farmer declined without offering a reason.
C. The farmer knew that the gardener was detrimentally relying on the farmer's offer to save the equipment.
D. The gardener and farmer were old friends who often helped one another on the farm and in the garden.

Correct answer: C. Absent a special relationship or other exception, tort law generally imposes no duty to act such as to come to the rescue of another, unless one's actions created the need for rescue. The farmer's offer to help, and the gardener's detrimental reliance on that offer, and the farmer's knowledge of the detrimental reliance, would establish a special relationship. Option A is incorrect because the farmer did not owe the gardener a duty. Option B is incorrect because one person cannot create a duty on the part of another simply by asking. A person need not give reasons for refusing to come to another's rescue. Option D is incorrect because it does not describe the kind of special relationship that would give rise to a duty of aid or rescue.

NEGLIGENCE—DUTY—ECONOMIC-LOSS DOCTRINE
61. A boat captain negligently rammed the boat into bridge pilings. The bridge was closed to vehicular traffic for three days while the pilings were repaired. A manufacturer's outlet store near one end of the bridge had virtually no sales for the three days that the bridge was closed. The store usually had brisk sales that time of year. The manufacturer's chief operating officer sought advice from a lawyer regarding whether the manufacturer could sue the boat captain and company for negligence to recover the lost sales. Which of the following is the best evaluation?

A. The manufacturer has a claim.
B. The manufacturer has no claim.
C. The manufacturer has a claim only if the lost sales can be proven to a certainty.
D. The manufacturer has no claim unless the captain knew sales would be lost.

Correct answer: B. The economic-loss doctrine limits tort duties to those instances where there is some direct injury and bars pure economic loss claims by those who have suffered no physical impact. The doctrine bars the manufacturer's claim because the manufacturer had solely economic loss without physical impact. Option A is incorrect because there is no claim, the only plausible claim being barred by the economic-loss doctrine. Option C is incorrect because the claim is barred by the doctrine whether or not the lost sales were certain. Certainty of loss is not the proof burden in any case. Option D is incorrect because the captain's knowledge of the lost sales would not create a duty to prevent them, when the claim is barred by the economic-loss doctrine.

Negligence—Duty—Contracts: A cabler had a contract to run wire for a new fire alarm system in a building. The cabler got busy with other jobs and did not complete the work according to schedule. A fire occurred resulting in damage to equipment stored in the building. The fire would not have damaged the equipment, and would have been extinguished, if the cabler had completed his cabling contract timely. Explain whether the cabler owed the equipment owner a duty, the breach of which would give rise to a negligence claim against the cabler. *Model Answer:*

The question requires determining whether a cabler who failed to complete his cabling work for a new fire alarm system owed an equipment owner a duty cognizable in negligence, when the fire would not have damaged the equipment and would instead have been extinguished if the cabler had finished the cabling contract timely.

A claimant proves negligence with evidence of duty, breach, causation, and damage. The question focuses on the duty element of a negligence claim. Ordinarily, one owes a duty of reasonable care whenever acting in a way that gives rise to a risk of injury or loss. The mere omission to act, rather than careless action, generally does not give rise to a duty unless other circumstances are present. One of those circumstances can be a contract duty. However, a tort duty generally arises out of a contract only when the contract obligor begins performance, not when the obligor completely fails to perform. The rule is one for duty arising on misfeasance in performing a contract, not for mere nonfeasance in failing utterly to perform.

Here, the facts give no direct indication of any affirmative act on the cabler's part that might create a risk of harm to the equipment owner. From the given facts, we must look instead to the possibility of the cabler's tort duty arising out of the cabler's contract to run wire for the alarm system. If the cabler failed to do any work at all on the contract, that is, in nonfeasance, then we would still not have a basis for a tort duty. If on the other hand the cabler did at least some work but was careless in that work or in not completing that work timely as the contract required, then the equipment owner would have a good argument for a tort duty based in misfeasance of the contract obligation. The facts are not crystal clear on whether the cabler began to perform the contract to run wire for the new fire alarm system, although the facts twice state that the cabler had not *completed* the cabling, at least suggesting some work (a dispositive point to investigate). Assuming then that failure to *complete* cabling means some performance of the work, the equipment owner would have a good case for a tort duty in the cabler's misfeasance in performing the work or performing it untimely.

In conclusion, while the case requires further investigation, it appears from the given facts that the equipment owner would have a contract-based duty on which to sue the cabler for failure to perform the contract reasonably, fully, and timely.

Negligence—Duty—Omissions: A trucker had his vehicle skid off the road in an ice storm in a remote area. Within minutes of the accident, a hunter drove by and saw the motorist waving for help in the freezing cold by the crumpled vehicle. The hunter did not stop. It was several hours before another motorist drove by and saved the trucker, who suffered severe frostbite, hypothermia, and shock because of the delay in his rescue. Explain whether the hunter owed the trucker a duty of care the violation of which would give rise to a claim for negligence. *Model Answer:*

The case requires determining whether a hunter who drove by a stranded trucker had a duty to rescue the trucker from the freezing cold of an ice storm to prevent the trucker's severe frostbite, hypothermia, and shock due to delayed rescue, cognizable in a negligence claim.

A negligence claim requires proof of duty, breach, causation, and damages. The question focuses on the duty element of a negligence claim. Duty generally arises from affirmative acts that create risk of injury or loss rather than from mere omissions. Ordinarily, one has no duty to rescue, particularly for those who did not create the need for rescue and have no status and obligation as professional rescuers. One has no duty to act absent a contract obligation (at least partially performed) or special relationship imposing such a duty.

Here, the facts indicate no particular duty. The trucker slid from the highway of his own accord rather than due to any action by the hunter who drove by minutes later. The mere fact that the hunter observed the stranded trucker waving does not give rise to a legal duty. Surely, the hunter should have either stopped or called for rescue as a moral matter, but tort law does not generally impose that duty to rescue under these circumstances. While the facts clearly indicate that the trucker suffered injuries as a direct consequence, causation and damages alone do not create a duty. The hunter was not a professional rescuer and was not on the given facts in any other relationship to the trucker that might impose a duty. The case does not fit into any of the other exceptions to the no-duty rule such as for active operations, control of a dangerous instrumentality, advertised safety, misrepresenting one's intent causing reliance, or voluntarily undertaking a duty.

In conclusion, the hunter owed the trucker no duty cognizable in tort. This case appears to fit most squarely within the no-duty rule rather than any of its several exceptions.

Negligence—Duty—Economic Loss: A delivery truck broke down due to its driver's negligent maintenance. A part to repair a die-casting machine was stuck on the delivery truck for 24 hours while the driver repaired the truck. The 24-hour delay in delivery of the part caused the machine's owner to lose production of 600 parts at a profit of $10 per part. Explain whether the machine's owner has a negligence claim against the driver for the $6,000 loss. *Model Answer:*

The question requires determining whether a machine owner has a negligence claim against a driver for the driver's negligent maintenance of the driver's delivery truck, when the truck broke down delaying the delivery of a repair machine part and causing the machine owner a $6,000 economic loss.

A negligence claim requires proof of duty, breach, causation, and damages. The question raises an issue of duty. Generally, one owes a duty for affirmative acts that create risks of injury or loss. However, that duty must have reasonable limits. The economic-loss doctrine holds that the duty does not extend beyond those whose loss is due to direct physical impact, to cover pure economic loss by others who can show no direct physical impact. The doctrine keeps the scope of loss to manageable risks short of pure business loss from inability to continue operations.

Here, the facts make it clear that the delivery driver was negligent in maintaining his vehicle, causing its breakdown, which in turned caused delay in delivery of the machine owner's repair part. Thus it might at first appear that the delivery driver's affirmative act of delivering machine parts was the sort of affirmative loss-creating act giving rise to a duty to the machine owner waiting for delivery of the part. However, here the machine owner cannot show any direct physical impact to the owner's machine or even its delivered part. Rather, the owner's loss accrued because of the inability to continue machine operations due to the delay in part delivery. The machine owner could conceivably have some contract remedy against the delivery service (an unlikely scenario given that contracts would more likely provide for the opposite limitation on damages), but the machine owner would not be able to establish a tort duty.

In conclusion, the economic-loss doctrine bars the machine owner's claim against the delivery driver who caused no direct physical impact to the owner's machine or part.

WEEK 7

NEGLIGENCE—DUTY—EMOTIONAL DISTRESS ONLY
62. A mother was tossing a softball in the yard with her daughter when a car careened into the yard and struck and seriously injured the daughter. Police investigating the incident determined that the car's drunk driver had been speeding. Mother and daughter sued the drunk driver, whose lawyer moved to dismiss the mother's claim. Which of the following would be the most likely additional fact to affect the court's ruling on the motion?

A. The mother was so upset over witnessing her daughter's serious injury that she had to get psychological help for her nightmares and medical care for her gastric distress.
B. The mother was so upset over witnessing her daughter's serious injury that she threatened to harm the drunk driver if he was not criminally convicted for the incident.
C. The mother and daughter were so socially and emotionally close that they were often seen together and mistaken for sisters.
D. The daughter was so severely distressed by her serious injury that she needed the mother's love, society, and companionship more than the usual daughter.

Correct answer: A. Courts may require those who claim negligently caused emotional distress (without physical impact) to also show that they were contemporaneous witnesses, were a family member of the person physically injured, and suffered severe distress with physical manifestation. Psychological help indicates severe distress, and gastric distress may qualify as physical manifestation. Option B is incorrect because threats by the mother would have no relevance to whether she had a claim against the drunk driver. Option C is incorrect because the social and emotional closeness of mother and daughter would only be relevant to the extent that it contributed to the mother's severe distress over her daughter's injury. Direct evidence of the severe distress (Option A) is better than evidence of a reason for it (Option C). Option D is incorrect because the daughter's distress would only increase the daughter's damages, not give rise to a claim by the mother.

NEGLIGENCE—DUTY—MISHANDLING CORPSE/DEATH NOTICES

63. A woman resided in a home into which a plane crashed, destroying the home. The woman was not at home at the time of the plane crash and was not hurt. A reporter covering the plane crash obtained contact information for the woman's son and sent the son an erroneous message stating that his mother had been killed in the plane's crash. The son was severely distressed when he received the erroneous email message that his mother was killed in the house into which the plane had crashed. The son later sued the reporter, whose lawyer moved to dismiss for lack of duty. Which of the following is most likely the correct ruling?

A. Grant the motion if the son was an adult rather than a minor.
B. Grant the motion.
C. Deny the motion.
D. Deny the motion unless the reporter apologized to the son.

Correct answer: C. Traditionally, courts will allow pure-emotional-distress claims for the negligent mishandling of corpses and negligent transmission of death notices. Although the facts do not expressly indicate that the reporter was negligent, there was likely a duty owed not to transmit the erroneous death notice. Option A is incorrect because the traditional rule does not distinguish between minor and adult children. Option B is incorrect because the traditional rule recognizes a duty not to negligently transmit erroneous death notices. Option D is incorrect because an apology would not bar liability.

NEGLIGENCE—DUTY—PRENATAL HARM

64. A pregnant woman was in a motor-vehicle accident which was the fault of another driver. The accident permanently damaged the woman's unborn child. The mother and father consulted a lawyer regarding whether the child, when born, would have a claim against the at-fault driver. Which of the following additional facts would most likely help the lawyer resolve any duty issues in favor of a claim?

A. The child was not viable at injury and was not born alive.
B. The child was viable at injury and was born alive.
C. The child was viable at injury but was not born alive.
D. The child was not viable at injury but was born alive.

Correct answer: B. Most courts allow claims for prenatal harm so long as the child is born alive or was viable at injury but reject claims when the child was not born alive or viable at injury. Option A is the least likely situation in which a court would recognize a claim on behalf of the child. Options C and D would involve claims recognized in some but not the most jurisdictions, when compared with the correct Option B.

NEGLIGENCE—DUTY—WRONGFUL CONCEPTION

65. A couple sought medical counseling to prevent the woman's pregnancy. The man underwent a sterilization procedure. The woman later conceived. The couple was initially disappointed that the woman had conceived after the man's sterilization. Disappointment gave way to excitement. The couple remained concerned, though, at the cost of pregnancy and delivery. The couple consulted a lawyer. Which of the following is the most reliable advice regarding the couple's legal rights against the medical-care provider performing the sterilization procedure?

A. Depending on the law of the jurisdiction, there may be recovery for the cost of pregnancy and delivery.
B. Depending on the law of the jurisdiction, there is likely to be recovery for the cost of raising the child.
C. Depending on the law of the jurisdiction, there is likely to be recovery for the child's pain and suffering.

D. There is no prospect of any recovery in any jurisdiction because children are always considered to be a benefit.

Correct answer: A. Although there is significant variation in this area, some courts allow claims for wrongful conception, but where those claims are recognized, courts tend to limit them to the cost of pregnancy and delivery. Option B is incorrect because jurisdictions tend not to recognize claims for the cost of raising the child. Option C is incorrect because wrongful-life claims are generally not recognized except in rare cases for extraordinary expense, and there is no indication in this case that there will be any such extraordinary expense. Option D is incorrect because there is some prospect of recovery of costs of pregnancy and delivery in some jurisdictions.

NEGLIGENCE—BREACH—PROOF—DIRECT OR CIRCUMSTANTIAL
66. A shopper was inspecting the baking goods on the shelves of a grocery store. The shopper did not notice that cooking oil had leaked from one of the goods onto the aisle floor. The shopper slipped and fell in the oil, injuring herself. The shopper retained a lawyer who filed a negligence action against the grocery store. The grocery store's counsel moved to dismiss the action for no evidence of breach of duty. Which of the following facts should the shopper's lawyer offer as evidence of breach?

A. The oil on the floor appeared from its stickiness to have evaporated in part.
B. The shopper had never slipped and fallen before in any other store.
C. The grocery store had several clerks on duty at the time the shopper fell.
D. The grocery store had wet-floor signs posted near the entrance to the store.

Correct answer: A. Proof of breach may be by direct or circumstantial evidence, including (for instance) constructive notice as to how long an unreasonably dangerous condition existed. The oil's stickiness from evaporation would tend to show that it had been on the floor long enough for the grocery store personnel to observe it and clean it up before the shopper slipped. Option B is incorrect because it would not tend to prove the grocery store's breach. Constructive notice is the breach issue, not the shopper's reasonable care. Option C is incorrect because it tends to show adequate staffing levels and thus work against breach of duty. Option D is incorrect because the wet-floor signs at the store's entrance would not have alerted the shopper to the oil on the floor of an aisle and would, if anything, tend to show the store's reasonable care rather than lack thereof.

NEGLIGENCE—BREACH—PLAINTIFF'S BURDENS
67. An employee of a convenience store mistook a customer for a thief. The employee training manual instructed to call 911. The employee instead tackled and held the customer while others called police. The customer, who was injured in the incident, sued the employee for negligence. At trial, the jury received the training manual as an exhibit, saw the store's video-recording of the incident, and heard the employee's judicial admission that the customer was not a thief. The employee's lawyer moved for directed verdict, arguing that the customer had failed to satisfy her burden to produce evidence of duty and breach. Which of the following is the customer's best argument in response?

A. Duty from the video and breach from the admission.
B. Duty from the admission and breach from the manual.
C. Duty from the manual and breach from the admission.
D. Duty from the manual and breach from the video.

Correct answer: D. The plaintiff has the burden of pleading breach, producing evidence of it, and proving it by a preponderance of the evidence. The manual's instruction would be evidence of the duty owed a customer when suspected of theft (to call the police), and the video recording showing the employee's failure to follow the instruction would be proof of breach. Option A is incorrect, because the video would not establish any duty or standard, and the admission that the customer was not a thief does not establish breach of duty in a suspected thief's restraint. Option B is incorrect because the admission that the employee mistook a customer for a thief is not a statement of duty or a standard of care, and the manual does not establish breach. Option C is incorrect because although the manual establishes a duty, the admission does not establish a breach. It may have been reasonable to restrain a suspected thief.

Negligence—Duty—Emotional Distress: A mother watched from the kitchen window as her seven-year old son jumped from the day-camp van. Suddenly, she noticed her son struggling with his coat that appeared to catch when the van door closed. The van started to drag the son who fell and flipped over repeatedly as the van pulled away from the curb. The negligent van driver brought the van to a sudden halt when he noticed the mother running screaming from the house. The son survived, but the mother suffered post-traumatic stress disorder including severe gastric distress and weight loss, and sleep disorder. Explain whether the van driver owed the mother a duty of care and whether she would have a negligence claim for her emotional distress as a bystander to the incident. *Model Answer:*

The question requires determining whether the negligent driver of a van who drove away dragging a child whose coat caught in the van door as the door closed after dropping off the son, owed a duty to the child's mother who watched the incident from her home's window before running after the van in rescue of her child.

Negligence claims require proof of duty, breach, causation, and damages. This question focuses on the duty issue. Duty generally arises from affirmative acts that create risk of injury or loss. Certain rules though limit the duty. One of those rules has to do with recovery for pure emotional distress. A claimant can recover for emotional distress when accompanied by physical impact and injury. However, various state rules may bar recovery when the claimant suffers only emotional distress with no impact, as in the case of bystander witnesses to the injury of others. One exception to the no-duty-to-bystanders rule is when the bystander is a close family member who as a contemporaneously present witness suffers severe distress with physical manifestation. Other exceptions can be for being in the zone of danger (near-miss cases) and for fear of disease where a transmission route is present.

In this case, the mother was a bystander to her son's injury. The negligent van driver would obviously have owed a duty to the physically impacted son. Yet here we must analyze whether the van driver owed a duty to the mother so as to give the mother a tort claim for her understandable distress. Because the mother suffered no physical impact, we must look to an exception to the no-duty-to-bystanders rule. The exception for close family members would clearly apply. The mother is a close family member of her son, as close as one can get. She saw the whole incident from her kitchen window and ran out to wave down the van, making her a contemporaneous and even participating witness. Her distress also satisfies the severity and physical manifestation requirements in that she had diagnosed PTSD including severe gastric distress, weight loss, and sleep disorder. The zone-of-danger and fear-of-disease exceptions do not apply.

In conclusion, depending very much on the particular state's law (given that state laws vary on this rule), the mother would have a claim for her pure emotional distress under a state-law exception to the no-duty-to-bystanders rule for severe, manifested distress by a close family contemporaneous witness.

Negligence—Proof of Fault: An angler borrowed a motorboat to go fishing. The motorboat's balky engine quit. The angler had a heart attack from the stress of trying to paddle the motorboat with a seat cushion. Others later found the angler dead in the motorboat the next day. Identify the direct and circumstantial evidence you would seek to support the estate's proof of duty and breach in its negligence claim against the motorboat's owner. *Model Answer:*

The case requires determining the direct and circumstantial evidence to support an estate's negligence claim against a boat owner when the boat's balky engine quit, requiring the decedent angler who borrowed it to try paddling the boat with a seat cushion, from which the angler died of heart attack due to stress.

Claimants prove negligence claims by satisfying elements of duty, breach, causation, and damages. Here, the question focuses on direct and circumstantial evidence supporting a claim. A claimant proves breach of the standard of care using direct or circumstantial evidence. Direct evidence can involve eyewitness observation and testimony. Circumstantial evidence can include reconstruction of events from the physical evidence remaining after the event occurs. Circumstantial evidence can include expert testimony by reconstruction experts.

In this instance, the facts indicate that the defendant motorboat owner loaned the boat with a balky engine to the decedent angler. The angler's estate may present direct evidence that the boat was not properly equipped with paddle or other safety equipment. In particular, the estate may present direct or circumstantial evidence of the boat owner's knowledge of the engine's balkiness. If in fact the engine was balky when the owner loaned the boat to the angler, then the estate may present direct or circumstantial evidence that the owner unreasonably failed to warn the angler of the balkiness. The estate may also present direct evidence that the owner failed to equip the boat with a paddle, radio, or other means of avoiding a stressful effort of getting the boat back to safety attempting to use a seat cushion as paddle. The estate may also present circumstantial evidence of the additional stress of the event, including medical testimony as to the cause of the heart attack and the connection between stressful effort of the seat-cushion-paddling kind and the angler's heart attack and death. The estate may also present circumstantial evidence of the time of the angler's death and the connection between the engine's quitting and the discovery of the angler dead the next day, to support a theory that the owner's careless failure to warn the angler and properly equip the boat with paddle, radio, or other means caused such delay in rescue and medical treatment as to contribute to the angler's death.

In conclusion, this case is of just the type as to require substantial direct and circumstantial evidence in order for the angler's estate to maintain any negligence claim against the motorboat's owner. The case does not present a simple motor-vehicle accident but rather a series of events under circumstances that the estate must establish fairly precisely in order to prove this unusual negligence claim.

WEEK 8

NEGLIGENCE—BREACH—RES IPSA LOQUITUR
68. A vehicle owner had the vehicle's tires rotated by an experienced mechanic. On the owner's way home from the mechanic's shop, the vehicle's wheels fell off causing an accident that injured the owner. Damage to the vehicle left it unclear why the wheel had come off. The vehicle owner consulted a lawyer regarding whether the owner had a negligence claim against the mechanic. Which of the following is the best evaluation?

A. No claim because no duty.
B. No claim because no breach.
C. Plausible claim.
D. Certain liability.

Correct answer: C. The doctrine of res ipsa loquitur provides an inference of negligence when the injury-causing event speaks of negligence, the plaintiff cannot obtain evidence of negligence, and the circumstances are within the defendant's control. There is likely an inference that the mechanic negligently failed to secure the wheel's lug nuts or otherwise contributed to the occurrence. Option A is incorrect because the mechanic clearly had a duty. Option B is incorrect because of the effect of the doctrine of res ipsa loquitur. Option D is incorrect because res ipsa loquitur provides an inference of negligence, not certain liability.

NEGLIGENCE—BREACH—VIOLATION OF STATUTE—EFFECTS
69. A lawyer presented the plaintiff's proofs in a motor-vehicle negligence case involving a rear-end collision. The lawyer's only witness as to duty and breach was a police officer who testified to the violation of a statute requiring drivers to maintain an assured clear distance ahead. The defense lawyer moved for a directed verdict at the close of the plaintiff's proofs. What should the plaintiff's lawyer argue in response?

A. A police officer is the most credible witness available to any plaintiff, and the court must give such an impressive witness great deference.
B. The police officer was the only witness available to this plaintiff, and the court must respect that the plaintiff was at a loss to provide other evidence.
C. Courts construe the violation of a safety statute as evidence that the defendant must have done something wrong, which means that the defendant automatically loses.
D. Courts construe the violation of a safety statute as negligence per se or allow a presumption or inference of negligence, which satisfy the plaintiff's burden of production.

Correct answer: D. Courts construe the violation of a safety statute as negligence per se (the majority position) or allow a presumption or inference of negligence. Any of these positions satisfy the plaintiff's burden of production. Option A is incorrect because officers, though often credible, are not necessarily the most credible witnesses for any plaintiff, and deference to impressive witnesses is not the directed-verdict standard. Option B is incorrect because the facts do not indicate that there were no other witnesses, and whether there were other witnesses or not is irrelevant to the directed-verdict standard. Option C is incorrect because the violation is not construed as the defendant doing something wrong or that the defendant must lose. The proper terms are negligence per se or a presumption or inference of negligence, each of which permit the defendant to offer explanations.

NEGLIGENCE—BREACH—VIOLATION OF STANDARD

70. A die-cast operator was running a die-cast machine when the machine malfunctioned. The operator called for a repair person. The operator then went to the back of the machine to look for problems. The operator was leaning on the machine's railing at the back when the repair person cycled the machine from the front. The cycle of the machine crushed the operator's fingers between the die and the railing. The operator later retained a lawyer to investigate whether the operator had a cause of action against the machine's manufacturer for negligent design. Which of the following discoveries would most aid that cause of action?

A. A plant inspector's report that a supervisor had failed to train the operator.
B. An industry standard that die-cast machine manufacturers guard all pinch-point.
C. The repair person's admission that he was unaware of the operator's presence.
D. An OSHA citation for failure to lock out the machine while under repair.

Correct answer: B. Violation of industry standards may give rise to an inference of negligence. Option A is incorrect because the employer's failure to train would not help an action against the manufacturer of the die-cast machine, nor would it give rise to a negligence action against the employer because of the worker's compensation exclusive-remedy provision. Option C is incorrect because the repair person's not knowing about the operator would not aid the action against the manufacturer of the machine. Option D is incorrect because it tends to place responsibility on the repair person and employer rather than machine manufacturer.

NEGLIGENCE—CAUSE-IN-FACT ELEMENT

71. A vehicle driver was on the road for several hours late in the day. The driver's eyes adjusted as the sun gradually set, so that the driver did not turn on his vehicle headlights as state law required. A second driver drove her vehicle through a stop sign without stopping and directly into the side of the vehicle driven by the first driver without the headlights on. The second driver admitted that she would not have seen the first driver's vehicle and been able to stop in time, even if its headlights had been on. A vehicle passenger injured in the collision consulted a lawyer about the probable liability of the first and second drivers. Which of the following is the best evaluation?

A. The first driver and second driver are each liable.
B. The first driver and second driver are each not liable.
C. The first driver is liable and the second driver is not liable.

D. The first driver is not liable but the second driver is liable.

Correct answer: D. The causation element of a negligence claim requires that the plaintiff show a cause-and-effect connection between the negligence and the injury. Here, the first driver's negligence in not having his lights on was not a cause-in-fact of the collision and passenger's injury because the second driver would not have seen the first driver's vehicle even if the first driver had his vehicle's headlights on. Options A and B are incorrect because the first driver is not liable. Options B and C are incorrect because the second driver is liable.

NEGLIGENCE—CAUSE-IN-FACT—EGGSHELL SKULL RULE
72. A motor-vehicle passenger was in an accident caused by the negligence of the vehicle driver. At the moment of the accident, the passenger had braced her hand and arm against the dashboard, sustaining trauma. The passenger fully expected her bruising and soreness from the accident but was surprised at a persistent numbness of the hand that doctors connected with the accident trauma. The passenger further developed an unusual reflex sympathetic dystrophy that resulted in the amputation of her hand. How should the court treat the passenger's amputation in the passenger's negligence action against the driver?

A. Prohibit evidence of it as indirect and unforeseeable.
B. Prohibit evidence of it given no direct and foreseeable harm.
C. Allow evidence of it given some direct and foreseeable harm.
D. Allow evidence of it only if amputation was a common result.

Correct answer: C. Under the eggshell-skull rule, defendant will pay for all of the harm, even that which is not foreseeable, if at least some harm was the direct and foreseeable result. Because the passenger had some direct trauma including bruising and soreness, the eggshell-skull rule provides that the passenger recover for even the unusual dystrophy and amputation. Options A and B are incorrect because the evidence should be allowed under the eggshell-skull rule. Option B is also incorrect because there was direct and foreseeable harm involving the bruising and soreness. Option D is incorrect because uncommon results are recoverable so long as there is some direct and foreseeable harm.

NEGLIGENCE—CAUSE-IN-FACT—EXPERT TESTIMONY
73. A woman saw an oncologist to determine if she had cancer. The oncologist misread a lab report, incorrectly reporting to the woman that she had no cancer. When the woman's symptoms persisted and she returned to the oncologist months later, a second lab report confirmed the cancer. The woman also discovered the misread lab report. The woman died shortly later despite heroic efforts at treatment. The woman's estate sued the oncologist for misreading the first lab report and failing to diagnose the woman's cancer. Which of the following would be the most helpful additional information in evaluating whether the oncologist is liable?

A. Expert opinion on the woman's probability of surviving with a prompt diagnosis.
B. Expert opinion on the standard of care for the oncologist reading the lab report.
C. Information on how many heirs or beneficiaries the woman left following her death.
D. Information on the cost of treatment if the woman had been promptly diagnosed.

Correct answer: A. Expert testimony may be required to establish cause-in-fact on medical, legal, technical, and scientific matters. To establish cause in fact, the estate must have expert opinion on what difference a prompt diagnosis would have made in the woman's survival. Option B is incorrect because although expert testimony on the standard of care may ultimately be required, the facts state that the oncologist misread the lab report, which is an obvious breach, making the causation issue the critical issue. Option C is incorrect because information on heirs or beneficiaries may be relevant at most to damages, not liability, depending on the jurisdiction's wrongful-death act. Option D is incorrect because treatment costs may be relevant at most to damages, not liability.

Negligence—Res Ipsa Loquitur: A man let a woman use his woodworking shop one weekend afternoon for the woman's project. The woman started the table saw near a propane space heater along one side of the shop. There was a flash and explosion severely burning the woman. Because of the fire, investigators were unable to determine just what had caused the explosion. Recall and apply the elements of res ipsa loquitur to determine whether the woman has a negligence claim against the man. *Model Answer:*

The case requires determining whether a woman injured by an explosion from operating a table saw near a space heater has a negligence claim against the shop's owner when fire investigators were unable to determine the explosion's cause because of the ensuing fire.

Negligence requires proof of duty, breach, causation, and damages. The question focuses on the proof of breach. Claimants ordinarily prove breach by direct and circumstantial evidence. Direct evidence would include eyewitness testimony as to conditions at the time of the injury-causing event. Circumstantial evidence would include reconstruction, often by experts, of events from evidence remaining after the incident. When evidence is beyond the claimant's reach through no fault of the claimant's own, the event itself speaks of negligence, and the respondent had exclusive control over the conditions, then the claimant may find support in state law for relying on the doctrine of res ipsa loquitur, which would create a presumption of negligence requiring the respondent to disprove negligence rather than the claimant to prove negligence.

Here, the shop owner would have owed the woman who borrowed the shop and its equipment a duty of reasonable care as to the reasonable safety of the premises. However, absence of evidence as to the cause of the explosion would make it difficult to impossible for the woman to prove the shop owner's breach of that duty of reasonable care. The woman simply cannot establish (that is, fire investigators were unable to establish, unless the woman finds a better expert) the explosion's cause. Fire destroyed that evidence. The woman must therefore attempt to rely on the doctrine of res ipsa loquitur if the state's law makes that doctrine available to her, to shift the proof burden to the shop owner. The woman is probably able to satisfy the first two conditions for res ipsa loquitur including that the evidence is not available to her through no fault of her own and that the event speaks of negligence. Explosions simply do not happen under these circumstances of equipment operation with some extraordinary cause likely the result of some careless action. Query whether state law would allow an expert to articulate the res ipsa theory. It is less clear whether the woman can satisfy the third condition that the shop owner have had exclusive control over the circumstances. To the contrary, the woman was present at the explosion, not the shop owner, thus suggesting the woman's greater control. On the other hand, the shop owner controlled the shop generally, not the woman who had just borrowed it one weekend afternoon. This third condition may or may not be satisfied, making for a close call. I would lean toward the shop owner *not* having exclusive control and thus believe that the woman would not have the benefit of res ipsa to prove the claim, depending on research into how strictly the state applies that third condition.

In sum, the woman would need the benefit of the doctrine of res ipsa loquitur to be able to prove her negligence claim against the shop owner, which would be problematic in that she may have had control or shared control over the circumstances with the shop owner, thus not meeting all of res ipsa's three conditions.

Negligence—Violation of Statute: A 17-year old girl piled four other girls in her convertible and headed for the cruising strip. State law prohibited any driver the 17-year-old's age from having more than one other person her age or younger in the vehicle if no adults were also present in the vehicle. The girl's vehicle collided with a tree that had fallen across the road resulting in the injury of one of the other girls when force threw her from her perch atop the backseat of the vehicle. Assess and describe the effect of the girl's violation of the state law on a negligence claim against her by the injured girl. *Model Answer:*

The question requires determining the effect of a state statute prohibiting 17-year-old drivers from having more than one other young person in the vehicle if no adults are also present, on the negligence claim of a girl against a 17-year-old driver who struck a tree throwing the girl off the backseat of the driven convertible.

A negligence claim requires proof of duty, breach, causation, and damages. This question focuses on breach of duty, in particular the effect of violation of statute. Violation of a safety statute can give rise to a presumption of negligence, negligence per se, or an inference of negligence depending on the applicable state law. A presumption of negligence requires the defendant to come forward with contrary evidence to defeat the presumption effectively shifting the burden of proof, whereas an inference of negligence simply satisfies the plaintiff's burden of production. Negligence per se establishes negligence except in the event of extraordinary excuse. For any particular rule to apply, the statute must be a safety statute, and the legislature must have intended the statute to protect the claimant's class against the risk that injured the claimant.

In this case, the statute prohibiting 17-year-old drivers from driving with other young persons in the car unless accompanied by an adult is surely a safety statute. Young drivers cause an inordinate number and percentage of motor-vehicle accidents. Distraction of young drivers by other young persons in the vehicle contributes to those high accident rates. Statutes of this kind have reduced those high accident rates. Legislatures also mean to protect the youthful occupants of vehicles by these statutes. The statutes protect others on the roads as well, but they do reduce youth accident injuries and deaths. Hitting a tree in the roadway is potentially the kind of risk against which these statutes protect. The girls in the accident vehicle may have distracted the 17-year-old driver, a point definitely to investigate. Query also the effect of the claimant girl having voluntarily occupied the vehicle and whether the girl knew of the statute and was contributorily or comparatively negligent. Yet on the issue of the statute's violation alone and its effect on the 17-year-old driver's negligence, that violation would likely give rise to a presumption or inference of negligence, or negligence per se (which of those options depending on the particular state's law), on the driver's part, thus supporting the injured girl's claim.

In conclusion, the injured girl likely has the support of the statute's violation in establishing her negligence claim against the 17-year-old driver, whether that violation presumes or infers negligence or establishes negligence per se depending on the applicable state law.

Causation—Cause in Fact: A secretary negligently left the key in the door when leaving for the evening. The tenant of the next office noticed the key and decided to see if the secretary was in the office. While groping for the light switch inside the door, the tenant's hand touched a plug plugged into an outlet that an electrician had negligently installed against code immediately above the light switch. A cleaning-service employee had negligently loosened the plug while vacuuming. The tenant received a severe burn from the plug. Determine and explain whether causation in fact is satisfied as to the negligence of the secretary, cleaning-service employee, and electrician for the tenant's injury. *Model Answer:*

The question requires determining and explaining whether causation in fact is satisfied in a tenant's claims against a secretary, cleaning-service employee, and electrician, when the secretary carelessly left the key in an office door when leaving for the evening, the tenant noticed the key and looked inside for the secretary, groping for a light switch but touching a plug that the cleaning employee had carelessly loosened from an outlet that the electrician had negligently installed.

Negligence requires proof of duty, breach, causation, and damages. This question focuses on the first of two aspects of causation, which is causation in fact. The other aspect is proximate or legal cause. Causation in fact is logical or scientific cause, usually under the but-for test requiring proof that but for the negligence, the injury would not have happened. An alternative test when but-for causation fails as to multiple causes requires proof that the breach was a substantial factor in bringing about the harm.

These facts support a straightforward application of the but-for test for causation. But for the secretary's carelessness in leaving the key in the door, the tenant would not have entered the office where the tenant got hurt. So the proofs readily satisfy but-for causation as to the secretary's negligence even if those proofs might not satisfy proximate or legal cause. Also, but for the cleaning employee's leaving the plug loosened, it appears that the tenant would not have come into contact with the plug prongs and suffered shock and burn. Thus, the proofs also satisfy cause in fact as to the tenant's claim against the cleaning employee. The proofs are also reasonably clear as to the electrician's fault being a cause in fact of the tenant's injury. When the electrician put the outlet right above the light switch, which was the negligence against the code, the electrician's negligence set in motion the event that brought the tenant's hand into contact with the exposed plug. But for the electrician's negligence, the plug would have been away from the switch where the tenant's groping hand would not have come into contact with it.

In conclusion, although the events present an odd combination of circumstances that might not satisfy proximate or legal cause as to each potential defendant, the facts readily satisfy cause in fact under its but-for test as to the negligence of the secretary, cleaning employee, and electrician, for the tenant's claims.

WEEK 9

NEGLIGENCE—CAUSE-IN-FACT—SUBSTANTIAL-FACTOR TEST

74. A local river guide took two tourists canoeing in the tourists' own canoe. The guide carelessly navigated the tourists' canoe over some falls resulting in the canoe getting wedged by strong current among logs and boulders. A man who was clearing timber along the riverbank helped force the canoe free but in doing so carelessly applied too much force to it, cracking the canoe's bottom. The canoe instantly swamped when freed, causing the canoe and its contents to be lost to the river. Which of the following best describes the relative liability of the guide and the man along the riverbank?

A. Neither is liable because it took each of their actions to combine to cause loss of canoe and contents.
B. Only the guide is liable as the first to carelessly set events in motion to cause loss of canoe and contents.
C. Only the man is liable as the last to carelessly complete events causing loss of canoe and contents.
D. Both are liable if each of their actions were substantial factors in the loss of canoe and contents.

Correct answer: D. When two or more causes would each have brought about the harm independent of the other, a substantial-factor test will determine whether any one of those defendants contributing to the harm is liable. The actions of the guide and man appear to each have been a substantial factor in the loss of canoe and contents. Option A is incorrect because negligent actions that are substantial factors can result in liability even if it took other actions to cause the loss. Options B and C are incorrect because cause in fact does not follow first-action or last-action tests. The order of the actions is unimportant so long as each was a substantial factor.

NEGLIGENCE—CAUSE-IN-FACT—SHIFTING BURDEN

75. A restaurant's kitchen manager left rat poison in a plastic container similar to a container that waiters used for sugar. Two waiters each negligently mixed a spoonful of the rat poison into glasses of iced tea one of which was then served to a patron who was poisoned. Both waiters had mistaken the poison for sugar, but the patron was unable to show which of them had made the glass from which the patron had been poisoned. Which of the following best describes the waiters' potential liability to the patron?

A. Each is potentially liable, shifting the burden of proof to them to disprove liability.
B. Neither is potentially liable because the burden of proof remains on the patron.
C. Only one is potentially liable, depending on whether the patron can prove which one.
D. Each is potentially one-half liable, provided that the patron rules out other causes.

Correct answer: A. When two individuals both act negligently, and only one has brought about the harm, but the plaintiff cannot determine which one, then the courts may shift to the defendants the burden of disproving causation. Each waiter is potentially liable, with the burden of proof shifted to them to disprove their liability. Options B and C are incorrect because the courts may shift the burden of proof to the two waiters. Option D is incorrect because the liability would not be divided equally but shifted to the waiters to disprove.

NEGLIGENCE—PROXIMATE CAUSE

76. Several hikers decided to take an early spring hike up a mountain that others knew to have occasional late-spring snowstorms. An outfitter worked with the hikers to prepare for the hike up the mountain. The outfitter was among the many who knew that the mountain had late-spring snowstorms. The outfitter negligently failed to warn the hikers, as did several friends, family members, park rangers, and other acquaintances. After several days of successful hiking, the hikers were trapped by a snowstorm. Several suffered severe frostbite injuries requiring amputation of toes and fingers. Those hikers sued the outfitter. Which of the following is the outfitter's best argument for dismissal of the hikers' action?

A. No duty.
B. No breach.
C. No proximate cause.
D. No damages.

Correct answer: C. Proximate cause asks whether, as a policy matter, the cause-in-fact connection between the negligence and the injury is close enough to hold the defendant liable. There may have been too remote and tenuous of a connection between the outfitter's failure (among the failure of several others) to warn the hikers and the eventual occurrence of the snowstorm. Option A is less likely correct because the outfitter may well have owed a duty on the basis of superior knowledge and expertise, and the special relationship. Option B is incorrect because the failure to warn would be a breach of a duty to warn. Option D is incorrect because there were severe frostbite injuries and amputations.

NEGLIGENCE—PROXIMATE CAUSE—SPREADING FIRES

77. A mechanic negligently spilled gasoline behind a shop while refueling an engine for testing. The gasoline caught fire from a spark of static electricity as the mechanic attempted to clean up the spilled gasoline. The fire spread across a field to a rancher's barn, where it destroyed the barn and equipment inside it. The rancher consulted a lawyer about whether to sue the mechanic for the loss of the barn and equipment. What issue must the lawyer resolve before advising the rancher?

A. The jurisdiction's duty rules for professionals like mechanics.
B. The jurisdiction's standard-of-care rules for spilling gasoline.
C. The jurisdiction's proximate-cause rule for spreading fires.
D. The jurisdiction's damages rules for losses due to fire.

Correct answer: C. Proximate-cause tests for spreading fires vary from adjoining-property and first-building rules to much larger distances in rare cases. The outcome of this claim may well depend on which of those rules the jurisdiction recognizes. Option A is incorrect because no special professional-duty rules apply to the mechanic spilling gasoline. Option B is incorrect because the facts already state that the mechanic negligently spilled the gasoline, meaning that standard of care is not an issue. Moreover, there are no particular standard-of-care rules regarding spilling gasoline. Option D is incorrect because there are no special damages rules for losses due to fire.

Causation—Proximate or Legal Cause: A man loaned his fishing boat to a homeowner one evening, negligently forgetting to tell the homeowner that its gas tank was nearly empty. No sooner had the homeowner gotten the boat out on the lake, than its engine died with the gas tank empty. As a result, the homeowner was unable to get home in time to take his dinner out of the oven. Fire personnel responded to thick smoke from the burned dinner while the homeowner floated helplessly on the lake. Repairs from smoke and fire-personnel damage cost the homeowner several thousand dollars. Evaluate whether proximate cause is satisfied on the homeowner's negligence claim against the boat owner for those damages. *Model Answer:*

The case requires determining whether a homeowner can establish proximate or legal cause in the homeowner's negligence claim against a man who loaned his fishing boat to the homeowner while negligently forgetting to tell the homeowner that its gas tank was nearly empty, resulting in the homeowner being stranded on the lake too long to get his dinner out of the oven, further resulting in a fire for which the homeowner wishes to claim damages.

Proximate or legal cause is one of two conditions to satisfy causation as one of four elements duty, breach, causation, and damages in a negligence claim. While cause in fact tests the but-for or logical/scientific basis for causation, connecting the defendant's breach to the plaintiff's loss, proximate or legal cause is a policy question judging the fairness of holding the defendant liable and keeping negligence damages to a reasonable, insurance rated scope. The two primary tests for proximate cause are the traditional direct-sequence test and the modern foreseeability test. The direct-sequence test asks if the breach led in natural, probable, and close connection to the damages, usually close in time and place. The foreseeability test asks if the objective observer could foresee or predict damage from the breach in advance of the damage occurring.

In this case, the homeowner's fire-loss damage was not so close in time or place to the boat owner's breach as to satisfy the direct-sequence test. The boat owner forgetting to tell the homeowner that the boat was low in gas may (depending on investigation to confirm) have occurred as much as hours before the fire, at the time that the boat owner first loaned the boat. The boat loan and breach also may have occurred some distance from the fire loss, again depending on investigation. The sequence of acts between the boat owner's agreement to loan the boat and the fire loss was then relatively extensive, requiring the homeowner's putting his dinner in the oven, operation of the boat, running out of gas, and remaining out on the lake while the dinner burned in the oven, resulting in fire loss. The sequence was not natural, probable, immediate, or direct, but instead seems unnatural, improbable, remote, and speculative. The foreseeability test may be a closer call. An objective observer could potentially see some harm coming from the homeowner getting stranded on the lake, perhaps exposure to the elements, although the category of property loss and specific harm of the homeowner leaving dinner in the oven would be hard to predict and therefore probably not quite foreseeable.

In conclusion, on the whole, the unfairness of extending a large home fire-loss liability to a boat owner who forgets to tell the boat borrower that the boat is low on gas tends to confirm that the borrower's claim would not satisfy either the direct-sequence or foreseeability tests for proximate cause in the borrower's negligence claim against the boat owner. This case would not make a good case.

WEEK 10

NEGLIGENCE—PROXIMATE CAUSE—SUPERSEDING CAUSES
78. A feed mill stored fertilizer in a locked and secure shed. A worker negligently left the shed unlocked. Finding the shed conveniently unlocked, a thief stole the fertilizer and made a bomb out of it, destroying a business with the bomb. The business' owner consulted a lawyer over whether to sue the feed mill in negligence for leaving the shed unlocked. Which of the following is the best evaluation?

A. Strong on breach, strong on cause in fact, strong on proximate cause.
B. Strong on breach, strong on cause in fact, weak on proximate cause.
C. Weak on breach, weak on cause in fact, strong on proximate cause.
D. Weak on breach, weak on cause in fact, weak on proximate cause.

Correct answer: B. Extraordinary, unforeseeable, independent events that bring about the harm will supersede prior negligence and cut off proximate cause. There was clearly fault in leaving the shed unlocked. The facts state that the worker was negligent. There was also actual cause in the thief's convenience of finding the shed unlocked, so as to be able to steal the fertilizer and make a bomb out of it. Proximate cause is problematic at best, given the intentional and extraordinary nature of the act. Options A and C are incorrect because proximate cause is not strong. Options C and D are incorrect because breach is not weak. Options C and D are incorrect because cause in fact is not weak.

NEGLIGENCE—PROXIMATE CAUSE—FORESEEABLE CRIME

79. An art museum hired a security company to protect its new building and grounds from vandalism. Vandals caused substantial damage to the museum's new building and grounds on a day that the security company's guard had failed to show up for work at the museum. The museum filed a negligence action against the security company for the damage. The security company's lawyer moved to dismiss the action on the basis of superseding cause. Which of the following is the best evaluation of the merits of that motion?

A. It will be denied because the vandalism's foreseeability was what made the company negligent.
B. It will be denied because the substantial nature of the damages due to vandalism warrants compensation.
C. It will be granted because the vandalism was intentional and criminal, and therefore less likely foreseeable.
D. It will be granted because security companies cannot prevent every act of vandalism and should not have to pay for the loss.

Correct answer: A. If the occurrence of a foreseeable criminal or intentional act is what makes the other person negligent, then the criminal or intentional act is less likely to cut off proximate cause. The museum hired the company to prevent foreseeable vandalism, making negligent the company's failure to do so notwithstanding that the vandalism was intentional and criminal, and therefore potentiality superseding. Option B is incorrect because the substantiality of the damage does not make proximate cause more likely. Option C is incorrect because although intentional and criminal acts are more likely to cut off proximate cause, the security company was specifically hired to prevent vandalism, which was specifically foreseen. Option D is incorrect because the security company was hired to prevent vandalism. That not all vandalism can be prevented would go to the standard of care and whether the company breached it, not whether it was a superseding cause when it actually occurred.

NEGLIGENCE—PROXIMATE CAUSE—RESCUE DOCTRINE
80. A novice climber negligently trapped himself on a precipitous ledge in severe weather through lack of skill, preparation, and proper equipment. An expert climber quickly reached the novice climber leading to the novice's heroic rescue. The expert climber was injured in the rescue process through no fault of her own. The expert climber missed several months of work in her job in the construction trades and had many thousands of dollars in lost income as a consequence. The expert climber consulted a lawyer regarding whether the expert climber had any way of recovering her lost income. Which of the following is the best evaluation?

A. The expert climber has no recourse against anyone for the lost income.
B. The expert climber has recourse against her construction trades employer.
C. The novice climber is liable only if the novice climber has insurance.
D. The novice climber is liable to the expert climber for the lost income.

Correct answer: D. An actor whose negligence creates a need for rescue may be held liable for injury to the rescuer. The facts state that the novice was negligent and that the expert was not but was injured as a result of the rescue. Option A is incorrect because the novice is liable to the expert. Option B is incorrect because employers have no liability for injuries that occur to employees unrelated to the employment. Option C is incorrect because the existence or non-existence of insurance has no bearing here on the novice's liability. The rescue doctrine would apply independent of the availability of insurance.

NEGLIGENCE—PROXIMATE CAUSE—FORESEEABLE MALPRACTICE
81. A motorist ran her vehicle through a red light, hitting a pedestrian who was in the intersection's crosswalk. The pedestrian suffered fractures to both wrists when she put both hands forward to brace herself at the last instant before the collision. The pedestrian was taken to a hospital where an emergency physician overlooked the pedestrian's wrist fractures while treating other serious injuries. The physician's malpractice increased the pedestrian's wrist pain and disability resulting from the motor-

vehicle accident. In the pedestrian's negligence claim against the motorist, the motorist's lawyer requested a jury instruction prohibiting the jury from including the increased wrist pain and disability from the physician's malpractice. Which of the following is the best evaluation of whether the jury instruction should be given?

A. Yes, because malpractice is not foreseeable and is a superseding cause as to prior negligence.
B. Yes, because malpractice is not foreseeable, although if it were, it would not be a superseding cause.
C. Yes, because although malpractice is foreseeable, it is a superseding cause as to prior negligence.
D. No, because malpractice is foreseeable and not a superseding cause as to prior negligence.

Correct answer: D. An actor whose negligence creates a need for medical care may be held liable for injury from that medical care. Malpractice is ordinarily held to be foreseeable. Options A, B, and C are incorrect because the jury instruction should not be given. The extra damages from the malpractice should be allowed against the negligent motorist. Options A and B are also incorrect because malpractice is ordinarily held to be foreseeable. Options A and C are incorrect because malpractice is ordinarily not held to be a superseding cause.

NEGLIGENCE—PROXIMATE CAUSE—VOLUNTARY INTOXICATION

82. A host had several friends over to his home for an evening. The host offered beer and wine to his friends. Near the end of the evening, the host urged a departing guest, who was already slurring her words and acting tipsy, to have one last beer, which the guest did. The guest left in her car an hour later but only made it a few blocks before running a stop sign, striking and seriously injuring a pedestrian who was in the crosswalk. In a state with no dramshop act, what is the most likely evaluation of the pedestrian's negligence claim against the host?

A. Liability due to the host negligently offering more beer to a drunken departing guest.
B. No liability due to no negligence offering more beer to a drunken departing guest.
C. No liability due to no cause in fact between the drinking and running the stop sign.
D. No liability due to no proximate cause with respect to the guest voluntary imbibing.

Correct answer: D. An intoxicated person's voluntary drinking ordinarily, in the absence of dramshop legislation, cuts off proximate cause as to the negligent server of the alcohol. Social hosts are not ordinarily liable in the absence of statute. Option A is incorrect because there would be no liability in the absence of statute. Option B is incorrect because offering more beer to a drunken departing guest may well be negligence. Option C is incorrect because drinking may well have been a cause in fact of running the stop sign.

NEGLIGENCE—PROXIMATE CAUSE—FORCES OF NATURE

83. A developer purchased farmland for residential development. The farmland had an old barn on the property that wind and weather had seriously damaged over the years and looked to be in the process of falling down. A strong wind carried a section of the barn onto an expensive motor home parked on a neighbor's property, nearly destroying the motor home. The neighbor sued the developer, who retained counsel to defend. Which of the following facts would be most helpful to the developer's defense?

A. Expert investigation determined the barn to have been unsafe for occupation.
B. Expert investigation determined the strong wind to have been of tornado force.
C. Neighbors had previously asked the developer to take down the unsightly barn.
D. The developer had scheduled the barn for demolition the day after the strong wind.

Correct answer: B. Wholly unpredictable forces of nature will cut off proximate cause as to prior negligence, but proximate cause remains where the force was foreseeable. Strong winds may well be foreseeable, but tornado-force winds would ordinarily not be foreseeable. Option A does not help and may hurt the developer because the barn not being safe for occupation would tend to make its removal more compelling. Option C is incorrect because, again, it makes the barn's removal more compelling. Option D shows care on the part of the developer but would also tend to show the developer's knowledge of the risk and ability to remove it, so it could go either way depending on why the developer had not removed the barn earlier.

Causation—Proximate or Legal Cause—Intervening Causes: An apartment management company hired a maintenance person. The maintenance person had a criminal history of thefts that the company negligently failed to discover. The maintenance person used a master key to enter an apartment one night, thinking mistakenly that the tenant was away. When the maintenance person entered the bedroom, the tenant awoke and screamed. The maintenance person ran out. The tenant grew so upset by the incident that she suffered a miscarriage. Evaluate and discuss whether these events satisfy proximate cause in the tenant's claim against the company for harm related to her miscarriage. *Model Answer:*

The case requires determining whether a tenant who suffered a miscarriage from stress over a maintenance person entering her apartment bedroom attempting to commit a theft can satisfy proximate cause in a negligence claim against the apartment management company for negligent hiring.

Proximate or legal cause is one of two conditions to satisfy causation as one of four elements duty, breach, causation, and damages in a negligence claim. While cause in fact tests the but-for or logical/scientific basis for causation, connecting the defendant's breach to the plaintiff's loss, proximate or legal cause is a policy question judging the fairness of holding the defendant liable and keeping negligence damages to a reasonable, insurance rated scope. The two primary tests for proximate cause are the traditional direct-sequence test and the modern foreseeability test. A third test applies when after the breach other events intervene to result in the damage. When those subsequent intervening events are extraordinary, they may supersede the prior breach and cut off the chain of proximate cause. Intentional acts and especially criminal acts are more likely than negligent or innocent acts to constitute superseding causes, depending on the defendant's responsibility to predict and prevent those intentional or criminal acts.

In this case, the tenant may be able to establish proximate cause in her negligence claim against the apartment complex despite that the maintenance person's intervening act was both intentional and criminal. While the intervening-cause rule would ordinarily provide that a criminal act like the maintenance person's attempted theft would be a superseding cause cutting off proximate cause and defeating the tenant's negligence claim, apartment managers likely owe a clear duty to ensure that maintenance persons with access to apartments do not present a theft or assault risk to tenants. The theory of negligent hiring is not unusual. When an employer places an employee in a position of trust especially with respect to personal security and property loss, the employer should foresee those risks and should ensure the employee's fitness. This maintenance person had a criminal history of thefts, and yet the management company gave him a master key to apartments. Under the modern foreseeability test, the maintenance person's using the master key to attempt theft would not be so unusually unpredictable as to defeat proximate cause and would instead be reasonably foreseeable. The same analysis would apply to the intervening-cause test that the maintenance person's intentional and criminal wrong in attempting theft would not under the circumstances of his prior theft convictions and possession of the master key be such an extraordinary act as to constitute a superseding cause.

In sum, the tenant should be able to satisfy proximate cause in her negligence claim against the apartment management company despite that her negligent-hiring theory relies on the maintenance person's intervening criminal act. The maintenance person's criminal act was not so extraordinary and unpredictable as to cut off proximate cause.

WEEK 11

NEGLIGENCE—PROFESSIONAL

84. A homebuyer contracted with surveyors for a survey of property that the homebuyer was considering purchasing. The surveyors had surveyed the property just the previous year. Instead of

performing a complete survey, the surveyors provided the homebuyer with a copy of the previous survey. Unknown to the homebuyer or surveyors, a neighbor had recently built a driveway and carport on the property. The homebuyer discovered the neighbor's encroachment only after purchasing the property because the survey did not disclose it. The homebuyer made a demand on the surveyors for damages and expenses relating to the undisclosed encroachment. Which of the following facts would most support the surveyors' liability?

A. The homebuyer paid the surveyors' charge at the time of the closing on the sale of property to the homebuyer.
B. The neighbor did not have a survey performed before having the encroaching driveway and carport constructed by a builder.
C. The surveyors usually did a visual inspection of the site to avoid these kinds of costly errors but had neglected in this instance to do so.
D. The surveyors usually charged less for a survey based on a recent previous survey but had neglected in this instance to do so.

Correct answer: C. Malpractice claims hold professionals liable for harm resulting from their negligence, under special rules. Those rules include that the standard of care is established by professional customs. If the surveyors usually did a visual inspection of the site, then that practice would tend to support the custom and standard of care, which was then breached in this instance. Option A is incorrect because the timing of the payment does not bear on the responsibility of the surveyors to perform to professional standards. Option B is irrelevant as to the care taken or not taken by the neighbor, on the issue of the surveyors' liability to the homebuyer. It is not even relevant to the trespass liability of the neighbor. Option D is incorrect because the pricing would not affect the duty with regard to damages from undisclosed encroachments. Perhaps the homebuyer should have had the lower price, but in either case, the surveyors should have performed within the customary practices.

NEGLIGENCE—PROFESSIONAL—DUTY TO RESCUE
85. An elderly woman had multiple minor health problems. She frequently sought help for those minor health problems from a neighbor physician, who would tell her where she could obtain medical assistance. On one occasion, the elderly woman called and left a telephone message asking the neighbor physician for help, but the neighbor physician did not respond. Family members later found the elderly woman comatose in her home, due to a condition the symptoms of which she had reported to the physician in her telephone message. The family members, who were distraught that the neighbor physician had not helped the elderly woman, consulted a lawyer regarding the neighbor physician's liability to her. Which of the following is the best evaluation?

A. No liability.
B. No liability unless the physician had the special knowledge and skills to have helped the elderly woman based on her telephone message to him.
C. Liability unless the physician did not get the telephone message before the elderly woman lapsed into a coma.
D. Liability.

Correct answer: A. A professional does not owe a duty to come to the aid or rescue of another unless employed at that time for that purpose or having negligently created the need for rescue. Option B is incorrect because possessing special knowledge and skill does not mean that the professional must use it when there is no duty to do so. Option C is incorrect because there would have been no duty whether or not the physician got the message in time to help the elderly woman. Option D is incorrect because there was no duty.

NEGLIGENCE—PROFESSIONAL—NO DUTY TO THIRD PARTY

86. A lawyer prepared a will for an elderly client that bequeathed the client's estate to a charity. The lawyer had his daughter, a high-school student who was shadowing his secretary, sign the client's will along with the secretary. After the client subsequently died, heirs at law proved that the will was invalid because the lawyer's daughter was too young to act as witness. The charity sought legal advice regarding the lawyer's malpractice liability to it for losing the bequest. Which of the following statements is most accurate with respect to the lawyer's liability?

A. The lawyer is not liable to the charity because the only duties the lawyer owed were to the elderly client, not the charity.
B. The lawyer is not liable to the charity because the lawyer did his best to carry out the elderly client's wishes, and the elderly client is deceased.
C. Depending on the law of the specific jurisdiction, the lawyer may be liable to the charity as the direct beneficiary of the lawyer's services.
D. Depending on the law of the specific jurisdiction, the lawyer may be liable to the charity but only if the charity paid for the lawyer's services.

Correct answer: C. Professionals ordinarily do not owe duties to third parties, except where their service is for the direct benefit of the third party, as, commonly, in a lawyer's preparation of a will. Option A is incorrect because many jurisdictions would recognize liability to a third party for whom the lawyer was providing a direct benefit when acting for the client. Option B is incorrect because doing one's best is not sufficient. Professionals must conform their conduct to the customary practice of a competent professional in the same field under the same circumstances. The client's decease does not end the duty. Option D is incorrect because payment is not necessary for there to be a duty to a third party whom the client intends the service to benefit.

NEGLIGENCE—PROFESSIONAL—DUTY TO WARN FORESEEABLE VICTIMS

87. A patient struggling with relationship problems visited a therapist. The patient described for the therapist problems that the patient had with his girlfriend. "I bought a gun and plan to use it on her," the patient calmly told the therapist. The therapist noted the statement in the patient's records. Two weeks later, the patient shot and killed his girlfriend. Police located the therapist's record and confirmed with the therapist that the patient had threatened the girlfriend. A lawyer for the girlfriend's estate learned of the threat. Which of the following statements best describes the therapist's liability to the girlfriend's estate?

A. No liability because the therapist had no way to stop the patient from killing.
B. No liability because a duty of confidentiality bound the therapist not to disclose.
C. Liability to an identifiable victim of a particularized threat of imminent violence.
D. Liability to anyone the patient harmed within two months of treatment.

Correct answer: C. Mental-health care providers owe duties to warn foreseeable victims of patients' particularized threats of imminent violence likely to seriously injure or kill. The therapist will be liable if the therapist could have warned the girlfriend in a manner that would have saved her life. Option A is incorrect because a warning to the girlfriend, a report to the police, or treatment of the patient, or some combination of those actions, may have saved the girlfriend's life. Option B is incorrect because the duty of confidentiality is waived in these circumstances. Option D is incorrect because the duty to warn extends only to identifiable victims regarding particularized threats of imminent violence.

NEGLIGENCE—PROFESSIONAL—DUTY TO PREVENT SUICIDE

88. A psychiatrist admitted a patient with severe depression to a hospital's observation unit. The psychiatrist noted "suicidal ideation" in the patient's chart intending the customary suicide-prevention measures. The hospital put none of those measures in place, even though it was customary in the observation unit to do so for patients suffering with thoughts of suicide. As a result, the patient committed suicide shortly after admission to the observation unit. Hospital administrators consulted a

lawyer regarding liability to the patient's estate. Which of the following statements is the best evaluation?

A. Liability because breaches of customary measures resulted in the suicide.
B. Liability because no one should die an unnatural death in the hospital.
C. No liability because suicide is an intervening and superseding act.
D. No liability because persons are entitled to do as they please with their own life.

Correct answer: A. A medical-care provider or other professional having charge of a person may owe a duty to prevent that person's suicide. The psychiatrist admitted the patient for observation regarding severe depression and suicidal thoughts. Both the hospital and the psychiatrist failed to follow customary measures for suicide prevention, resulting in the patient's death. Option B is incorrect because the duty is to take customary measures, not to prevent all unnatural death. Option C is incorrect because suicide would not be a superseding act as to the liability of professionals trained in suicide prevention. Option D is incorrect because the right to do as one pleases does not extend to suicide in these circumstances. The patient sought and accepted psychiatric care which the hospital should have provided according to custom.

NEGLIGENCE—PROFESSIONAL—EXPERT TESTIMONY

89. An internist performed abdominal surgery on a patient with clear indications of appendicitis. The internist used cottonoids to pack the surgical site and keep the operative field clear of blood during the surgery. The patient developed an infection and continued to have abdominal pain after the surgery. Follow-up radiographs of the area showed a cottonoid's radiopaque marker, indicating that the internist had mistakenly left the cottonoid in the patient when completing the surgery. The internist's mistake made a second surgery necessary. In a trial of the patient's malpractice case against the internist, the patient presented these proofs without expert testimony as to the customary practice to ensure removal of cottonoids. The internist's lawyer moved for directed verdict. Which of the following is the most appropriate ruling?

A. Motion denied because jurors determine reasonableness under all circumstances.
B. Motion denied because no expert testimony is required for obvious breaches.
C. Motion granted because expert testimony is required to establish the custom.
D. Motion granted because the internist did what was necessary in the second surgery.

Correct answer: B. The professional's standard of care ordinarily requires expert testimony by a similarly qualified professional, except in the rare case when the breach is obvious. Mistakenly leaving a surgical tool or material in the patient is an obvious breach that does not require expert testimony as to the custom for ensuring its removal. Option A is incorrect because reasonableness is not the professional's standard. Customary practice is the standard. Jurors are not generally permitted to determine the professional's custom without expert testimony from similarly qualified professionals. Option C is incorrect because the breach was sufficiently obvious not to require expert testimony as to the custom. Option D is incorrect because a second surgery, although then necessary, would not have been necessary if the internist had not mistakenly left the cottonoid in the patient.

NEGLIGENCE—PROFESSIONAL—BREACH—TORT, NOT CONTRACT

90. A woman consulted a cosmetic surgeon to improve the appearance of her nose. The surgeon drew pictures of her anticipated new nose. The woman agreed to the surgery. An office manager then met with the woman to have her sign a consent form saying that nothing was guaranteed as to the final appearance of her nose. The surgeon then performed the surgery. The result was nothing like the pictures the surgeon had drawn. A second cosmetic surgeon told the woman that she got a bad result because the first surgeon had not done the surgery according to the custom. The woman consulted a lawyer who assigned an associate to draft a complaint against the first surgeon. What claims should the associate include?

A. Breach of contract.
B. Breach of contract and malpractice.
C. Malpractice.
D. Malpractice and battery.

Correct answer: C. Professionals who breach the standard of care causing injury are ordinarily sued in tort (malpractice), not contract, unless guaranteeing the result. The surgeon departed from the custom causing the bad result. The surgeon did not guarantee the result. The consent form said nothing was guaranteed. Options A and B are incorrect because the claim is not for breach of contract. Nothing was guaranteed. Professionals are generally sued in tort (malpractice), not breach of contract. Option D is incorrect. There is no indication of an intentional harmful or offensive contact. The surgeon had the woman's consent to perform the surgery, and nothing indicates that he exceeded that consent.

NEGLIGENCE—PROFESSIONAL—LOCAL OR NATIONAL STANDARD
91. A board-certified neurologist misdiagnosed a patient's neurological condition. The misdiagnosis resulted in delayed treatment and a serious worsening of the patient's condition. The patient consulted a lawyer about a malpractice claim against the neurologist. The lawyer hired another board-certified neurologist expert from a distant city to testify to the standard of care and breach. At trial, defense counsel sought to prove the expert's distant residence to establish that the expert did not know the neurologist's standard of care in the locale where the misdiagnosis occurred. The lawyer objected to the questioning. Which of the following is the most accurate ruling on the objection?

A. Objection overruled because distant experts are less credible.
B. Objection overruled because the local standard is what matters.
C. Objection sustained because the expert may know the local standard.
D. Objection sustained on the basis of a national standard.

Correct answer: D. An expert testifying in a malpractice case may be required to show knowledge of the practice in the same or a similar locale, unless the defendant is a specialist, in which case the standard is likely to be national. Neurology is a specialty certification under a national board examination. There is no local standard. The court should sustain the lawyer's objection and bar the inquiry. Option A is incorrect because defense counsel sought to prove the distant residence to establish that the expert did not know the standard, not that distant experts are less credible. The court should sustain the objection when the evidence is offered for that irrelevant purpose. Option B is incorrect because there is no local standard for specialties under national board certifications. Option C is incorrect because there is no local standard, whether or not the expert knows the local standard is irrelevant, and if it were relevant then the objection should be overruled, not sustained, so that defense counsel could investigate it with the expert.

NEGLIGENCE—PROFESSIONAL—CAUSATION—EXPERT TESTIMONY
92. An earthquake destroyed a building. Investigation showed that when the building was built, an architect had failed to specify structural steel as was the custom. The building was built with ordinary steel. The building owner consulted a lawyer about suing the architect for the building's collapse. What further opinion does the lawyer need from an architect expert to sustain a malpractice action against the architect who failed to specify structural steel?

A. What was the custom with respect to specifying structural steel in these circumstances.
B. What were the architect's qualifications to design a building in these circumstances.
C. Whether quakes were common enough that this building was sure to collapse.
D. What would have happened in the quake if the architect had specified the structural steel.

Correct answer: D. Causation issues in malpractice cases ordinarily require expert testimony as to what would have happened if the professional had complied with the standard of care. The building owner needs support from an expert that the structural steel would have made a difference. Option A is incorrect because the facts already state that specifying structural steel was the custom. Option B is incorrect because whether or not the architect was qualified, the architect must conform practice to the custom of competent professionals in the field. Option C is incorrect because liability does not depend on a building being sure to collapse. Some probability of collapse would be sufficient.

NEGLIGENCE—LAWYER MALPRACTICE—CASE-WITHIN-A-CASE

93. A patient consented to surgery on her right foot. With the patient under a general anesthetic, the surgeon mistakenly performed the surgery on the patient's left foot and then, realizing the mistake, also completed the right-foot surgery. The surgeries benefited both of the patient's feet, although the patient had consented to surgery on only one foot. The patient consulted a lawyer about claims against the surgeon. The lawyer negligently ignored the patient's matter until after the limitations period had expired for the patient's battery claim but not the medical-malpractice claim. Which of the following is the best evaluation of the patient's legal-malpractice claim against the lawyer?

A. Substantial based on the lawyer's reprehensible conduct.
B. Substantial based on the medical-malpractice claim.
C. Nominal based on the battery claim.
D. Non-existent because the lawyer did not hurt the patient.

Correct answer: C. In a legal malpractice case of this kind, the plaintiff must prove causation by showing what would have happened in the underlying case if the defendant had not committed malpractice. The only underlying claim that was barred by the lawyer's negligence in not timely filing was the battery claim. Because the patient's other foot benefited from the surgery, the only damages would be for the affront to the patient's autonomy, which in this instance appears nominal. Option A is incorrect because damages are not based on the reprehensibility of the lawyer's misconduct. They are based on the loss or injury in the underlying action lost because of the lawyer's malpractice. Option B is incorrect because the medical-malpractice claim was not barred. It could still be filed. Option D is incorrect because the lawyer's malpractice prevented the patient from recovering in battery against the surgeon, which would have brought at least nominal damages.

NEGLIGENCE—PROFESSIONAL—INFORMED CONSENT

94. A woman consented to a vein-stripping procedure by a physician. The woman suffered a stroke as a result of the procedure. The woman did not know that stroke is a common risk of vein stripping about which physicians ordinarily advise patients. The woman would not have consented to the procedure if she had known of that risk. The woman consulted a lawyer regarding potential claims against the physician. Which of the following is the best evaluation of the claim?

A. Valid claim for negligently causing a stroke.
B. Valid claim for failure to obtain informed consent.
C. No claim because stroke is a common risk.
D. No claim because the procedure worked.

Correct answer: B. Medical-malpractice cases may be based on the physician's failure to obtain the patient's informed consent. The physician did not advise the woman of stroke risk when physicians ordinarily do so. That failure was a breach of the standard of care. The woman would not have had the procedure had she known, meaning that causation is also satisfied. Option A is incorrect because there is no indication that the stroke was the result of negligence. Rather, it was a common risk of the procedure. Options C and D are incorrect because there is a valid claim. Option C is also incorrect because just because the risk is common does not mean that there is no claim. The physician should have advised of the risk. Option D is also incorrect because the facts do not say that the procedure worked and because whether it worked or not, the woman realized a risk as to which she was not advised when she should have been.

NEGLIGENCE—PROFESSIONAL—BATTERY

95. A diabetic woman saw a physician regarding deep infection and circulation loss in her small toe. The woman consented to the physician's debridement of the deep infection to see if the toe could be saved from amputation. With the woman under general anesthetic, the physician attempted debridement but decided to amputate the toe. The woman was mortified when she discovered the amputation. She retained a lawyer to sue the physician. The lawyer contacted several physicians all of whom declined to testify as liability experts in the matter. Which of the following is the lawyer's best course?

A. File suit without expert testimony on liability.
B. Do not file suit until a liability expert is found.
C. Terminate the representation for lack of a claim.
D. Consult another lawyer who might find an expert.

Correct answer: A. A medical-care provider's failure to obtain any consent at all may be treated as a battery in addition to malpractice. No expert testimony is necessary to establish liability in a battery claim. Option B is incorrect because the woman has a battery claim without expert testimony as to liability. The only claim may be the battery claim, if the standard of care as to advise and perform amputation. Option C is incorrect because there is a battery claim. Option D is incorrect because no expert testimony on liability is required, and none may be available.

NEGLIGENCE—PROFESSIONAL—CONFLICT OF INTEREST

96. A physician sent a patient to a lab for special testing. The physician advised the patient that the testing could worsen the patient's condition but was advisable to diagnose the patient's condition. The patient's condition worsened as a result of the testing. The patient made a demand that the physician compensate the patient for the worsened condition. The physician consulted a lawyer regarding the physician's potential liability to the patient. Which of the following facts, none of which the patient knew at the time of consenting to the testing, would the lawyer most want to know in order to properly advise the physician?

A. That the patient was suffering from another disease that required treatment.
B. That the lab had an average incidence of success and failure with the testing.
C. That the physician owned substantial assets to protect from liability in these cases.
D. That the physician owned the lab to which he had sent the patient for the testing.

Correct answer: D. Medical-care providers must ordinarily disclose conflicts of interest that may affect their judgment and about which the patient would want to know. The physician owned the lab may have influenced the physician's judgment, and the patient may have been entitled to know of the physician's ownership before consenting to the testing. Option A is incorrect because the presence or absence of other treatable diseases does not change the physician's potential liability to the patient for failure to advise regarding this testing. Other diseases are irrelevant. Option B is incorrect because the incidence of the lab's success and failure is of no consequence when the issue is the physician's failure to advise of his ownership. The physician told the patient that the condition might worsen. Option C is incorrect because the amount of assets the physician owned would not alter the lawyer's opinion on the physician's liability to the patient. Liability is unrelated to the wealth of the defendant.

Negligence—Professional—Duty—Standard of Care: A pediatrician treated a child patient's fractured wrist resulting in the fracture's disunion after eight weeks in a soft splint. The patient's parents retained a lawyer to pursue a malpractice claim, but the lawyer did not file one within the statutory limitations period. The lawyer's accountant did not file the lawyer's tax return by the deadline. The accountant's plumber left a drain line uncapped resulting in the flooding of the accountant's basement. Identify the applicable standard of care for each professional. *Model Answer:*

The question requires identifying the applicable standards of care for a pediatrician treating a child's fractured wrist, a lawyer filing a malpractice claim, an accountant filing a tax return, and a plumber installing or inspecting an uncapped drain line.

Professional negligence or malpractice requires proving duty, breach, causation, and damages as in ordinary negligence claims. However, the law treats the professional's standard of care differently from the standard of care in ordinary negligence cases. The claimant must prove the custom or practice within the professional's field, that is, to establish what competent practitioners in the professional's field would do or not do under the same circumstances. Juries are generally not competent to determine reasonable care for a professional because they lack the professional's training, skill, and experience. So other professionals serving as expert witnesses must in the usual professional-negligence case establish the standard of care based on customary practice within the same field.

Here, the pediatrician was treating a child's fractured wrist using a soft splint to bad result that the fracture remained in disunion. While expert consult would be necessary to establish what the pediatrician should have done or not done, the standard of care may well have been to apply that manner of fixation, such as hard cast, that competent pediatricians would use in customary practice for fixing a child's fracture to allow for bone knitting and solid healing within 8 to 12 weeks. The lawyer reviewing that malpractice claim would have a standard of care that competent lawyers would establish through customary practice, likely to calculate, calendar, notice, and file complaint due dates so as to comply with applicable limitations periods. The accountant filing the lawyer's tax return would have a standard of care that competent accountants would establish through customary practice, likely to calculate, calendar, notice, and file tax return due dates so as to comply with those dates rather than file late. The plumber installing or inspecting the uncapped drain line would have a standard of care that competent plumbers would establish through customary practice, likely to install, inspect, complete, or repair drain lines with caps, traps, or back-flow devices so as to prevent flooding through an uncapped drain line.

In conclusion, while each of these professional standards of care requires expert consult and testimony, one can draw the above preliminary inferences as to these specific medical, legal, accounting, and plumbing standards of care so as to further investigate through expert consult.

Negligence—Professional—Informed Consent: An orthopedist recorded in medical records that she consulted with a patient about the risks and benefits of soft splinting of the patient's fractured wrist. The patient will testify that the orthopedist said only that soft splinting was the recommended treatment and that there were no other viable alternatives. Apply the principles of informed consent to determine whether, or under what circumstances, the patient would have a malpractice claim for failure to obtain informed consent. *Model Answer:*

The question requires applying informed-consent principles to determine the circumstances, if any, under which the patient would have a malpractice claim against an orthopedist saying that a soft splint was the only recommended and viable treatment for wrist fracture.

Failure to gain informed consent is a special type of professional negligence or malpractice claim. Ordinarily, a physician is not liable when the patient suffers a known risk of treatment and the physician has otherwise conformed the treatment to the standard of care. Not every medical procedure works. The mere fact that a procedure does not work does not mean that the physician has committed malpractice. However, physicians owe patients the duty to inform the patient of treatment options and foreseeable treatment risks about which the reasonable patient would want to know, so that the patient can make an informed decision whether to proceed with the treatment, select other treatment options, or forgo treatment. When the physician fails to do so, the patient can show that the patient if informed would have pursued alternative treatment or no treatment, and the patient suffers the treatment risk as a result, then the patient has a failure-of-informed-consent claim.

Here, the patient will testify that the orthopedist said only that soft split was a viable and recommended treatment, even though the orthopedist recorded advising the patient about risks and benefits. If the patient's testimony is credible and the jury believes it, which may be doubtful in light of the medical records to the contrary, then the patient would have a failure-of-informed-consent claim if the patient's expert medical witness can establish that the patient had viable and recommended alternative treatments to soft splint, for example, hard cast, internal fixation, or no treatment (self-restriction). The patient would further have to show that the reasonable patient would want to know of those alternatives *and* that the patient would have selected one of those alternatives if so informed.

In conclusion, the patient would have a difficult informed-consent claim given the contrary medical records, and only if the patient can establish alternative treatments through expert testimony that the reasonable patient would want to know and this patient would have accepted. The case does not sound like the easiest or best case.

WEEK 12

NEGLIGENCE—PREMISES LIABILITY—CLASSIFICATIONS
97. A man asked a store clerk if the farm-supply store the man was visiting had a public restroom. The store clerk showed the man to an employee area, saying that he was welcome to use the restroom there. The man cut himself badly on a broken piece of metal corner-beading when he tripped over a cat sleeping in the darkened employee area on the way to the restroom, and reached to catch himself. The man consulted a lawyer regarding whether he had a claim against the store for his injury. What additional evidence would most help the man in his claim, in a jurisdiction following traditional premises-liability rules?

A. The store clerk was unaware that the cat was sleeping in the darkened backroom.
B. The restroom was ordinarily reserved only for employees, not customers.
C. The man had been inspecting riding mowers at the store for a possible purchase.
D. The man had been waiting to find a restroom since he left home an hour earlier.

Correct answer: C. Premises-liability claims in most states require classifying the plaintiff as an invitee, licensee, or trespasser. Landowners owe the highest duty to invitees, who are on the premises for the owner's pecuniary benefit. If the man was inspecting a mower for possible purchase, then he was an invitee whom the landowner would owe a higher duty. Option A is incorrect because it adds nothing to the liability of the store. It would make the store less responsible rather than more so. Option B is incorrect because it is probably irrelevant in this instance. The store clerk allowed the man to use the restroom, so the fact that it was ordinarily off limits to customers probably makes no difference. Option D is incorrect because it would make the man only a licensee there for his own personal benefit.

NEGLIGENCE—PREMISES LIABILITY—RECREATIONAL USES
98. A hunter using lands with the owner's permission found an old tree stand. The hunter climbed into the tree stand to hunt. The tree stand broke, seriously injuring the hunter in a fall. The hunter sued the landowner for his injury. The landowner's insurer assigned the case to defense counsel, who undertook to research affirmative defenses. Which of the following should defense counsel research?

A. Whether tree stands are reasonably safe for hunting.
B. Whether hunters are ordinarily reasonably prudent.
C. Whether there is a rescue-doctrine in the jurisdiction.
D. Whether there is a recreational-use statute in the jurisdiction.

Correct answer: D. Most states have recreational-use statutes that grant landowners limited immunity from negligence claims by individuals using the land for recreational purposes. Under the statute, the landowner may owe the hunter only a duty not to commit gross negligence or some other, higher duty, barring the claim. Option A is incorrect because the research would not lead to a legal defense pled as an affirmative defense. Option B is incorrect because it is a non-sequitur and would not establish a legal defense pled as an affirmative defense. Option C is incorrect because the claim would not have to do with the landowner causing the need for rescue, which is the nature of the rescue doctrine. The rescue doctrine does not apply to this case.

NEGLIGENCE—PREMISES LIABILITY—LESSOR LIABILITY

99. A company leased land from its owner to operate a gas station. The company installed gasoline pumps and operated the station for half of the 30-year lease. A gasoline pump exploded, seriously injuring several customers at the station. Investigation established that the pump exploded due to poor maintenance. After the company went bankrupt, a customer who was injured in the explosion sued the landowner. The landowner's lawyer moved to dismiss the case. How should the court rule?

A. Grant the motion based on no causation.
B. Grant the motion based on no duty.
C. Grant the motion based on no jurisdiction.
D. Deny the motion.

Correct answer: B. The one who controls the land (generally meaning the tenant, not landlord) owes the tort-based duties with respect to its reasonable safety. On the given facts, the landowner would owe no duty, the company having installed and operated the pumps for 15 years. Option A is incorrect. The duty analysis would precede any causation analysis and dispose of the case. Causation arguments tend to assume duty and breach, of which there is no evidence here. Option C is incorrect because the facts implicate no jurisdiction issue. Landowners are generally subject to jurisdiction in a court of the state where the land is located.

NEGLIGENCE—PREMISES LIABILITY—INVITEES—DUTY

100. A crowd gathered outside of a store early in the morning on Black Friday, the day after Thanksgiving, the busiest shopping day of the year. When the store opened at 9 a.m., a man rushed in to be the first shopper to purchase sale merchandise. An employee had left an extension cord on the floor from last-minute vacuuming. In the crush of shoppers, the man tripped over the extension cord and injured himself. Which of the following allegations best describes how the man's lawyer should plead his negligence action in a jurisdiction following the traditional premises-liability classifications?

A. The store breached its duty, owed an invitee, of reasonable care.
B. The store breached its duty, owed a licensee, to cure hidden defects.
C. The store breached its duty, owed a licensee, to warn of hidden defects.
D. The store breached its duty, owed anyone, to warn of known hidden danger.

Correct answer: A. Invitees, who enter another's premises with permission for pecuniary purposes or accompany another who does so, are owed duties of reasonable care. The man was a shopper whom the store owed a duty of reasonable care as an invitee. Option B is incorrect because the man was an invitee, not a licensee, and the duty to a licensee is to warn of known hidden dangers, not to cure them. Option C is incorrect because the man was an invitee, not a licensee, and the invitee duty is higher and more applicable to this condition, which was not a hidden defect. Option D is incorrect because the man was owed a higher duty as an invitee, and landowners do not owe a duty to anyone to warn of hidden dangers. Trespassers are owed no duty.

NEGLIGENCE—PREMISES LIABILITY—CHANGING STATUS

101. A farmer looked over used farm equipment on a sales lot. The farmer inspected a combine he thought he might purchase. The farmer knew from signs and prior conversations with sales agents that the sales lot's strict policy was that customers should stay out of equipment unless accompanied and authorized by a sales agent. The farmer nonetheless climbed into the combine to inspect the cab. Climbing out of the combine, the farmer fell and injured himself due to the combine's broken handrail. The farmer sued the sales lot for his injury. The sales lot's insurance company assigned the defense to a lawyer for answer. The lawyer's research disclosed that the jurisdiction would treat the farmer under the traditional classifications for premises liability. Which of the following best describes how the lawyer should treat the farmer's status at the moment of his injury, in the sales lot's answer?

A. As a customer owed a duty of reasonable care.
B. As an invitee owed a duty of reasonable care.
C. As a licensee owed a duty to warn of known hidden dangers.
D. As a trespasser owed no duty.

Correct answer: D. A person's status can change from invitee to licensee to trespasser, depending on their activities and purpose, and scope of permission. The farmer was violating the sales lot's policy at the moment of his injury and was a trespasser owed no duty. Option A is incorrect because traditional jurisdictions require classifying the plaintiff as invitee, licensee, or trespasser. Option B is incorrect because the farmer was no longer an invitee once he entered the combine without permission. Option C is incorrect because the farmer was not a social guest but a customer who was violating the scope of permission to be on the premises, once he entered the combine against the signs and policy.

NEGLIGENCE—PREMISES LIABILITY—INVITEE—STANDARD OF CARE
102. A customer approached the entrance to a store during a light rain in cold weather. The customer slipped and fell on a thick layer of ice that had formed in front of the store's entrance as rain ran off the roof onto the concrete at the store entrance. The customer was seriously enough injured in the fall that she required hospitalization. The customer retained a lawyer to sue to get the store's insurer to pay for her medical bills. Which of the following best describes the standard of care the lawyer should allege in the complaint?

A. The store owed the customer the duty to reasonably inspect the premises so as to warn the customer against weather conditions.
B. The store owed the customer the duty to reasonably design and construct the premises so that rain did not freeze from run-off.
C. The store owed the customer the duty to reasonably design, construct, inspect, and maintain the premises, and to reasonably warn and protect the customer.
D. The store owed the customer the duty to keep all rain, ice, and snow off of the store entrance under any weather conditions.

Correct answer: C. The duty of reasonable care that a landowner owes an invitee may include the duty to design, construct, maintain, repair, warn, and protect against unreasonably dangerous conditions on the premises. Option A is incorrect as too limited an allegation of duty. The allegation should include aspects of the store's design and construction, and the need to maintain the premises in a reasonably safe condition. Option B is incorrect as too limited an allegation of duty. The allegation should include aspects of inspecting, warning, and protecting, such as by salting and sanding while placing warning cones or signs if necessary. Option D is incorrect as too broad an allegation of the standard of care, not limited by reasonableness.

NEGLIGENCE—PREMISES LIABILITY—DUTY TO PROTECT AGAINST CRIME
103. A casino advertised lighted, secure parking. The secure parking was so limited that on any given night most customers had to use a dark and unguarded back lot. A casino customer parked her vehicle in the dark and unguarded back lot because the lighted lot was full one late night. On her way in to the casino, the customer was robbed and assaulted in the darkness of the lot. The customer sued the casino. The casino's lawyer moved to dismiss the case based on no duty. How should the court rule?

A. Grant the motion based on the event happening outside of the casino.
B. Grant the motion based on no duty to protect against criminal acts.
C. Deny the motion based on the money the casino would make from the customer.
D. Deny the motion based on the advertised and assumed duty.

Correct answer: D. Landowners may have limited duties to protect against the criminal acts of others on the premises, based on the landowner's assuming or advertising a duty, special relationship, or special knowledge. The casino advertised lighted, secure parking, meaning that it may have assumed a duty to provide it to most customers including the woman. Option A is incorrect because even though it happened outside, it still happened on the casino's premises, in its parking lot. Option B is incorrect because although there may ordinarily be no such duty, when the casino advertised lighted, secure parking, it probably assumed a duty at least in that respect. Option C is incorrect because the money the casino expected to make would have made the customer an invitee, but invitees are owed reasonable care, not necessarily the duty to prevent crime. You need the advertising and assuming of a duty.

NEGLIGENCE—PREMISES LIABILITY—LICENSEE—DUTY
104. A young woman loved visiting with her neighbor while her neighbor worked in her garden. On one of those occasions, the young woman broke her ankle when a loose walkway plank in her neighbor's garden suddenly twisted. The neighbor knew, but the young woman did not know, that the plank was loose. The young woman asked a lawyer to contact the neighbor's homeowner's insurer regarding liability for the young woman's medical expense and wage loss due to her ankle injury. Which of the following best describes how the lawyer should state the neighbor's duty to the young woman, in a jurisdiction that follows the traditional premises-liability classifications?

A. The neighbor owed the young woman the duty to warn of known hidden dangers creating unreasonable risk of harm.
B. The neighbor owed the young woman a duty of reasonable care to keep the premises in reasonably safe condition.
C. The neighbor owed the young woman a duty to make sure that planks in the walkway were safe on which to walk.
D. The neighbor owed the young woman a duty not to allow her to come over and talk if the young woman was going to get hurt.

Correct answer: A. Licensees, who enter another's premises with permission but for their own non-pecuniary purposes, are owed a duty to warn of known hidden dangers creating unreasonable risk of harm. The young woman was a licensee on her neighbor's premises with her neighbor's permission but not for pecuniary purposes. Option B is incorrect because the young woman was not an invitee, and only invitees are owed a duty of reasonable care in traditional-classification jurisdictions. Option C is incorrect because it states the duty owed a licensee too broadly. The neighbor would first have to know of the hidden danger. There is no duty to guarantee safe planks. Option D is incorrect because it does not describe a legal duty but a conclusion. There is no duty to foresee and prevent all injury.

NEGLIGENCE—PREMISES LIABILITY—TRESPASSERS
105. Several boys dug small caves at the base of a cliff cut into the wall of an unused portion of a gravel pit. Workers from another part of the gravel pit occasionally chased the boys out of their caves, but the boys would return after a few days. The boys never realized that the cliff under which they were digging could come down at any moment. A portion of the cliff collapsed, killing one of the boys. The boy's parents made a demand on the owner of the gravel pit, who consulted a lawyer regarding liability. Which of the following best describes the duty the gravel pit owner owed the boys?

A. No duty because the boys were trespassers and the workers chased them off.
B. No duty because a cliff is a natural condition and who knew it would fall?
C. A duty with respect to concealed artificial conditions and discovered peril.
D. A duty with respect to dangerous instrumentalities under the owner's control.

Correct answer: C. Trespassers are generally owed no duty, except perhaps as to active operations, tolerated intruders, concealed artificial conditions, and discovered peril. The cliff was artificial and the cave-in probability known to the pit workers, such that a duty was owed as to concealed artificial conditions and discovered peril. Option A is incorrect because although the workers occasionally chased the boys off, the workers knew that the boys were returning and digging at the base of the cliff. Option B is incorrect because the cliff was not natural but artificial dug in the gravel pit, and the workers probably did know that cliffs fall. Option D is incorrect because the cliff would not have been an instrumentality in the nature of an operating piece of equipment to which this doctrine usually applies.

NEGLIGENCE—PREMISES LIABILITY—ATTRACTIVE NUISANCES
106. An exclusive development constructed a shallow pond to advertise as a lake. The development constructed a dock in the pond to make the lake look more authentic. Late one night some visiting young boys snuck out to dive into the pond from the dock. The first boy to attempt the dive injured his neck in the shallow water. His parents sued the development, whose lawyer moved to dismiss the action. Which of the following best describes the court's most likely ruling on the motion?

A. Grant the motion on the obviousness of the risk to boys on escapades like this one.
B. Grant the motion on foreseeability, tender years, and attractive nuisance.
C. Deny the motion on the exclusive nature of the development and affordability.
D. Deny the motion on foreseeability, tender years, and attractive nuisance.

Correct answer: D. Landowners traditionally owed children of tender years a duty to protect against an attractive nuisance, but the modern formulation looks to the landowner's knowledge of the risk and the child's inability to recognize the danger. The development may have owed a duty to protect children of tender years a duty to protect against unreasonable dangers about which the development knew but the child would not recognize. Option A is incorrect because the risk was likely not obvious to the boys, or they would not have been attempting to dive. Option B is incorrect because each of those rules and doctrines argue for denying, not granting, the motion. Option C is incorrect because the development's exclusive nature and its ability to afford liability are not factors in establishing duty.

NEGLIGENCE—PREMISES LIABILITY—OUTSIDE THE LAND
107. The owner of a residence planted an ornamental tree to hide a stop sign from the view from his living-room window. The branches of the ornamental tree gradually grew to hide the stop sign from motorists using the lane on which the residence was located. A motorist touring the lane ran the stop sign because it was hidden by the tree. A collision ensued in which another person was injured. That person sued the motorist, who retained a lawyer to answer and defend. The lawyer asked her law clerk to draft a research memorandum on whether the motorist should third-party in the owner of the residence. What should the memorandum conclude?

A. Yes because landowners usually have liability insurance that should cover a portion of the losses due to the motorist's own negligence.
B. Yes because landowners may owe limited duties to protect passersby from artificial conditions on the premises creating unreasonable dangers.
C. No because landowners owe duties only with respect to conditions on their own premises that injure individuals on their own premises.
D. No because landowners have nothing to do with the safety of motorists driving by the lands and accidents that they may cause.

Correct answer: B. Landowners may owe limited duties to protect neighboring landowners and passersby from artificial or unreasonable dangers on the premises. The owner of the residence planted the tree that hid the stop sign, creating an unreasonable danger. Option A is incorrect because the existence of liability insurance is not a basis on which to allege the liability of a landowner. The landowner would have a duty or not have a duty independent of the question of insurance. Option C is incorrect because although landowners usually face liability for injuries on the premises, there would also be a duty to passersby from artificial conditions creating unreasonable risks. Option D is incorrect because there can be circumstances, like here, where landowners owe duties to passing motorists.

Premises Liability—Classifications: A local pizzeria paid a boy to tuck pizza-delivery advertisements in the doors of units at an apartment complex, where a sign at the entrance to the complex said "no advertising or soliciting." The boy tripped and fell on a loose piece of carpet the apartments had installed and maintained on one of its stairways. The following week after the boy's injury, an apartment tenant was injured tripping and falling on the same piece of loose carpet. The following week, an apartment guest was injured tripping and falling on the same piece of loose carpet. Classify the boy, tenant, and guest for purposes of their premises-liability claims against the apartment, applying the standard of care for each to determine whether they would prevail, consistent with this chapter. *Model Answer:*

The question requires classifying a boy tucking advertising in apartment doors, apartment tenant, and apartment guest, each of whom suffered injury tripping and falling over a loose piece of apartment-stairway carpet, and each maintaining premises-liability claims against the apartment.

Premises liability is a special form of negligence action. In most jurisdictions, the standard of care requires classifying the plaintiff as invitee, licensee, or trespasser. Some jurisdictions follow a general reasonable-care rule without regard to status, but the question asks for classifications, directing the answer to the traditional form of premises liability. An invitee or business visitor is one who is on the premises for the financial benefit of the premises owner or controller. The classic invitee would be a paying customer at a retail business. A licensee is one who is on the premises for his or her own benefit without financial or business interest of the premises owner or controller. The classic licensee is a social guest. A trespasser is one who does not have permission to be on the premises and has made an unauthorized entry. The owner or controller of the premises owes invitees a duty of reasonable care as in the usual negligence case. The owner or controller owes a licensee only the duty to warn of dangers hidden from the licensee but known to the owner or controller. The owner or controller generally does not owe a duty to a trespasser except as to active operations, dangerous instrumentalities, discovered peril, and tolerated intruders.

In these three cases, the boy is likely a trespasser, the tenant an invitee, and the guest a licensee. The boy was on the premises contrary to the no-advertising-or-solicitation sign. The apartment probably had no financial or business interest in pizza delivery, although query whether the apartment gains indirectly in delivery services to tenants and may also have tolerated pizza delivery and advertisements for pizza delivery. The boy would have no claim if a pure trespasser and might have only a difficult claim if a tolerated intruder especially given that the boy was the first of the three plaintiffs to fall. The apartment might not have had prior notice of the loose carpet as a trip hazard, which is a point for investigation. The tenant though would have a reasonably strong claim. The tenant would have been the apartment's invitee given that the tenant was presumably paying rent for the tenancy, a business interest of the apartment. The apartment would have owed the tenant reasonable care and may well have breached the standard of care to construct, maintain, and inspect the premises reasonably so as to avoid trip hazards. The apartment may have had prior notice or constructive notice from the boy's prior trip (another point to investigate). The apartment would then have breach its duty of reasonable care owed to the tenant, causing the tenant's trip injury. The guest may also have a claim. The guest would clearly have been a licensee, on the premises for the guest's own benefit as a classic licensee, with no financial or business benefit to the apartment. Yet the apartment would still have owed the duty to warn the guest of known hidden dangers. Depending on investigation, the apartment may by then have known of the loose-carpet trip hazard from the prior trips of the boy and tenant. The loose carpet was apparently a hidden danger because all three plaintiffs tripped over it and fell to their injury within a reasonably short period.

In sum, the boy likely has no claim because of his probable status as a trespasser, while the tenant probably has a claim as an invitee owed a duty of reasonable care, and the guest may also have a claim as a licensee owed a duty to warn of known hidden dangers. I would take the tenant and guest claims, not the boy's claim.

WEEK 13

NEGLIGENCE—DEFENSES—CONTRIBUTORY NEGLIGENCE

108. A motor-vehicle collision occurred at an intersection where one driver faced a stop sign and the other driver had a through route. The accident report showed that although the first driver had not stopped at the stop sign, the second driver had been speeding, contributing to the cause of the accident. The first driver, who was injured, consulted a lawyer regarding making a claim against the second driver based on the second driver's speeding. Which of the following is the best evaluation of the first driver's claim, in a contributory-negligence jurisdiction?

A. Valid claim because the second driver's speeding contributed to the accident.
B. Valid claim because the accident report is the best evidence of what happened.
C. No claim because the second driver's speeding probably had nothing to do with it.
D. No claim because barred by the first driver's running the stop sign.

Correct answer: D. The traditional contributory-negligence defense bars a plaintiff's negligence claim if the plaintiff was at fault in part in the plaintiff's own harm, unless the defendant acted wantonly. The first driver's running the stop sign was contributory negligence that would bar the first driver's claim against the second driver even though the second driver was also negligent. Option A is incorrect because of the contributory-negligence defense that the second driver would have to the first driver's claim. Option B is incorrect because the accident report, although some evidence, is not necessarily the best evidence, and because the claim would be barred by the contributory-negligence defense. Option C is incorrect because the accident report indicates otherwise, that the speeding contributed to the accident. Speeding could have made it harder to slow, brake, evade, and yield.

NEGLIGENCE—DEFENSES—COMPARATIVE NEGLIGENCE
109. A daycare worker left her purse with her wallet, cell phone, photographs, and other valuables inside a storage unit while she worked. A custodian from another company using the same storage unit left the storage unit's door wide open. In a rush to get other things done, the daycare worker did not notice the children go inside the storage unit. The children got water and paint all over the daycare worker's purse, destroying its contents. The daycare worker consulted a lawyer regarding possible claims to recover the value of the purse and its contents. In a comparative-negligence jurisdiction, which of the following best evaluates the daycare worker's negligence claim against the custodian?

A. The worker has a claim against the custodian, the value of which will be reduced by the percentage of the worker's own negligence.
B. The worker has a claim against the custodian, the value of which will be reduced by the percentage of the custodian's negligence.
C. The worker has no claim against the custodian because the worker's comparative negligence will bar her claim.
D. The worker has no claim against the custodian because the custodian's negligence depended on the worker's negligence.

Correct answer: A. Comparative negligence does not bar a plaintiff's action but reduces the plaintiff's claim by the percentage of plaintiff's fault compared to defendant's fault or wanton misconduct. The worker was comparatively negligent in letting the children go unattended and play in the storage unit in her rush, while the custodian was negligent in leaving the storage-unit door open. The negligence of one would be compared to the negligence of the other, and the worker's claim reduced by her own percentage negligence. Option B is incorrect because comparative negligence reduces the award by the plaintiff's, not the defendant's, negligence. Option C is incorrect because comparative negligence does not bar, but only reduces, a claim. Option D is incorrect because the negligence of two or more actors can combine to cause harm, and both will be liable (or, in this case, the negligence of the plaintiff will reduce the recovery by comparative-negligence rules).

NEGLIGENCE—DEFENSES—COMPARATIVE NEGLIGENCE—STATUTES

110. A retired professor drove his vehicle to the corner store every evening to purchase a soda pop. The professor had grown into the habit of not wearing his seatbelt for the little jaunt to the corner store. On one of those occasions, a driver ran a stop sign, causing the professor to drive into the side of the driver's vehicle. Unrestrained by any seatbelt, the professor was thrown into the windshield by the collision, resulting in seriously disabling head injuries. The professor consulted a lawyer regarding a negligence action against the other driver. Which of the following should the lawyer know before advising the driver?

A. Whether the other driver was licensed to drive, what his driving record was, and whether his driving record included running stop signs.
B. Whether the vehicle the other driver was driving was registered, and whether the professor's vehicle was in good repair.
C. Whether the professor really needed a soda pop each evening, or whether he would have been better off without it for his health.
D. Whether there is a statute limiting fault for not wearing a seatbelt, whether the state has a no-fault act, and if so, what are its terms.

Correct answer: D. Statutes may further alter comparative negligence rules, such as by limiting the plaintiff's failure to wear a seatbelt to 5% comparative negligence. No-fault acts of various forms in 12 states may also limit liability actions to certain circumstances. Both might affect the outcome here. Option A is incorrect because running a stop sign is negligence whether or not one has a license and has a record of previously running stop signs. Option B is incorrect because the registration or non-registration of the other vehicle would not affect liability, and neither would whether the professor's vehicle was in good repair, except for its brakes, but there is no indication of brake failure affecting the collision. Option C is incorrect as a matter of personal option unrelated to liability.

NEGLIGENCE—DEFENSES—COMPARATIVE NEGLIGENCE—OTHER REFORM

111. A landowner hired a contractor to add on to the landowner's house. The landowner agreed to keep the worksite clean so as to lower the construction costs. A sub-contractor was seriously injured falling into a debris pile filled with old boards with nails. The sub-contractor sued the landowner. The landowner was adamant that the contractor should reimburse the landowner for what he had to pay the claimant because the contractor was more to blame. Which of the following courses should the landowner's lawyer pursue to give the landowner the greatest opportunity for the contractor to share in the liability, in a comparative-negligence jurisdiction?

A. Settle with the sub-contractor and seek contribution from the contractor.
B. Bring the contractor in as a third-party, seeking allocation of fault.
C. Allege the sub-contractor's comparative negligence as an affirmative defense.
D. Contact the contractor's liability insurer seeking coverage for the landowner.

Correct answer: B. States adopting comparative negligence may abolish the last-clear-chance doctrine, joint-and-several liability, defendants' rights of contribution, and related doctrines. The landowner should third-party in the contractor seeking allocation of fault. Option A is incorrect because contribution rights may require joining the non-party in the action, or may be abolished in favor of allocation of fault to parties and non-parties, or may require that the landowner prove that he tried to get the contractor to participate in the settlement and that the settlement was in good faith. Option C is incorrect because, although possibly an appropriate action depending on more facts, it would not increase the landowner's opportunity to get the contractor to share in the liability. Option D is incorrect because the contractor's liability insurer would insure the contractor, not the landowner. Coverage demands are not a way of allocating fault to another party.

NEGLIGENCE—DEFENSES—ALLOCATION OF FAULT TO NON-PARTIES

112. A vehicle without brake lights stopped suddenly on the road for no apparent reason. A following vehicle that was speeding swerved to avoid the first vehicle, causing the following vehicle to roll over. A passenger in the following vehicle was seriously injured. The first vehicle left the scene of the accident. The passenger sued the young man who was the driver of the following vehicle. No one was able to determine who the other driver had been, leaving the young man the only defendant in the passenger's case. The young man's motor-vehicle insurer assigned the case to a lawyer. Which of the following should the lawyer know before pleading the young man's defense, in a comparative negligence jurisdiction?

A. Whether the state's law allows comparative negligence against passengers.
B. Whether the state's law allows allocation of fault to unidentified third parties.
C. Whether the state's law includes a statute requiring operating brake lights.
D. Whether the state's law prohibits drivers from leaving the scene of an accident.

Correct answer: B. Some states allow the factfinder to allocate fault to non-parties, reducing the plaintiff's damages accordingly. The state's law may allow allocation of fault to unidentified third parties, which could significantly reduce the young man's liability to the passenger. Option A is incorrect because there is no indication of the passenger's comparative negligence and the facts already state that it is a comparative-negligence jurisdiction. Option C is incorrect because whether there was a statute or not, the fleeing vehicle should have had brake lights, and it would not matter if the driver could not be identified and the jurisdiction did not allow non-party fault, as Option B sought to determine. Option D is incorrect because a leaving-the-scene statute would not make the young man's liability to the passenger any lesser or greater.

NEGLIGENCE—DEFENSES—ASSUMPTION OF RISK

113. A woman had wanted to shoot the rapids on a river since she was a little child. She was pleased to learn that some young men had started a company that offered rides down the rapids. The woman did not hesitate to hire the company for a ride down the rapids, even though she had seen many rafts flip on the rapids. The woman was injured when her raft flipped. She sued the company. The company's liability insurer assigned defense counsel. What affirmative defense should defense counsel plead?

A. Implied assumption of risk.
B. Express assumption of risk.
C. Contributory negligence.
D. Comparative negligence.

Correct answer: A. The assumption-of-risk defense bars plaintiff's negligence claim if plaintiff voluntarily encountered and accepted the hazards of a known risk. Assumption of risk was implied here from the woman's having observed many rafts flip. Option B is incorrect because there is no indication of the woman having expressed her acceptance of the risk by, for instance, signing a liability waiver. Options C and D are incorrect because there is no indication of the woman's contributory or comparative negligence or of which of those defenses would apply in this jurisdiction.

NEGLIGENCE—DEFENSES—ASSUMPTION OF RISK—EXPRESS

114. A young woman decided to have elective cosmetic surgery under general anesthetic. Just before the surgery, the anesthetist asked the young woman to sign a consent form. The consent form surprised the young woman as she read that the risks of the elective surgery included stroke and even death. The woman suffered a mild stroke during the surgery. She sued the anesthetist, whose malpractice insurer assigned defense counsel to the case. What affirmative defense should defense counsel plead?

A. Contributory or comparative negligence.
B. Failure to mitigate damages.
C. Express assumption of risk.

D. Implied assumption of risk.

Correct answer: C. Express assumption of risk involves the plaintiff's express agreement, usually by words or writings, to accept a disclosed risk. The young woman signed a consent form that expressly disclosed the stroke risk. Option A is incorrect because there is no indication of the woman's fault contributing to the stroke. Option B is incorrect because there is no indication of the young woman's failure to mitigate her damages. Option D is incorrect because the assumption of risk was expressed, not implied. Given the woman's surprise at the form, there is no indication outside of the consent form that the woman otherwise voluntarily encountered a known risk.

NEGLIGENCE—DEFENSES—ASSUMPTION OF RISK—IMPLIED
115. A leadership camp created a timed obstacle course for voluntary participants. A competitor was confident that he could complete the obstacle course, even though he had seen all of his associates fall from its rope-swing element. The competitor fell from the rope-swing element, injuring himself. The competitor sued the camp, alleging that the rope-swing element was negligently designed to guarantee failure and falls. The camp retained a lawyer to defend the action. Which of the following is the best way to end the action?

A. Move to dismiss based on implied assumption of risk.
B. Move to dismiss based on express assumption of risk.
C. Move to dismiss based on contributory or comparative negligence.
D. Allege each of the above defenses for resolution at trial.

Correct answer: A. Assumption of risk may also be implied from circumstances showing the plaintiff's voluntary acceptance of a known risk. The competitor saw all other competitors swing and fall. He voluntarily encountered a known risk. Option B is incorrect because there is no indication that the camp expressly disclosed the risk in a way that the competitor expressly accepted. Implied assumption of risk is the better defense. Option C is incorrect because there is no indication of contributory or comparative negligence, which would likely be a jury question, not a question of law for the court to decide on motion, if there was some such evidence. Option D is incorrect because there is no evidence at present for Options B and C, and allowing the case to go to trial would take more time and expense than testing the claim by motion to dismiss.

Negligence—Defenses—Comparative Negligence: A hunter stepped outside his cabin with his rifle to walk down a lane for a few minutes in the plain clothes he happened to be wearing. Another hunter on an overlooking ridge, who had just seen two does walk down the lane, was sure that a buck would follow. He fired at and hit what he thought was a good-sized buck but turned out to be the other hunter. Evaluate the effect of each hunter's negligence under the doctrines of contributory and comparative negligence. *Model Answer:*

The case requires evaluating the effect of the negligence of two hunters, one of whom wore plain clothes and the other of whom shot that hunter, under the doctrines of contributory and comparative negligence.

The several negligence defenses begin with contributory or comparative negligence, which involve consideration of the plaintiff's own fault. Just as defendant wrongdoers owe duties of reasonable care to the plaintiffs whom they injure, plaintiffs owe themselves duties of reasonable care for their own safety. When a plaintiff sues a defendant in negligence claiming the defendant's lack of reasonable care, the defendant may defend using the doctrine of either contributory or comparative negligence if the plaintiff failed to use reasonable care for the plaintiff's own safety. Contributory negligence, surviving in only four states, bars a plaintiff's claim if the plaintiff exhibited any degree of negligence, however large or small. Comparative negligence, the favored modern doctrine, allocates percentage fault between the plaintiff and any defendants so that the judge can apportion damages accordingly, with adjustments peculiar to each state's law. Contributory or comparative negligence is an affirmative defense that the defendant must plead and has the burden to prove.

In this case, the plain-clothes hunter would be bringing a negligence claim against the shooting hunter. The shooting hunter certainly owed the plain-clothes hunter a duty of reasonable care and breached that duty in failing reasonably to identify the other hunter so as to avoid shooting him. However, the shooting hunter would maintain a defense of contributory or comparative negligence against the plain-clothes hunter who likely exhibited some lack of care for his own safety when leaving the cabin with a rifle presumably to hunt while not wearing bright-orange or other distinguishing clothing. Hunting safety probably requires such bright clothing, depending on the customs and practices of the area. If the jurisdiction applies the doctrine of contributory negligence, then that lack of care, however large or small, would bar the plain-clothes hunter's negligence claim. If the jurisdiction applies the comparative-negligence doctrine, then the factfinder would fix the percentage of the plain-clothes hunter's negligence against the percentage of the shooting hunter's negligence. Probably, wearing plain clothes while walking down one's lane outside one's cabin exhibits only a small degree of lack of care compared to shooting a person walking down the person's own lane, which exhibits a large or even extraordinary degree of lack of care. I would estimate the shooter's negligence to be 90% and the plain-clothes hunter's negligence to be 10%, but reasonable jurors could certainly assign other percentages.

In sum, the plain-clothes hunter's failure to wear orange clothing while walking down his lane with a gun presumably hunting probably exhibits a small degree of contributory negligence, which would bar his claim, or comparative negligence, which would reduce his claim, depending on the law of the jurisdiction, while the shooting hunter would bear the brunt of the negligence in a comparative-negligence jurisdiction.

Negligence—Defenses—Assumption of the Risk: An outdoor-recreation enthusiast insisted on renting a canoe despite warnings that the river was running high from snowmelt and spring rains. The rental agreement stated the risks of canoeing. At the first bend in the river, the enthusiast broke an old paddle in the swift current, leaving the enthusiast helpless to prevent the canoe's swamping. Witnesses were unable to save the enthusiast from drowning. Discuss and evaluate the effect of the assumption-of-risk defense on the wrongful death claim of the enthusiast's estate against the canoe-rental company. *Model Answer:*

The question requires discussing and evaluating the effect of an assumption-of-risk defense in a wrongful-death claim after a canoeing enthusiast insisted on taking out a canoe on a snowmelt-swollen river despite specific warnings and a rental agreement stating the risks of canoeing.

Assumption of risk is one of several available negligence defenses in most jurisdictions, although some jurisdictions have discouraged or abandoned the defense when adopting comparative negligence as a defense. Assuming that the defense remains available in this jurisdiction, assumption of risk involves voluntarily encountering a known risk. Assumption of risk can be either express or implied, or in some cases both. Express assumption involves written or verbal communication and acknowledgment of the known and accepted risk, while implied assumption involves circumstances demonstrating that the plaintiff knew of the risk and yet voluntarily accepted and encountered it. Assumption of risk is an affirmative defense that the defendant must plead and has the burden to prove.

Here, the estate of the canoeing enthusiast pursues what must be a negligence claim against the canoe-rental company, in which the company asserts an assumption-of-risk defense. Assumption of risk presents a strong but not necessarily complete defense for the company. The facts indicate that the enthusiast had warnings that the river was running high from snowmelt and rains. The fact that the enthusiast nonetheless insisted on renting a canoe would imply assumption of the risk from snow-and-rain-swollen fast waters. The facts also state that the rental agreement stated the risks of canoeing, suggesting express assumption of risk, particularly if the enthusiast signed the agreement in a way that confirmed express acknowledgment and assumption, which is a point to investigate. However, the facts do not say what risks the rental agreement disclosed other than risks of canoeing, which presumably include swollen fast waters, swamping of a canoe, and potential drowning. Investigation should confirm the details of the rental agreement to determine whether this event falls within the disclosed risks. On their face, implied and express assumption of risk appear to make for strong defenses for the company. On the other hand, the facts state that the enthusiast broke an *old* paddle in the swift waters. For the rental company to supply unfit equipment, if by *old* the facts mean to imply that the paddle was aged and potentially defective, could take the claim out of the risk assumption. Presumably, the rental agreement and warnings said nothing about risks of unfit equipment. Yet this question is one for investigation, and the paddle did break *in the swift current* implying that the swollen waters (about which the enthusiast had ample warning) were a contributing factor.

Thus on a relatively close call, the canoe-rental company may well have an assumption-of-risk defense based on both express and implied assumptions, depending on the question of the condition and fitness of the old paddle that broke in the swift current. This case warrants further investigation.

www.ingramcontent.com/pod-product-compliance
Lightning Source LLC
Chambersburg PA
CBHW080037100526
44584CB00023BA/3256